Nonprofit
Bookkeeping & Accounting
FOR
DUMMIES®

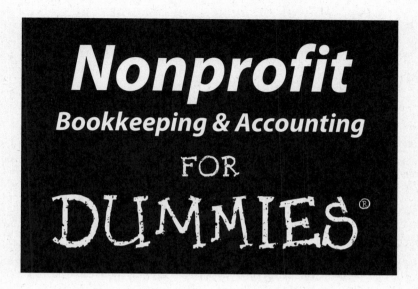

by Sharon Farris
President of Farris Accounting &
Consulting Training Services (FACT$)

WILEY

Wiley Publishing, Inc.

Nonprofit Bookkeeping & Accounting For Dummies®

Published by
Wiley Publishing, Inc.
111 River St.
Hoboken, NJ 07030-5774
www.wiley.com

For general information on our other products and services, please contact our Customer Care Department within the U.S. at 877-762-2974, outside the U.S. at 317-572-3993, or fax 317-572-4002.

For technical support, please visit www.wiley.com/techsupport.

Wiley also publishes its books in a variety of electronic formats. Some content that appears in print may not be available in electronic books.

Library of Congress Control Number: 2009925029

ISBN: 978-0-470-43236-5

Manufactured in the United States of America

10

WILEY

About the Author

Sharon Farris, president of Farris Accounting & Consulting Training Services (FACT$), is an accountant and grant consultant. She is a Certified Grants Manager (certified by Management Concepts) and received her bachelor's degree in accounting from Troy University of Montgomery, Alabama.

During the past ten years, she has provided training and consultation to more than 100 public and private organizations in fields such as accounting, business writing, grant writing, and proposal development. She has developed and taught training certification programs for Auburn University Montgomery and Alabama State University in Montgomery, Alabama.

Sharon's clients have included the U.S. Department of Education, United Way of Alabama, State of Alabama Council for Developmental Disabilities, Montgomery County Board of Education, Montgomery County Sheriff's Office, Council on Aging, Alabama A&M University, 100 Black Men of Montgomery, Alabama, Faith in Action Outreach Ministries, Grace Christian Academy, and the Montgomery County Historical Society.

Sharon provides on-site training in all aspects of accounting, budget analysis, and proposal development. She works with organizations to assess their current funding streams and organizes and develops funding plans to stabilize and sustain the organizations. In addition, Sharon serves as the keynote speaker at meetings for organizations and professional associations.

To discuss this book or understand how Sharon can work with you to establish, develop, and expand your organization, please contact her at FACT$, P.O. Box 242143, Montgomery, AL 36124, phone (334) 224-6541, e-mail thatsfacts@gmail.com, or Web site www.thatsfacts.org.

Dedication

To my beautiful daughter, Keisha, and my mother, Beatrice Rembert. May we continue to share laughter together.

Author's Acknowledgments

This final product took a consortium of friends from my inner circle to write and publish. I want to thank many people for making this book possible. First, I want to thank Dr. Beverly Browning for the referral. Thanks to her for connecting me to Acquisitions Editor Stacy Kennedy. I received the e-mail proposal from Stacy Kennedy about the vision for this book on my birthday. Thanks for making that day one to remember.

Thanks to Chad Sievers, my project editor, and Vicki Adang, my copy editor, for their guidance, support, and the endless hours they spent working to make this book a complete product.

Finally, thanks to my inner circle of friends and professional associates, who helped me cross the finish line. Norell Carter, an associate of FACT$, took time away from studying for the CPA exam to work on this book. Thomas Gaither spent countless hours encouraging me to press forward. Thanks also to Wayne "Turkey Leg" Jones, my business partner, for moral support.

Finally, I have to thank my family for their continued help and inspiration. Thanks to my sister, Earsie Mack, for understanding and encouraging me. Thanks to my dear sister, Odessa T. Lee, for talking the talk and motivating me to see this book through to its completion.

Publisher's Acknowledgments

We're proud of this book; please send us your comments through our Dummies online registration form located at http://dummies.custhelp.com. For other comments, please contact our Customer Care Department within the U.S. at 877-762-2974, outside the U.S. at 317-572-3993, or fax 317-572-4002.

Some of the people who helped bring this book to market include the following:

Acquisitions, Editorial, and Media Development

Project Editor: Chad R. Sievers

Acquisitions Editor: Stacy Kennedy

Copy Editors: Vicki Adang, Amanda Gillum

Assistant Editor: Erin Calligan Mooney

Editorial Program Coordinator: Joe Niesen

Technical Editor: Robert Harveywebster, CPA

Editorial Manager: Michelle Hacker

Editorial Assistant: Jennette ElNaggar

Cover Photos: © JUPITERIMAGES/Creatas/Alamy

Cartoons: Rich Tennant
   (www.the5thwave.com)

Composition Services

Project Coordinator: Katherine Key

Layout and Graphics: Reuben W. Davis, Sarah Philippart, Christine Williams

Proofreader: Toni Settle

Indexer: Christine Karpeles

Publishing and Editorial for Consumer Dummies

   Diane Graves Steele, Vice President and Publisher, Consumer Dummies

   Kristin Ferguson-Wagstaffe, Product Development Director, Consumer Dummies

   Ensley Eikenburg, Associate Publisher, Travel

   Kelly Regan, Editorial Director, Travel

Publishing for Technology Dummies

   Andy Cummings, Vice President and Publisher, Dummies Technology/General User

Composition Services

   Debbie Stailey, Director of Composition Services

Contents at a Glance

Table of Contents

Introduction

Counting the money in your wallet or purse is an act of accounting. If you ever make a note of how much you have, you're even performing a bookkeeping function. You count things all the time in everyday life without thinking twice about accounting. For example, you count the plates before setting the table at home. You count the number of e-mails you receive while you're out of the office. Even a gesture such as looking at your watch and thinking about how much time you have before your next appointment is a form of accounting.

Bookkeeping and accounting are service activities that involve auditing, tax services, management advisory services, general accounting, cost accounting, budgeting, and internal auditing. Even though your organization is a nonprofit, these services are essential parts of your daily activities. Without them, your nonprofit can't survive the long haul.

In the wake of increased accountability, understanding how to track and account for the everyday activities of your nonprofit is important. Keeping the books for a nonprofit is exciting. Getting federal grant money to fund your programs relieves financial stress. Getting a clean bill of health from your financial audit adds credibility. I devote this book to all nonprofits that add credibility to the sector by keeping their books in order.

About This Book

Bookkeeping and accounting for an organization involve several fundamental steps. Beginning with a simple transaction such as a donation and ending with financial statements, you go through an accounting cycle of 12 months. The cycle repeats as long as your nonprofit continues to operate. To help you with the normal day-to-day transactions — as well as any sticky situations you may find along the way — I wrote this book for the nonprofit director and manager (as well as the nonprofit bookkeeper and accountant).

Feel free to use this book as a quick reference. It's designed to help you with everything you need to know to operate your nonprofit according to generally accepted accounting principles (GAAP). It covers information about the steps to file your own payroll taxes and tax information Form 990. It also explains how to account for almost every situation that may come up in your nonprofit.

This book serves as a tool that you can pick up from time to time during your accounting cycle to brush up on the following steps:

1. **Your nonprofit enters into a transaction with a second party.**

2. **You or your employee prepares a business document, such as a sales invoice, that leaves a paper trail.**

3. **You or your employee records the transaction in the book of first entry, your journal.**

4. **You post the transaction to the general ledger.**

5. **You balance the general ledger and prepare a trial balance.** Your trial balance tests the accuracy of account (debit and credit) balances.

6. **You prepare your financial statements.**

This book serves as a reference tool, no matter where you are in the accounting process, by helping you reach your ultimate goal of well-prepared and accurate financial statements.

Conventions Used in This Book

Throughout this book, I use the following conventions to help you find your way:

- ✔ Every time I introduce a new word, I *italicize* it and then define it.

- ✔ **Boldface** text is used to indicate keywords in bulleted lists or to highlight action parts of numbered steps.

- ✔ Monofont is used for Web site addresses.

What You're Not to Read

I understand that you're a very busy person working in a small- to medium-sized nonprofit. Every day throws different and unique challenges at you. You won't hurt my feelings if you don't read every word I've written. So if you're strapped for time, feel free to skip the sidebars (the gray boxes). In sidebars, I include some real-world examples that you can skip — don't worry, you won't miss anything essential to understanding my point.

Foolish Assumptions

While writing this book, I made the following assumptions about you, my dear reader. Some may be more relevant than others.

- ✔ You're the executive director of a newly formed, small nonprofit, and you want to know how to manage your own books.
- ✔ You direct or manage a midsize nonprofit and want to understand a little more about how to manage day-to-day operations and take care of your own books.
- ✔ You're interested in keeping the books of a nonprofit organization.
- ✔ You're interested in bookkeeping and accounting as a profession.
- ✔ You've been performing the functions in this book, but you're not sure if you've been doing them right.
- ✔ You're thinking about starting your own nonprofit and want to know how an effective nonprofit keeps track of its bookkeeping and accounting needs.

Finally, I assume you know that you can read this book over and over again and discover something new every time. You can refer to this book as a quick reference whenever you need to know the how-to of managing your financial records for your organization. I assume this book takes the guesswork out of bookkeeping and accounting and provides some peace of mind about how the system is designed and how you can work it to benefit your organization.

After reading this book, I hope you're confident that you can take care of most of your bookkeeping and accounting needs yourself. At least, you can get a better handle on how your accounting cycle functions.

How This Book Is Organized

This book is organized into five parts. You don't have to read it from cover to cover; you can dip in for reference at any point that interests you and jump from part to part if you like. I won't tell anyone.

Part 1: Accounting and Bookkeeping Nonprofit Style

This part talks about basic bookkeeping and accounting terminology. You can also find a chapter that helps you understand financial statements.

And when you're ready to get your hands dirty, you can read about record keeping and then decide whether to design your own computer system or use store-bought software.

Part II: Balancing Your Nonprofit Books

This part covers the nuts and bolts of setting up and balancing your nonprofit books. I cover how to set up a chart of accounts, how to record transactions in the bookkeeping journal, and how to make entries in and balance your nonprofit's checkbook. Balancing your cash flows and planning your budget are two important aspects discussed in this part. If you're not sure how to stay in compliance with federal nonprofit guidelines, follow the tips suggested here for help.

Part III: Accounting for Nonprofit Situations

I should have named this part "Documentation 101" because that's what the chapters here seem to boil down to. Part III focuses on grants, payroll, and accounting for Form 990, all of which are extremely important for keeping your nonprofit up and running. This part covers information about federal grants management and the grant audit. Everything you need to know about payroll taxes and filing Form 990 also is summarized here to keep you in good standing with the IRS and Uncle Sam. All of these tasks come back to staying organized and keeping a good paper trail.

Part IV: Wrapping Up the Books

Part IV shows you how to create your own financial statements. It also describes the steps you have to take to close one accounting period and prepare the books for the next cycle. Finally, in this part, I cover what you need to do to prepare your books for an audit of your financial statements.

Part V: The Part of Tens

This is the famous _For Dummies_ Part of Tens. You can find out how to keep your books in good standing and how to stay out of hot water with the federal government using the helpful tips in this part. After reading these chapters, you can feel confident that you're indeed going about your books in the right way.

Icons Used in This Book

For Dummies books use little pictures, called icons, to get your attention in the margins. Here's what they mean:

This icon highlights techniques or draws your attention to something noteworthy.

This icon highlights important information to keep in mind and points out things you shouldn't forget.

This icon points out pitfalls and signals red flags of caution.

This icon points out real-life anecdotes from my years of experience and mistakes.

Where to Go from Here

Like every *For Dummies* book, each chapter stands alone, so you can jump from chapter to chapter and read whichever ones pique your interest. Glance at the table of contents and go to the topic that interests you. You can read this book in many ways, depending on your needs. If you're new to the nonprofit arena, start with Part I. If you're a veteran, I suggest you brush up on some info about filing your tax information in Part IV. Make plans to read the information more than once. You don't have to remember this stuff; just pull your book out and use it as a reference as you need it.

This book is organized in an order logical to the accounting process, but you don't need to read it from front to back to gain important insight and wisdom about the tricks of the trade. Feel free to read it cover to cover if you're just biting at the bit to uncover everything you can about nonprofit bookkeeping and accounting.

Part I
Accounting and Bookkeeping Nonprofit Style

The 5th Wave

By Rich Tennant

"Maybe it wasn't clear on my resume when you hired me as your bookkeeper, but my previous experience was as a beekeeper... a beekeeper."

In this part . . .

*B*efore you can dive into the pool of nonprofit bookkeeping and accounting, you have to be familiar with
basic accounting terminology and financial statements.
After grasping the fundamentals, you can account for your
nonprofit activities. You may want to use a manual
record-keeping system, or you may opt for a sophisticated
computerized system instead. Which style you use
doesn't matter as long as you understand the mechanics
of the trade.

As you put your toes in the water, you may be asking
yourself a few questions: What is a debit? What is a
credit? What is an asset? How do I begin keeping my
accounting books in order? This part helps you answer
these early questions and gives you a basic understanding
of the bookkeeping and accounting processes you need to
master to get an approved audit.

Chapter 1

The Nuts and Bolts of Nonprofit Bookkeeping and Accounting

*Y*our accounting year indicates the beginning of your accounting period and the end of your accounting period. This period may reflect the calendar year from January to December or some other 12-month period. If you use the calendar year, then the first transaction after January 1 starts your accounting cycle, and your last transaction on December 31 ends the cycle. You compile your financial statements after the cycle ends, get your financial statements audited, and start the cycle over again. It always feels good to finish something, doesn't it? If you start with the end in mind, you have audited financial statements that summarize your accounting activities for the accounting period.

Now more than ever people are calling for accountability in the world of nonprofits. Long gone are the days when you can assume that your stakeholders will just take your word that you're successful at your mission and are spending their donations wisely. People want to see proof — cold, hard numbers in black and white. So you must dot every i and cross every t in your day-to-day operations.

Being accountable for your nonprofit requires that your books adequately reflect your activities. You need sound financial management by qualified individuals to keep your head above water. I wish you could focus only on your programs and the people whom you help, but you need a penny pincher and a number cruncher to keep up with the money coming in and going out. This chapter serves as a jumping off point into the world of nonprofit bookkeeping and accounting and touches on the important concepts. Throughout this book, I then dive deeper into these topics.

Getting Started with Your Nonprofit's Books

Before you can fully get going with your books, you first need to know where to begin. Start by identifying your destination: to have audited financial statements. You begin with a journal entry of a transaction, in which you record the exchange of something (money or time) for something else (products or services). Every financial transaction creates a record or document to support its occurrence. For example, if you buy a pen, you either give up cash or add to your charge account.

Adapting the habits of a packrat isn't a bad idea when it comes to keeping up with your paperwork. Hold on to every receipt and record it in the proper location by posting to the right accounts. The central location of most transactions starts with your checking account in which you make deposits from donors and write checks to pay the bills. The key to properly tracking your steps starts with your checkbook. (Check out Chapter 7 for more on getting a checkbook going.)

Of course, lots of things happen during the course of an accounting year. This section outlines the basics of nonprofit bookkeeping and accounting and what you need to understand before you can delve into your books.

Identifying the difference between bookkeeping and accounting

Before you can make sure your nonprofit's books are okay, you need to have a firm understanding of bookkeeping and accounting. Here are the main differences. Chapter 2 provides more insight on the two.

A bookkeeper records day-to-day activities by recording one side of the transaction. They usually record transactions when cash changes hands (called the *cash basis* of accounting; see the next section for more details). Usually bookkeepers pass the books to the accountant at the end of the year to generate financial statements.

Accountants balance both sides of a transaction (the debit and credit sides) by evaluating how one transaction affects two or more accounts. Accounting isn't complicated mathematics; it's adding, subtracting, dividing, and multiplying, with some analysis thrown in based on principles and rules written by the profession. Accountants dig a bit deeper into understanding the treatment of accounts or the right way to handle financial situations based on principles. A bookkeeper may not be able to analyze accounts, but she can record the transaction.

You may say, well, what's the real difference here. Accountants understand the why of everything that takes place, whereas a bookkeeper may not grasp the concept behind the action. I'm not saying that bookkeepers function like robots, but some bookkeepers haven't had the level of education as an accountant. Accountants have a minimum of a four-year degree, whereas a bookkeeper may be trained on the job to perform her duties.

Accountants also get paid more than bookkeepers. You're likely to have a bookkeeper on your payroll to perform day-to-day functions and an accountant on retainer to put together reports on a quarterly or annual basis.

Some accountants take a standardized test, called the CPA exam, to prove they know the mechanics and ins and outs of the profession. Accountants who pass the test are called *certified public accountants (CPAs)*. CPAs are the only individuals who can audit your financial statements.

Don't be intimidated by CPAs because they have passed this tough exam. By all means, show some respect for their devotion to analyzing your financial situation, but do use their knowledge and ask them some questions about your affairs. That's what you're paying them for!

Picking your accounting method

Your *accounting method* determines when you record activities. Your accounting method answers this question: Do you record a transaction when it happens or when cash exchanges hands?

You have two choices:

- ✔ **Cash basis:** This method records transactions only when cash is received or paid. Bookkeepers use this method.
- ✔ **Accrual basis:** This method records revenues when they are earned, expenses when they are used, and purchases when they take place. Accountants use this method.

For example, if you ordered copy paper over the Internet for your office and charged it to your account, when does the transaction take place? Does it happen when you charge the purchase to your account? Or does it transpire when you pay the bill? If you were using the cash method, you'd record the transaction when the bill is paid. If you were using the accrual basis of accounting, you'd record the transaction right after charging the purchase to your account. Check out Chapter 2 for more in-depth discussion about these two methods and which one may be best for your nonprofit.

Keep watch over your nonprofit's finances

Sometimes nonprofit directors and managers feel they don't have the knowledge to do their own books, so they turn everything over to a CPA. This book gives you the help you need to do some of your nonprofit's basic bookkeeping and accounting. However, you may rightfully need a licensed professional to help with the more technical aspects of keeping your nonprofits books. That's where a CPA can help. However, when using a CPA, don't put all of your eggs in one basket. Although most CPAs are trustworthy and knowledgeable, I strongly suggest you keep some checks and balances in place to prevent any potential fraud. *Checks and balances* are periodic times when you sit down with your CPA for a layman's analysis of what's going on with your finances. You can also check for ways to improve your accounting procedures. (Check out Chapter 2 for more info.)

Don't become a victim by trusting a CPA to handle everything without asking questions. All too often, the media reports on an accountant or CPA embezzling funds from organizations. Oftentimes employers trust them because they don't want the hassle of trying to understand the lingo. Therefore, many fall victim to situations that can be prevented. To avoid these problems, keep a close eye on your finances and ask your CPA questions. Also have someone in your office who works with the numbers so you're not leaving everything up to your outside CPA.

For example, I received a call from a small boating company that had been taken for $80,000 by its accountant. The woman on the phone was hurt because the accountant had robbed the company of its entire savings. The accountant took care of everything — made all the purchases, paid all the bills, wrote all the checks, balanced the books — and never missed a day of work.

This accountant also owned a check-cashing company. This allowed him to write checks to individuals and companies and cash them at his check-cashing store. This setup was a neat little scheme until the bottom fell out. One day the accountant took ill and couldn't report to work for a week. The owners had to take care of the payroll and accounts payable. When they reviewed the books, they found out that they were flat broke.

The owners could have prevented this situation by not allowing the accountant to collect the money and pay the bills. They needed to find someone else to handle one of those tasks. This is called *segregation of duties*.

Understanding the basic terms

Before jumping into bookkeeping and accounting, make sure you understand some basic terminology. Throughout this book, I use the basic language the professionals use. That's all you need to get a good grasp of processes and procedures. There's no need to add another nerd to the accounting profession. Here I only share the need-to-know information.

To break down the accounting process, start with the basic accounting equation:

Assets = Liabilities + Owner's equity

This equation needs to stay in balance. That's why some call it *double-entry accounting.* (Check out Chapter 2 for more info on double-entry accounting.) What happens on one side must take place on the other in order for everything to stay in balance.

To help you understand how you can use this equation, I cover the accounts found on your *statement of activities* (the nonprofit term for what the for-profit world calls the *income statement*) and your *statement of financial position* (the nonprofit term for the for-profit *balance sheet*). Walking through the equations used to complete these two statements gives you an accurate picture of your nonprofit's financial situation. Knowing these two equations can make you a better decision maker and better financial manager by understanding how every transaction affects your financial statements.

- ✔ **Statement of activities equation, also called the income statement equation:** Revenues – Expenses = Income

- ✔ **Statement of financial position equation, also called the balance sheet equation:** Assets – Liabilities = Equity or Assets = Liabilities + Equity (*equity* explains the difference between assets and liabilities)

Your statement of financial position summarizes how financially stable your organization is and how solvent it is. A quick eye can look at this statement and gain great insight into your future to determine whether your organization can sustain the forces of the market. (Check out Chapter 16 for more about how this statement works.)

Assets, liabilities, and equity

Think of *assets* as something that you own or that adds value. Think of *liabilities* as something you owe or that takes away. Think of *equity* as the difference between the assets and liabilities.

An asset adds value, whether it's monetary or not. Examples of assets are

- ✔ Accounts receivable
- ✔ Buildings
- ✔ Cash
- ✔ Equipment
- ✔ Furniture

- Homes
- Inventory
- Pledges receivable
- Prepaid expenses
- Property (land)
- Vehicles

A liability is something you owe or an obligation of time, money, or resources. Anything that must be paid is considered a liability. Some common liabilities are

- Accounts payables
- Accrued expenses
- Bills
- Car notes
- Mortgages
- Notes payable
- Short-term payables
- Utility bills

Equity is the difference between assets and liabilities. Equity is your *net worth* and is also referred to as *net assets*. When you have a list of all assets and all liabilities, you have everything needed to calculate your net worth. *Net* means the remainder after positive and negative amounts are combined.

Your goal at the end of the year is to have an increase in net assets and not a decrease in net assets. This means your net worth has increased.

Debits and credits

Accounting reflects what happens financially by increasing and decreasing accounts in the form of debits and credits. After you grasp the *normal balances* — what it takes to increase an account — for all accounts, you'll know when to apply debits and credits.

Accounts are like coins in that they have two sides:

- The left side is the *debit* side of an account.
- The right side is the *credit* side of an account.

Some people refer to this as *T accounting* because the record keeping is set up in the shape of a giant T. Imagine taking a piece of paper and drawing a horizontal line across the top and a vertical line down the middle. You've drawn a large T. On the left side of the vertical line you record debits, and on the right side is where credits go.

For example, take the statement of financial position with its assets and liabilities. Asset accounts normally have a debit balance, so the normal balance for assets accounts is a debit balance. *Normal* balance of any account is a positive amount or what is done to increase that account. So if you want to decrease an asset, you credit it. Asset accounts are debited for increases and credited for decreases. On the flipside, the normal balance for all liability accounts is a credit balance. To increase a liability account, you credit the account. To decrease a liability, you debit the account. Liability accounts are debited for decreases and credited for increases.

Debits and credits are done through double-entry accounting to keep your accounting equation in balance. Every transaction affects two or more items in your accounting equation. When you record entries in two or more places, you're doing *double-entry accounting*.

Throughout your accounting period, you make debits and credits not only to your statement of financial position accounts, but also to your statement of activities accounts. Understanding how to increase and decrease these accounts is important.

- ✔ Revenue accounts are debited to decrease and credited to increase.
- ✔ Expense accounts are debited to increase and credited to decrease.

These mechanics are part of double-entry accounting, and the basis of every transaction is knowing what to do to increase and what to do to decrease an account. Check out Chapter 2 for more on double-entry accounting.

Adhering to GAAP

Before you can play a game, you read the instructions, right? Well before you can fully understand bookkeeping and accounting for your nonprofit, you have to familiarize yourself with the ground rules. The ground rules of the accounting profession can be attributed to *generally accepted accounting principles (GAAP)*. GAAP are the standards that accountants follow when making decisions about how to handle accounting issues. Call them the rules of the profession.

GAAP were put in place to help accountants put their clients' needs first and behave ethically. The idea is to make sure that your accountant treats you and your nonprofit's business the same as he treats his other clients, and that all accountants are playing by the same rules. See Chapter 9 for more on GAAP.

Keeping a paper trail

Leaving tracks in the sand is essential to proper management of your nonprofit's books. You need documentation to prove why you did what you did. It adds credibility to your management of funds. Good housekeeping starts by keeping your checkbook register balanced (see Chapter 7) and continues with maintaining organized records (see Chapter 4).

It's best to keep copies of where every donation comes from and how each dollar is spent. Part of being a good steward is leaving marks in the sand to account for your nonprofit activities.

Watch out for your debit cards issued by your bank. Transactions for these cards are so easy to forget to record in your checkbook register. They're like the little foxes that catch you off guard.

Additionally, your auditor will want to backtrack in your steps to find the initial record that began a single transaction. Auditing is like looking for a needle in a haystack. Sometimes only your auditor knows what she's looking for and why, but you have to let her look. Getting an audit of your financial statements is a necessary part of keeping your nonprofit status. Chapter 20 tells you what to expect during an audit.

Auditing 101: It's a GAAS!

In addition to playing by the rules when keeping your nonprofit's books, you also need to follow other important rules concerning audits. *Generally accepted auditing standards (GAAS)* are rules or standards used to perform and report audit findings. *Auditing* is gathering and reviewing evidence about your organization to report on the degree between the way your nonprofit's financial information is presented and the standards set by rule makers. The American Institute of Certified Public Accountants (AICPA) sets the rules and requirements for audits, among other things.

Auditors give opinions by writing a report about your operating procedures, compliance with specific laws, and whether your financial statements are stated according to GAAP. As a nonprofit director or manager, you need to be concerned with three types of audits:

- ✔ An audit of financial statements, sometimes called an *accounting audit,* verifies whether statements have been prepared according to GAAP. Check out Chapter 20 for what happens during this type of audit.

- ✔ A compliance audit, sometimes referred to as a *grant audit,* reviews your financial records to determine whether your nonprofit is following specific procedures, rules, or regulations set down by some higher authority, like the IRS or some other government or rule-making body. See Chapters 9, 12, and 20 for more information about compliance.

> ✔ An operational audit (also called the *management audit* or *performance audit*) measures and evaluates how efficiently you're operating and how effectively you're managing your nonprofit's resources. Boards of directors often request this audit to evaluate organizational structure, computer operations, marketing, and so on.

Making Sure Your Books Are Balanced

Staying on top of your nonprofit's financial activities is important because as the director, you can be held accountable. The way to start is making sure you have balanced books. *Balanced books* are up-to-date current information about your accounts. Every transaction that takes place affects two or more items in accounting, and you have to make sure everything stays in balance. Whether you create your own manual system or take advantage of the software on the market, you need to keep your books in order.

This section walks you through some basics to help you ensure your books are balanced. Follow the chapters in Part II for tools to assist you in maintaining balanced books.

Establishing a chart of accounts

Your *chart of accounts* is your blueprint for assigning numbers to specify accounts and having a method to track all accounts. By having a chart of accounts, you can recognize what type of account it is based on the beginning number. For example, accounts beginning with 1 are usually assets accounts. After you get used to using the chart of accounts, you'll enjoy the benefits of coding transactions according to their classification. Chapter 5 has more on setting up your chart of accounts.

Tracking transactions

To have a firm grasp on your nonprofit's financial status, your records have to be accurate. The only way to have accurate records is to record transactions when they take place.

Tracking your revenues and expenses is like in-house overdraft protection. It helps you know when you're short on cash and when you've got plenty of money to pay the bills. For example, you know the feeling you get when someone doesn't cash a check you've written? That outstanding check sort of bugs you and leaves you wondering if the check is lost. Then, one day after a few months, the check clears. Without a good tracking device or accounting system, you can easily lose track of your true checking account balance.

So how can you keep track of transactions? Don't feel overwhelmed. You don't need a PhD in aeronautical engineering. The following are a couple of easy ways to track them. Check out Chapters 6 and 7 for more on recording transactions and using a checkbook.

> ✔ **Use online banking.** Online banking gives up-to-date current balances anytime, day or night.
>
> ✔ **Itemize your transactions when they happen.** When you swipe your credit card or bank debit card, write it down right away in your checkbook register.

One of the most important things you need to keep track of is your donors list. A donors list includes contributors' names, addresses, and phone numbers, as well as the donation dates. Your auditor will use this list to verify where the money came from and when.

Developing a budget

Your *budget* is your financial plan. It tells you how much money you have, how much you expect to receive, and how much you expect to spend. When you create a budget, you develop a formal plan for paying for your organization's future activities.

You not only need an operating budget for your organization, but you also need a separate budget for each and every program. Chapter 8 explains how to create a budget.

Always know how much money is needed to operate your nonprofit. If a private donor asks, you should know the exact amount needed to *break even* (the amount of money it takes to run all programs and pay all expenses within a given year).

Staying within the lines: Compliance

Only a few things can knock your nonprofit off the map. Not filing your paperwork with the IRS, operating as a for-profit entity, and playing political games can throw you out of the nonprofit loop. As long as you operate according to your bylaws, stay out of political activities, and jump through all of the IRS's hoops you'll be in compliance.

In addition, you have to mind some accounting standards: generally accepted accounting principles (GAAP), rules set by the Financial Accounting Standards Board (FASB), and laws established by the Sarbanes-Oxley Act (SOX). I explain the ins and outs of these guidelines in Chapter 9.

You're in the Money: The Lowdown on Federal Grants

Finding donations and revenue for your nonprofit may be frustrating at times. The good news: The federal government provides free money in the form of grants that you can apply for and not have to pay back. Grants come in all sizes, from preemies of $10,000 to supersizes of $1 million. And you don't need to be an established nonprofit to apply for funding. Even if you're small and new to the scene, you automatically qualify for a piece of the government grant pie. Take a slice and find viable solutions to your financial problems.

There is no way I would attempt to run a nonprofit without consulting with my rich Uncle Sam. Positioning your organization to receive grants requires four important things:

- ✔ **Organization:** You need to keep up with the paperwork involved to make the application and management process easier. I offer some steps in Chapter 10 that get you started in the right direction.

- ✔ **Reading:** In order to understand the dos and don'ts of how to put together your grant application, you need to carefully read all the paperwork. When you discover how many grants are available for you, it's gonna blow your mind.

- ✔ **Writing:** You need to put your plan on paper. Federal proposal writing is different from other writing you may do on a regular basis. I show you how to write about the facts and figures to prove your need, the steps to fulfill the need, the group of people who will carry out the plan, and how you will evaluate your results.

- ✔ **Accountability:** To fulfill reporting requirements, you need to be accountable. You successfully receive the grant; now you have to tell the government how you're spending the grant money and how many folks are benefiting from the funds.

This section gives you a snapshot of the federal grant process. Chapters 11, 12, and 13 provide an appetizing bite of what can become a buffet of federal money. Then you can stop worrying about how to fund your programs and focus on helping people.

Gleaning some grant basics

Grants are award instruments given by the federal government to implement programs that benefit people. You don't have to pay grants back — they're not loans. It's free money! Figuring out the grant application process is easy, and the benefits of receiving a grant are phenomenal.

Although many sources other than the federal government offer grants, I focus on Uncle Sam's jackpot. Billions of dollars are available from 26 federal agencies to:

- ✔ Help nonprofits implement programs to benefit communities
- ✔ Do work that government can't do
- ✔ Carry out a public purpose

Chapter 11 explores how grants can help your nonprofit's bottom line.

Following the rules

When your nonprofit gets federal grant money, you're not free to spend it as you wish. Grant money does have its red tape and paperwork, but you can't afford to overlook the number-one grant maker in the nation (other than Bill Gates). The federal government is the perfect place to research and secure grant funding.

It's a bit tricky to manage a grant, but after you get your first one behind you, managing others is like clockwork. Tick! Tock! Chapter 11 provides more insight to managing grant money.

The main challenge of managing a federal grant is submitting two reports in a timely manner. These reports tell the government

- ✔ What progress you've made toward your program goals to date
- ✔ How you've spent the federal money and how much is left

After you master the rules, you can play the grant game like a pro and become a grant guru.

Going through a grant audit

For many, the word *audit* brings to mind the freezing of assets and the endless search for paper trails that may lead to the discovery of something that wasn't handled properly. For the record, an *audit* verifies and confirms the accuracy of your financial records and your compliance with the grant requirements.

The grant audit is usually conducted by someone from the granting agency. Your grant auditor checks out the federal government's investment by seeing if you're a good steward of grant dollars. Basically, the auditor wants to view your accounting system to see how you separate your grant money from the rest of your money. Your auditor also looks at other areas, such as your organization's travel, personnel, and purchasing policies and procedures. Don't sweat it because I prepare you for the grant audit. I've been on both sides of the grant audit. I've audited others, and I've been audited. Chapter 12 walks you through what to expect during a grant audit.

Paying Uncle Sam: Employee Payroll Taxes

Although your organization is a nonprofit and is exempt from paying federal taxes, don't make this huge mistake: You're still responsible for paying federal payroll taxes for all of your employees. Unfortunately you can't avoid doing so (unless you want to end up in the clink for a while and have your nonprofit closed).

When you pay federal employee payroll taxes, usually on a quarterly basis, your payment consists of the employees' FICA withholdings. These taxes are for Social Security and Medicare and are taken out of employees' paychecks. Both Social Security and Medicare are financed primarily by employment taxes.

You are the steward of this money, and you need to submit it to the Social Security Administration and the IRS in a timely fashion. Hey, don't worry too much about this one, because you can do it yourself and save your organization some money.

After you've walked through this process a couple of times, you'll be able to calculate your payroll taxes yourself. Most payroll taxes are paid quarterly, and the feds will tell you when and how to pay. Chapter 13 gives you the lowdown on paying payroll taxes.

Getting a Grasp on Financial Statements

Financial statements are records of where your revenue comes from, where it goes, and where it is now. Your financial statements are important because they summarize your nonprofit's activities for a specific time period, as of a certain date. Check out the chapters in Part IV for more in-depth explanations on these statements and how you can create and use them to keep track of your organization's finances.

Soliciting donors

In a class I took a few years back at Auburn University in Montgomery, Alabama, the teacher talked about soliciting gifts and how Ida Bell Young had left land and a tremendously large gift to AUM. The teacher explained how he had visited Mrs. Young on numerous occasions, and she had never indicated that she was going to give the university a dime.

Mrs. Young, like so many others, was looking for a worthy cause to leave her fortune to. As the executive director or manager of a nonprofit, you're probably always looking for big donors like Mrs. Young. Soliciting a gift is a courtship, and you have to be persistent, patient, and exercise a lot of faith.

Your financial statements include

✔ **Statement of activities:** Also called the *income statement,* the statement of activities lists all revenues earned and all expenses paid for a time span of usually one year. It indicates whether your organization earned income by showing revenue collected, expenses incurred, and the difference between the two. The difference between revenue and expenses is net income or increases or decreases in equity or net assets. Refer to Chapter 15 for more info.

✔ **Statement of financial position:** Also referred to as the *balance sheet,* this statement reveals your solvency and stability by summarizing your assets (things you own) and liabilities (things you owe) and calculates your *net worth,* the difference between what you own and what you owe. Your statement of financial position reports your organization's assets, liabilities, and equity as of a certain date. The difference between assets and liabilities equals your equity. Check out Chapter 16 for more.

✔ **Cash flow statement:** This statement evaluates all inflows and outflows of cash for the accounting period according to the activity. The cash flow statement breaks activities into three categories: operating, financing, and investing. See Chapter 17 for more on the cash flow statement.

✔ **Statement of functional expense:** This statement breaks down your expenses by category. The three categories of expense are program expenses, management and general expenses, and fundraising expenses. After you've completed the income statement, your statement of functional expense takes your total expenses from activities and divides them by their functions. See Chapter 18 for functional expense classifications.

✔ **Notes to the financial statements:** The notes section tells the story behind the numbers. The notes describe your organization, explain your accounting methods, and explain any changes in those methods, potential lawsuits, or contingencies that threaten the livelihood of your existence. Plus they provide detailed information for some of the amounts in the financial statements.

In addition, the notes clarify all restricted assets. In the notes you find pertinent information about bonds and notes payable. Anything that can have a material impact on your organization should be disclosed in the notes to the financial statements. See Chapter 19 to understand the importance of completing the notes to your financial statements.

Figuring Out Where Your Nonprofit Is: Five Important Questions

So many executive directors and managers of nonprofits live on the edge. Some stay up nights worrying about how they're going to keep the lights on. Others wonder where they're going to find funding to keep their programs running. Wouldn't you like to relax a bit? Your relationship with your organization shouldn't be like fighting with your spouse about money.

Don't worry anymore. You don't have to live in crisis mode any longer. Here I provide five common questions you may have and give you some answers to make your life a little easier.

✔ **Why do I need a system to track and record revenues and expenses?** You need to do so because you're a good steward of the funds you manage, and you want to keep your supporters happy. A good steward is wise and prudent in the way he handles money. You first want to establish and then maintain a good reputation as being a good investment. You need a bookkeeping system that tracks and accounts for the funds you manage. Tracking and keeping up with the money that comes into your organization (revenues) and the money that goes out of your organization (expenses) makes you accountable and gives your nonprofit credibility.

✔ **I need more stable sources of income to fund my programs. How do I go about finding those?** I am glad you asked this question. Here is what you need to do. Get grant money! The most stable source of income for you is government grants. First do a little research. Then start reading. Now start writing. The final step is to manage your money. Don't hesitate; get your piece of the American pie today. See Chapters 10 and 11 for actual steps to take and where to turn.

✔ **What do I need to do with my records so I'm ready if I'm ever audited by the IRS?** One thing I've noticed about the government is how much it loves documentation. Record and store for safe keeping the transactions you make. Leave a paper trail that leads to every purchase. In other words, keep copies of everything pertaining to income received, expenses paid, and assets purchased. In real estate, it's all about location, location, location. With the IRS, it's document, document, and document. Chapter 4 can help you set up a record-keeping system.

✔ **My money is unpredictable so why do I still need an operating budget?** Whether you're flat broke and don't know where the next dime is coming from or have millions in the bank, you always need to have an operating budget. You need to know how much is needed to operate your organization on a weekly, monthly, quarterly, and annual basis. Your operating budget is your financial plan. Check out Chapter 8 for more advice.

✔ **What do I need to know about complying with IRS guidelines to keep my nonprofit status?** One thing that applies to all nonprofits, no matter how big or small, is filing information with the IRS annually through Form 990 or E-Postcard (Form 990-N). Which form you file depends on your annual gross receipts. Turn to Chapter 14 to find out more.

Chapter 2

Starting with Basic Bookkeeping and Accounting

In This Chapter

▶ Going over basic bookkeeping and accounting terminology

▶ Getting staffed: Bookkeepers, accountants, or doing it yourself

▶ Understanding your choices of accounting methods

▶ Taking steps to protect against employee theft

Sometimes when I talk to computer support people over the phone about problems I'm having with my computers, they start using words like PPPoE, ISP, and a bunch of other stuff that I don't have a clue about. When people talk over my head, my brain shuts down, and I can't understand anything. Every profession has its jargon, and accounting is no different. But the good news is that the jargon doesn't have to be an impenetrable wall separating you from the bookkeeping and accounting tasks you need to master.

In this chapter, I introduce you to accounting (including basic terms) and explain why you need to understand it and how it works. I also get you started down the path of managing your nonprofit's books — including deciding whether to handle the bookkeeping and/or accounting yourself or hire others to help you, selecting the most appropriate accounting methods for your organization, safeguarding against tax audits, and protecting your nonprofit's physical and financial assets from employee wrongdoing.

Understanding Bookkeeping and Accounting

Whether you're chief executive officer of a multibillion dollar corporation or the manager of your household, you use accounting every day. To *account* is to record and report a quantity of money or objects. *Accounting* is counting, recording, classifying, and summarizing transactions, events, and things in terms of money — and then interpreting the results. If you look inside your wallet and count your money, you have accounted for how much you have.

Bookkeeping, on the other hand, is the process of accumulating, organizing, and storing information about transactions on a day-to-day basis. When you write a check and record it in your checkbook register, you engage in bookkeeping.

Accounting and bookkeeping have several things in common, but the most basic is transactions. A *transaction* is an exchange of value between two or more parties. For example, you walk into a local store and purchase a pack of gum, handing the cashier a $5 bill. When you get your change back, you count it to verify that it's correct. Purchasing the gum is a transaction.

What's the difference between bookkeeping and accounting?

Bookkeeping is the starting point of the accounting process, and it tracks the day-to-day operations of an organization. A bookkeeper does *single-entry accounting,* which means that she may only record a transaction in one place. This bookkeeping system operates on the cash basis (which I explain in the section "Keeping track of the cash" later in this chapter), and the only entry may be in the checkbook. Bookkeepers maintain the following documents:

✔ Copies of invoices and receipts

✔ Copies of checks and bank statements

✔ All other paperwork required for accounting purposes

Bookkeepers perform daily tasks of recording, including:

✔ Dates of transactions

✔ Amounts of transactions

✔ Sources of donations

✔ Expenses and loss transactions

Accounting summarizes the day-to-day activities recorded by a bookkeeper. Based on this information, an accountant prepares financial reports used to make decisions. An accountant uses *double-entry accounting* to record every transaction because every transaction affects a minimum of two accounts. For example, if you write a check for a printer, your bookkeeper will write the check and record it in the check register. Your accountant realizes that writing a check increases your assets and reduces your cash — that's two things happening with one financial activity.

Accountants evaluate the overall results of economic activity by identifying, measuring, recording, interpreting, and communicating every transaction according to set rules and guidelines. They end the process by preparing financial statements that drive decision making within an organization.

Defining some common financial terms

Accounting is the language for business. As with all professions, it's the jargon that complicates things. In the following sections, I define the most common accounting and bookkeeping terms. (As you read through the book, you'll encounter many more accounting terms. I define those terms as you need to know them.)

Grasping assets, liabilities, and equity

I'll bet you've heard the terms "asset," "liability," and "equity" before, especially if you've made any major purchases, like a house. *Assets* are what you own and include things like cars, buildings, savings, and other items of value. A house is considered an asset, even when you don't yet own it outright.

Liabilities are what you owe, usually in the form of loan payments. Most people who say they're homeowners really aren't; as long as you're paying on a mortgage, the payment is a liability due every month.

Equity (sometimes called *net assets*) is the difference between what you owe and what you own. In the case of a house, the equity is the value of the home minus the amount you still owe on the mortgage. In other words, assets minus liabilities equals equity.

Eyeing donation revenues, expenses, and nonprofit income

Revenue is the inflow of assets received in exchange for goods and services, or from donations, investments, and other miscellaneous sources. Donations will probably be your primary source of revenue. *Donations* come from individuals, corporations, foundations, and government entities to help you fulfill your mission. Cash, grants, time, and services are examples of donations.

Expenses are the cost for goods or services. Your nonprofit encounters the same expenses as most for-profit corporations, except for income taxes. You have to account for overhead expenses (rent, utilities, and so on), program management expenses (salaries, fringe benefits, and office supplies), and other incidentals.

Some people have a misconception that nonprofits shouldn't make a profit or generate income, but no organization can operate without income. In the nonprofit arena, *net income* (revenues greater than expenses) increases net assets.

Thinking of a nonprofit in terms of *break-even analysis,* in which revenues equal expenses, is one way to understand the idea of a nonprofit acquiring income, and may motivate people to give to the organization.

Identifying cash flows and operating budgets

To stay afloat, you must identify new streams of cash flow to sustain your organization. *Cash flow* is the amount of money received in and paid out during a period of time. In the private sector, corporations are always looking for new ways to increase their cash flow, usually through new or improved products or services. (Think of how often the menu changes at fast-food restaurants!) As a nonprofit manager, you too must continuously look for new ways to appeal to your constituents and tap into new streams of cash flow. What you did last year may not appeal to them this year.

An *operating budget* is a financial plan with projections of what is expected and what is needed to operate. Even if you're low on funds, you still need to calculate a goal of how much you need. Otherwise, how will you know when you've reached your goal?

Getting a hold on debits and credits

Debits and *credits* are what's done to accounts to record transactions. To get a grasp on debits and credits, you must first know the normal balances of a few accounts. The *normal balance* is what it takes to increase an account.

Think of this as an equation that has two sides, a right side and a left side. What is done on the right must be balanced by recording the same amount on the left. For example, to debit an account is to charge the left side or left column of your journal or ledger. (A *journal* is a book of original entry where transactions are recorded in the order they occur; a *ledger* contains the transactions according to the account they belong to. Check out Chapter 6 for more info.) Asset and expense accounts are increased by debits. On the other hand, to credit an account is always done to the right side or right column of your journal or ledger. Revenue, liability, and equity accounts are increased by credits.

Asset accounts normally have a debit balance, so if you debit an asset account, you increase it. This transaction is placed on the left side of the journal or ledger. If you credit an asset account, you decrease it. Credits are shown on the right side of a journal or ledger.

Assets

Debit side	*Credit* side
shows *increases*	shows *decreases*

Asset accounts can be current or long term and include the following accounts: land, building, equipment, accumulated depreciation, cash, grants and accounts receivables, nonprofit inventory, prepaid rent, prepaid insurance, and supplies on hand.

Liability accounts normally have a credit balance, so if you credit a liability account, you increase it. If you debit a liability account, you decrease it. As with assets, debits are recorded on the left side or column of the journal or ledger, and credits are recorded on the right side or column. In fact, this holds true for all accounting processes.

Liabilities

Debit side
shows *decreases*

Credit side
shows *increases*

To decrease an account, you need to do the opposite of what is done to increase it.

Equity is handled the same as liability accounts. If you credit equity, you increase it. If you debit equity, you decrease it.

Equity

Debit side
shows *decreases*

Credit side
shows *increases*

Finding the Right People to Manage the Books and Monitor the Finances

Deciding whether to hire outside help to track your nonprofit's accounts or do it yourself is something that only you can decide. If you're busy with other things and it's within your budget to hire someone to do the job, then hire someone else to do it. This outside help can take a number of different forms, which I cover in this section. Of course, both options have advantages and disadvantages.

One advantage to hiring outside help is you get to delegate, which frees you up to do other things. Another upside is that you get an expert to manage your books and keep you on track. But the downside is that hiring someone to manage your books may cost you more than it would to pay someone on staff to handle the chore. You'll need to hire a reliable company, which may be expensive, or you can find a consultant, who may charge a bit more because he has to pay his own taxes.

Regardless of whether you or someone in your organization takes on your organization's bookkeeping and accounting or you hire outside help, you need to know some accounting. Also, you need to understand the basic principles accountants use when making decisions about how to record transactions. That's what the majority of this book helps you with. In the following sections, I explain who can do what when it comes to your nonprofit's finances.

Considering a bookkeeper or an accountant

Bookkeepers handle the day-to-day finances of your organization. There's no educational or training requirement to become a bookkeeper, but a person should be able to do basic math and be comfortable operating a 10-key adding machine. A bookkeeper passes the day-to-day transaction information on to the accountant. (See the "What's the difference between bookkeeping and accounting?" section for more on the specific duties of these positions.)

Accountants are required to have a minimum of a bachelor's degree to perform their duties and fully understand the accounting process. An accountant can perform the functions of a bookkeeper, but an accountant also looks at the big picture of your organization's finances and prepares the financial statements that help you determine whether you're on the right track or need to make some adjustments.

Accountants who pass the uniform Certified Public Accountants exam are called *CPAs*. CPAs are the only ones authorized to do a financial audit of your accounting records according to *generally accepted auditing standards (GAAS)*. An *audit* is an examination of your accounting records and financial statements that determines whether your records fairly represent your financial position according to *generally accepted accounting principles (GAAP)*. GAAP are the legal standards for measuring and reporting financial transactions that are the source of information used to prepare financial statements.

Since the Enron scandal in the early 2000s, organizations of all kinds must be aware of their CPA's activities and not necessarily sit back and trust their CPA to do the right thing. I'm not saying not to trust your CPA, but you shouldn't just take her word for everything. To protect your organization's finances, make sure you understand the basics outlined in this book.

Hiring a bookkeeper to record transactions and keeping a CPA on retainer can save you some money in the long run. A bookkeeper who communicates with a CPA makes the job easier for both. Plus, bookkeepers come a lot cheaper than accountants. Why pay an accountant's fees for a bookkeeper's task?

Doing it yourself

If your background isn't in accounting and you want to keep track of the day-to-day bookkeeping operations of your nonprofit, you can do most of the work yourself. If you opt to do it yourself, I hope you're a stickler for details. It helps if you're organized, too. You can figure out how to do this stuff if you're disciplined and use the information in this book. In the beginning, it may take a little longer to do a task because it will be new to you, but once you get it, you've got it.

However, one thing you can't do yourself is an independent audit of your own records. Well, you can audit your internal records, but performing the overall audit of financial statements doesn't give them an outsider's verification. An independent audit lends credibility to your organization based on the review of an outside CPA. Only a professional can offer such an opinion about your financial health.

GAAS state that only CPAs can perform an audit that provides an opinion on your financial statements. In addition, your auditor must be independent. The guidelines also recommend that you put your audit out to bid every three to five years or so.

Opting for a fiscal sponsor or agent

A *fiscal sponsor* or *agent* is a nonprofit organization that helps a smaller nonprofit by taking care of its financial responsibilities and allowing the smaller nonprofit to use the larger one's nonprofit status to get grants. Think of having a fiscal sponsor or agent as falling under someone's umbrella.

Usually your fiscal agent is an organization that

- Shares a similar mission as yours
- Has an accounting staff
- Has a proven track record of accomplishments
- Has years of experience

What type of relationship you have with your fiscal agent varies. Your fiscal agent may handle all of your money or just your grant money. You may approve the day-to-day transactions of your nonprofit and/or pass your bills and invoices on to your fiscal agent for processing and payment. Some fiscal agents process all payments and invoices as well as prepare financial status reports for your grants.

It all depends on your arrangement with your fiscal agent. Some fiscal agents receive an administrative fee of 5 percent or more for taking care of your accounting and reporting requirements. Some fiscal agents don't charge anything for the services they provide.

To qualify for most government and foundation grants, an organization must hold the IRS 501(c)(3) status of a nonprofit charitable organization. Some new organizations that haven't received their nonprofit status get a fiscal agent with 501(c)(3) status to help them qualify for grants until they receive their own nonprofit status.

If your organization is small, relatively new to the nonprofit scene (less than 3 years old), and needs someone to take care of its financial responsibilities, then finding a fiscal agent may be for you. To find a fiscal agent, contact

- Your state nonprofit resource center
- The community foundation in your area
- Your local United Way

Outsourcing the job

To *outsource* a job means to shift the responsibilities to someone outside your organization. There are some advantages and disadvantages to outsourcing work:

- **Advantages:** You don't have to pay payroll taxes or benefits for the employee, and if you're not satisfied with the services, you can always terminate the contract. You also use them on an as-needed basis.

- **Disadvantages:** You may not be able to terminate your contract if the contractor falls short on his duties. Most outsourcing arrangements involve contractual agreements for a certain amount of time for a set fee. Also, you may have to pay higher fees to the consultant, and you have limited control over the contractor.

You can outsource computer services, bookkeeping, accounting, grant writing, auditing, and legal services by hiring consultants in these areas.

When looking for people to outsource to it's best to get referrals from your peers. You can thumb through the phone book, do a search on the Internet, or run an ad in the newspaper, but referrals are best. Even if you outsource your accounting services, you still need to know and understand the basic steps of the accounting process. It's impossible to manage an organization without understanding the consequences of your financial actions.

Hiring an independent auditor

Hiring an independent auditor to audit your financial statement is a must if you want to qualify for government grants and lend credibility to your organization's financial statements. According to GAAS, all nonprofit financial statements must be audited by an outside independent auditor. Some states require nonprofits with a certain annual income to have their books audited. Plus, your board may want your books examined by an outside auditor.

Picking an auditor to give you a valid independent audit doesn't have to be a grueling process. Your board selects a committee to take care of this for you. Only a CPA can offer a professional opinion about your financial statements. Of course, you also can have your statements compiled and reviewed for in-house purposes, such as for staff and board meetings. Turn to Chapter 20 for what you need to know about having your financial statements audited.

Choosing Your Accounting Method

Before starting to keep track of things, you need to decide which of two methods you'll use to account for your activities. Will you use the cash basis or the accrual basis of accounting?

When you choose the *cash basis,* transactions are recorded only when cash changes hands, not when a purchase is made. When you make a purchase, you have several ways you can pay. Suppose, for example, you run to your nearest office supply store to stock up on pencils, paper, staples, sticky notes, and whatever other fun items you run across. You can pay for these goodies either with cash or a credit card, or you can have the goods charged to your account, which you will pay later. If you pay with cash or a credit card, the transaction shows up in your books immediately. ***Note:*** Although using a credit card is a cash transaction, you treat it as a payable transaction for simplicity and then adjust it at the end of the year. When you pay by writing a check, that's considered a cash transaction.

If you decide to charge the same stuff to your account, under the cash basis, you don't indicate the transaction until the bill is paid. If you're using the *accrual basis* of accounting, transactions are treated the same, no matter how they're paid for. You record transactions at the moment a purchase is made, whether you pay for it or charge it. So if you buy those nifty office supplies on credit and pay the bill four weeks later, the transaction is recorded when you bought the supplies.

You can choose to keep your accounting records on a cash or accrual basis, but your financial statements should be prepared using the accrual basis of accounting. The major difference between cash and accrual basis has to do with when transactions are recorded.

Keeping track of the cash

Cash is a medium of exchange. Cash is currency, and in accounting, cash is a current asset. Cash equivalents are instruments that can be immediately converted into cash and include

- Petty cash, usually kept to make small office purchases
- Checking account balances
- Certificates of deposits (CDs)
- Savings account balances

Recording transactions using the cash method means that you record revenues only when cash is received and record expenses only when they're paid. This is the easiest method to use because if you make a purchase on account, and the bill doesn't come out until next month, you don't record the transaction until you pay the bill. A bookkeeper may only know how to account for transactions using the cash method.

When preparing your organization's financial statements, a CPA can easily convert your cash basis accounting information into GAAP-required accrual basis information.

Accrual basis of accounting

The accrual basis of accounting dictates when revenues and expenses should be recorded on the books. To *accrue* means to accumulate or increase. Under the cash method, you record revenues and expenses at the moment cash exchanges hand. Under the accrual basis, revenues and expenses are recognized when a transaction takes place, whether cash exchanges hands or not.

For example, if you buy office supplies on account, you record the transaction in your accounting books when you make the purchase and again when the bill is paid. To record such a transaction, you debit your supplies and credit accounts payable for the cost of the office supplies. When the bill is paid, you debit accounts payables and credit cash.

The accrual basis gives you a more accurate account of what is owed at any given time. It also requires end-of-the-period adjustments for salaries and other expenses. Keep in mind, your accounting period may close, but you may have some expenses, such as prepaid subscriptions, prepaid insurance, or salaries, that cross more than one period. The accrual basis of accounting charges expenses to the period they are used.

Running Numbers on Your Assets

When you buy items such as printers, computers, cars, or other stuff that lasts more than a year, you need to place these items on your books as *assets*. To record an asset, you record it in your books at the price you paid for it.

Because some assets, such as computers, may last for several years, you need to write off the cost *(depreciate)* over the item's lifespan. For example, if a computer is expected to last three years, you'll need to depreciate it over three years. *Depreciable assets* are commonly referred to as *plant, property, and equipment (PPE)*. The following sections explain how to put a number to your assets and how to depreciate them.

When writing off the cost of assets, you never depreciate the cost of land. You need to depreciate the costs of all other assets classified as PPE that last longer than a year.

Evaluating assets by original cost or fair market value

Prices fluctuate just like the wind. You may pay $1,000 for something on Tuesday and then discover that it went on sale the next day for $500. When this happens, how much is the item worth? What amount should you record in your books? Maybe you should return the item, get a refund, and buy it again.

Don't go to any extra trouble because the answer is simple. All assets should be recorded at their purchased price. Think about this for a moment. If you purchased the item on Wednesday, it would be recorded on your books for $500; but if you bought the item on Tuesday, it would be recorded in the books at $1,000.

An *original cost* is the purchase price paid for an asset. *Historical cost* is also referred to as original cost, and it's an approach that keeps assets on the books at their purchased price with no regard for inflation or the economy.

If all assets are recorded on the books at their original cost, then unless an item depreciates, your books reflect your historic values. However, values can change due to market conditions or from an assets use. Accountants have been debating about recording assets at their original cost or market value for years. I don't expect the debate to stop anytime soon.

Presently, GAAP requires depreciable assets to be recorded at historic value. Depreciation is used to reduce an asset's value due to the asset's use over time. You can't take any additional adjustments for estimated changes in the asset's market value because market values for depreciable assets are only estimates. They aren't used to avoid the possibility of someone using the information to manipulate reported financial results.

In contrast to historical cost, *fair market value* is the price that an interested buyer would be willing to pay and an interested seller would be willing to accept for a particular asset. If you had to liquidate all of your assets tomorrow, then fair market value would be very important to you.

You record investments (marketable securities) at fair market value and adjust for changes in their value. These adjustments affect income. In this instance, market values aren't estimates; they're readily determined, and so there is no room to manipulate financial results.

Grasping depreciation methods

To *depreciate* means to write off the expense of an item over its expected useful life, less any *salvage value* (the amount that can be recovered after an asset's service life). When you purchase equipment or a building, you pay a set amount. As time passes, these assets lose some of their value. Accounting allows you to write off a portion of the cost by depreciating it as an expense. For example, suppose you buy a building for $450,000, and the building is expected to be useful to you for ten years, at which time its salvage value will be $50,000. You have $400,000 of depreciation expense to write off for the building over those ten years.

You get to choose which method you use to write off the cost of the building. The amount of depreciation expense you get to write off in any year depends on which depreciation method you choose. Because depreciation is an expense that's subtracted from revenue, it directly affects your bottom line.

The executive director and board, with the advice of an accountant, decide which depreciation method to use. You can use a different method for different assets. The most important thing to remember here is that you want to reflect the most accurate value of all of your assets. It's important for you to know the value of the assets you own.

In all that you do, you want to fairly present your financial information in the most accurate way. Some financial types have started discussing how assets are valued on the books compared to their market value. Some organizations have assets that are overvalued on their books, and then when those assets are evaluated, the previous value that has been indicated on the organization's statement of financial position isn't correct.

I suggest for most things that you use the straight-line method of depreciation because it equally writes off the cost over the years. For some assets, such as computers or cars, you may want to use an accelerated method to accurately reflect the asset's true value. You know how you've heard that the value of a new car depreciates the minute you drive it off the lot? Well, the same is true with computers because new technology is being invented all the time. (Keep reading to understand the differences between different depreciation methods.)

Employ the *consistency principle* by choosing a depreciation method and then being consistent with its use. This doesn't mean that you can never change from one accounting method to another. When you change methods, you need to disclose and explain the nature of the change and the effects on income in the notes to the financial statements.

Choosing declining depreciation

Declining depreciation, also called *accelerated depreciation,* is any method that writes off larger amounts of depreciation expense in the early years of an asset's life and smaller amounts in the later years. Declining depreciation can be used on any item classified as *plant, property, or equipment (PPE)*.

When to use this type of depreciation method depends on the use and life of the asset. Assets with shorter lives (less than ten years) usually lose most of their value in their earlier years, so declining depreciation methods are warranted. Longer lived assets tend to lose their value evenly over time, and straight-line depreciation is adequate for these assets (see the next section). Although the IRS and GAAP offer some guidance, use your professional judgment or solicit the advice of an accountant or CPA.

For tax purposes, the IRS has a declining depreciation system that provides useful lives for classes of assets and tables of depreciation percentages for various depreciation methods and asset lives. Computer software generally has a useful life of three years, most automobiles have a useful life of three to five years, other furnishings and equipment have useful lives of seven years, and you can depreciate a building over 39 years. The IRS system doesn't take salvage value into account, but the tables are useful and can be applied to amounts adjusted for salvage value. IRS Publication 946, How to Depreciate Property, is a good source of information about depreciation methods. You can find the publication online at www.irs.gov/publications/p946/index.html.

Going with straight-line

The most widely used method of depreciation is the straight-line method. The *straight-line depreciation method* allocates the same amount of depreciation for each year over the expected life of an asset.

When in doubt about which method to use, choose the straight-line method because it's the most conservative approach. The equation for the straight-line depreciation method is

(Cost − Residual value) ÷ Useful life

Residual value is the same as salvage value. It's the value placed on an asset after it's fully depreciated. For example, suppose you expect to use your computer system for three years, and you pay $30,000 with an expected salvage value of $3,000. Plug these numbers into the equation, and your depreciation expense using the straight-line method is $9,000 per year.

($30,000 − $3,000) ÷ 3 years = $9,000 depreciation per year for 3 years

Selecting double-declining balance

In a nutshell, the *double-declining balance depreciation method* is twice the rate of straight-line. The major difference between the double-declining balance and the straight-line method of depreciation is the amount of depreciation in each year of an asset's useful life. With double-declining balance, as opposed to straight-line, more depreciation is expensed in an asset's early years, and less is expensed in its later years.

Use the double-declining balance when depreciating assets that depreciate at an accelerated rate. For example, computer equipment depreciates faster than you can take it out of the box, so this is the perfect type of asset to apply the double-declining method to.

To calculate the double-declining balance method, you must first compute the rate of depreciation for the straight-line method. Then double this rate. You don't deduct the salvage value from the original cost of the asset when computing the asset's depreciable base. However, you stop taking depreciation expense when the asset's *net book value* (original cost less accumulated depreciation) reaches the asset's salvage value. GAAP doesn't allow a depreciable asset's net book value to be less than its salvage value.

Returning to the example from the previous section, suppose your computer system has a total cost of $30,000, a salvage value of $3,000, and is expected to last three years. Figure 2-1 shows a comparison of the straight-line and double-declining balance depreciation methods.

Straight-Line Depreciation Method		Calulating the Double-Declining Balance Method	
(Cost – Salvage value) divided by useful life		The straight-line rate is 1/3 or 33.33% per year	
$30,000 – $3,000 = $27,000/3 years = $9,000 per year for three years		Depreciation rate for double-decling balance method is 33% x 2 = 66.66%	
Depreciation for 2008 $27,000/3 = $9,000	$9,000	Depreciation for 2008 $30,000 x 66%	$19,800
Depreciation for 2009	$9,000	Depreciation for 2009 $30,000 – 19,800 = 10,200	$6,732
Depreciation for 2010	$9,000	$10,200 x 66%	
Total Depreciation	$27,000	Depreciation for 2010 Limited to amount that makes total depreciation taken = $27,000	$468
		Total Depreciation Cost – salvage value = total amount allowed for depreciation	$27,000

Figure 2-1: A comparison of the straight-line and double-declining depreciation methods.

The useful life of the computer is 3 years.

Keeping an Eye on Your Assets

It's virtually impossible to know if an employee will steal. You can do a background check on potential employees and give them assessment exams to find out what type of person they really are. Some of the major retailers ask a series of questions that gives them a good indication of a person's moral character. You can order or design a similar test for your staff. Also, you can install security cameras in your building that record everything that takes place.

In addition to implementing protective procedures regarding whom your nonprofit organization hires, you can institute internal controls that directly monitor your organization's financial holdings. A good system of internal controls puts some checks and balances in place to protect against employee theft. The following sections give you some ideas about how to keep your assets safe.

The next time you're ready to hire an employee, perform a background check on her. You can even get the potential employee to pay for the background check. Oftentimes this can be done through your state's attorney general's office or other law enforcement agencies.

Protecting your nonprofit's physical assets

Tracking and keeping up with inventory is a must to protect your nonprofit's assets. Portable equipment like a laptop computer is so easy to walk away with. To safeguard your valuables, require all equipment to be checked out before leaving the building. Furthermore, some organizations have their employees sign statements agreeing to have their final paychecks withheld until all equipment is returned in good condition.

Limiting access to certain areas of interest can protect your assets. Consider installing security cameras and key access cards, as well as keeping your petty cash drawer locked and a book handy to record all transactions with receipts to support them.

Setting internal controls

Internal controls are procedures and policies that you establish to limit the possibility of accounting errors, fraud, theft, or *embezzlement* (taking something of value from someone who trusts you).

Keeping some office doors locked and areas off limits is just one kind of internal control to protect important records and data from manipulation. Other internal controls are less obvious than locked doors.

Establishing checks and balances

The founding fathers of the United States knew that human nature is subject to error, and they established the system of checks and balances to provide constant oversight and accountability within the federal government. You can apply a similar system of internal control by which you have checkpoints to balance your books. For example, some organizations do a physical count of all inventories to see if anything is missing or unaccounted for.

Checks and balances in your organization not only can help you avoid an audit finding but also can protect your assets. Start with the following checks and balances and then expand upon them for protections that are even more specific to your organization and its operations:

- ✔ Require two signatures on all checks over a set amount (usually more than a typical payroll tax deposit amount)
- ✔ Separate duties between your record keeper and the person handling cash
- ✔ Record employees' hours daily on timesheets
- ✔ Require all invoices for payment to be reviewed and authorized

Your nonprofit's policies and procedures manual should present and explain your organization's checks and balances in such a way that all the steps are clearly defined. Most nonprofits have written policies about personnel, travel, and purchasing procedures. Put steps in writing about how to deal with personnel matters. Include the limits on travel pay for mileage, lodging, and so forth. Also, create rules to deal with large purchases of, say, more than $500. You need to have a plan for how these types of situations should be handled to bring structure to your organization.

Separating employees duties

You can place some roadblocks in your accounting system that prevent employees from stealing from your nonprofit (or at the very least, make it really hard). You can establish segregation of duties, which is a type of internal control. *Segregation of duties* assigns different steps of a process to different people. So, for example, you don't allow the same person who opens the mail to be responsible for making deposits. Think about how easy it would be for the person opening the mail to borrow cash payments.

Following are some examples of segregation of duties that you can apply to your nonprofit:

- ✔ **Accounts payable and receivable:** The person approving payments shouldn't be authorized to make purchases without some oversight by a second party. If yours is a large organization, your accounts payable office should be a separate entity from the accounts receivable unit.

- ✔ **Business mail and check deposits:** One person can open business mail and log in each check that's received, but someone else should be responsible for making deposits into your bank account.

Auditors write up many smaller nonprofits not because anything is wrong with their books but because they don't have adequate logical segregation of staff duties.

Insuring or bonding nonprofit employees

Checks and balances and segregation of duties establish some internal controls (refer to the preceding sections), but you can take your internal protections a step further with risk-management strategies. Insuring or bonding your nonprofit employees ensures that your nonprofit organization faces minimal risk of loss in case of mistakes or malfeasance by the people who manage your organization.

A *bond* is a debt security that guarantees to pay you for acts committed by board members or employees, and it protects you from employee or board theft. A bond is actually paid to you by the bonding company, but the person bonded reimburses the bonding company. Any reputable bonding entity will share some helpful tips about bonding your employees.

You determine the type and degree of insurance and bonded protections your nonprofit needs based on an assessment of your organization. First, you need to evaluate the potential risk and think about how much money is being handled. What is the value of what you own? How much equity do you have in your organization? How much money do you have in your savings and checking accounts? These are some of the questions you'll need to answer to determine how much insurance is needed. For example, your donors list is a valuable asset that you must safeguard (turn to Chapter 7 for an explanation of donors lists). You can protect your donors list by respecting those individuals who don't want to be disclosed to the general public. Your donors list should never be sold to another organization to solicit funds.

Do some research by consulting with a few insurance companies and comparing rates. Your board of directors is responsible for finding an insurance company and approving the purchase of bonding insurance. As with most things concerning the management of your nonprofit, your board is responsible for making key decisions.

Chapter 3

Introducing Financial Statements

If you've ever made a major purchase or tried to secure a large sum of money to purchase a home, the lending institution, mortgage company, or bank probably asked for personal financial information about what you earn *(income),* what you own *(assets),* and what you owe *(liabilities).* In essence, the lender wanted to know your true financial position. Although this example is on a personal level, for-profit businesses and nonprofit organizations need to access the same information in the form of financial statements.

Nonprofit organizations have similar financial transactions and needs as for-profit businesses. *Financial statements* describe and summarize operating activities, obligations, and economic resources for a given period, usually one year. A wide assortment of individuals and entities evaluate these statements to get a clear picture of your nonprofit's true financial position. Donors, investors, and creditors evaluate these reports when they're deciding whether to donate or lend money to your organization.

This chapter gives you a quick overview on why these financial statements are important and which statements your nonprofit needs to use. The chapters in Part IV then delve deeper into these statements and show you how your nonprofit can use them.

The Lowdown on Financial Statements: Why They're Important

Nonprofits are granted tax-exempt status by the government to enable organizations to provide services in the public's interest. In exchange for tax-exempt status (owing no federal corporate income taxes), these organizations are expected and required to perform and record financial functions in an effective, efficient manner. (See more about tax-exempt status in Chapter 14.)

Your nonprofit doesn't pay corporate taxes, but you're required to submit information to the IRS about your activities — annually. Your nonprofit will file a Form 990, Return of Organization Exempt from Income Tax, that tells where your money came from, who you paid, and how much you paid. Don't worry; no money is due, just information. You need to file this information every year by the 15th day of the fifth month after the end of a tax-exempt organization's fiscal year. For a calendar year, the deadline is May 15. (Refer to Chapter 14 for more info about Form 990.)

Not only is Big Brother watching over your shoulder, but the public has your organization under close watch because, in essence, the public is your employer. The very reason for a nonprofit's existence — to serve the public's interest — opens up financial information for public review. Therefore, your financial records are considered public domain. Because every move you make and every transaction you record are subject to public scrutiny, properly tracking every transaction by recording and keeping adequate books is essential.

If you want continued support from the public, then disclosing and reporting your organization's operating activities, economic resources, and obligations are in your best interest. Not only is it in your best interest, but it's required by law via a tax return.

A complete set of financial statements for nonprofit organizations includes the following:

- Independent auditor's report (see Chapter 20 for more info)
- Statement of activities, also called the *income statement*
- Statement of financial position, also referred to as the *balance sheet*
- Cash flow statement
- Statement of functional expenses
- Notes to financial statements

I explain each of these reports in more detail in this chapter.

When you have a small block of time, log on to www.guidestar.org and look up your favorite (or your own) nonprofit organization. You can find out where its money came from, who it paid, and how much. All Form 990s are open for public review.

In the following sections I give a brief overview of how you can use these statements to benefit and sustain your nonprofit. Tracking your income and spending helps you stay on track financially. Doing so is essential for you to know where your nonprofit's money comes from and where it goes.

Seeing the benefits of tracking the money

Financial statements summarize and describe nonprofit activity over a period of time. They should show that you have fulfilled your end of the bargain in being held accountable. They also indicate whether you've been a responsible steward or sloppy manager of nonprofit resources.

Sloppy management or inadequate accounting records can prove detrimental to your organization's reputation. The bulk of your support comes from contributions made by private donors, government entities, foundations, and corporate givers. If they see that you haven't been responsible with their money, they're likely to stop supporting you.

These statements also serve folks within the organization. People within your nonprofit use these financial statements to forecast the organization's needs and create plans to address those needs.

Who uses these statements

Without financial statements, planning and forecasting your organization's future needs is nearly impossible. Internal and external users rely on a nonprofit organization's financial statements to make important decisions. Managers of nonprofit organizations use financial statements to make decisions concerning the organization. People outside of the nonprofit use the documents to decide whether to make a donation. I go into more specifics about these uses in the following sections.

Internal users

The following individuals are examples of internal users of nonprofit financial statements:

- ✔ **Executive director:** This person is hired by the board of directors to preside over the day-to-day management of a nonprofit. She uses financial statements to see the big picture of the organization's finances.

- ✔ **Nonprofit executive manager:** This person oversees accounting, information systems, marketing, personnel, and fundraising. He is likely to follow the organization's finances more closely.

- ✔ **Nonprofit accountant:** He tracks and accounts for your financial activities. His work forms the basis of your financial statements.

- ✔ **Board members:** These folks are responsible for oversight of the entire operation. They use your financial statements to make sure the nonprofit is headed in the right direction.

Internal users have a greater need than external users do to review financial statements. Internal users must compare actual versus budget data on a month-by-month basis. *Actual* refers to results that have happened, and *budget* refers to anticipated results. A budget is a projection. It predicts future anticipated revenues and expenses that may change. Past financial information can be a good gauge of future revenues. (Check out Chapter 8 for more info on projecting a budget.)

Board members and executive directors rely on financial statements to guide their decision making. These reports tell how much money the organization received in the past year and how much it spent. They also reveal whether an organization can pay its debt. For example, the last figure on the statement of activities is either a positive or a negative number. This number reveals how well the organization performed financially over the last year. Information like this helps executive directors and board members do financial forecasting. Information from current statements can be compared to prior years.

External users

External users also rely on your nonprofit's financial statements. Those external users are

- ✔ **Bankers/creditors:** The first statement your banker will want to see is the statement of financial position. Just like all creditors, your banker wants to know if you have something of value to secure a loan.

- ✔ **Public donors:** They are public charities and government entities.

- ✔ **Private donors:** They are individuals, corporations, and private foundations that donate to your organization. They invest in your cause.

- ✔ **Independent auditors:** Your independent auditor needs copies of your financial statements to verify the fairness of representation of your finances. External auditors use financial statements from prior years to detect significant change. If a significant change is noticed, then you're required to explain. For example, if you have a large decrease or increase in cash without a clear explanation, then a red flag is raised. (See Chapter 20 for more about audits.)

- ✔ **Public watchdog groups:** These groups keep an eye on nonprofits. Their underlying motive is to expose your nonprofit to the general public as being a fraud or counterfeit if you're not being a good steward and doing

what you're supposed to be doing. Public watchdogs go to extreme measures to expose you if you're not doing the right thing. After the media
gets wind that you may not be doing what you should be doing with the
money, you may be tried in public.

Using Financial Statements to Your Advantage

Have you heard the phrase, "Everyone has to answer to someone"? Well, this
is true for nonprofits too. Life would be easier if nonprofits could just focus
on the people and causes they help and not have to worry about finances,
but this isn't the case. Call financial statements your financial scorecards; if
you don't keep score, someone else will tally it for you.

The quickest way to identify problems in an organization is to read the financial statements and notes to the financial statements. They can help managers identify and correct potential problems, and they can reveal to external
users whether your nonprofit uses its funds responsibly. The statements
should be accurate, easily readable, understandable, and done in a timely
fashion.

The headings on all financial statements answer the who, what, and when. The
who is the name of your organization; the *what* is the name of the statement;
and the *when* is the time period covered.

In the following sections, I list a few of the more important things that financial statements can be used for.

Assist with grant proposals

Whenever you submit a grant proposal, you're usually required to attach
copies of your organization's audited financial statements. Audited financial
statements must be compiled by an independent accounting firm or CPA. The
CPA provides an opinion on whether the information in the financial statements can be relied upon. (See Chapter 20 for more on audits.)

Government entities (federal agencies), corporate, and foundation grant
makers want an overview of your nonprofit's financial activities and its ability
to properly manage its finances. Many want to see if your organization has
the capacity to manage a grant. Trust me, grant makers know just what to
look for to determine if your organization is a wise investment. Being a good
steward of your organization's finances has its rewards.

A glance at the financial statements can either make you or break you. For example, if your organization has an operating budget of $25,000 and you're applying for a $150,000 grant, do you think it matters to the funder that you've never managed such a large sum of money? Yes, it does.

Allow you to track donations

Accurate financial statements allow internal users to project and anticipate potential changes in giving trends. You need to keep a close eye on changes in donations to properly project financial problems. Analyzing giving trends allows internal users to make decisions faster about increasing fundraising goals.

Keeping an accurate record of projected or pledged donations versus actual donations affects a nonprofit's ability to pay bills and meet payroll. Balancing the inflow with the outflow can feel like a juggling act. Your ultimate objective is to ensure you have enough cash to pay the bills.

All nonprofit organizations are required to keep a donors list on file. Your auditor will test your list by randomly contacting some of the donors. Tracking all donations isn't an option; it's a requirement. For more information about tracking donations, see Chapter 7.

Track nonprofit activities

Many nonprofit organizations receive income from government grants, foundations, corporate grants, fundraising activities, and donations. The financial statements, particularly the cash flow statement (refer to "Developing the cash flow statement" section later in this chapter for more info), let you keep track of important nonprofit activities, such as how much income will be allocated to pay for specific needs.

Nonprofit organizations must track income and expenses carefully to know and understand their financial situation. A good place to start is by balancing the nonprofit checkbook, which tracks expenses and deposits made into your checking account.

Record transactions in the checkbook register when transactions take place. Your checkbook register will contain records of every donation, all expenses paid, and a running balance of cash on hand. You'll know by your balance how closely you need to monitor your checkbook. (Chapter 7 covers how to balance your nonprofit's checkbook.)

Indicate lawsuits: Contingent liabilities

Accurate financial statements also provide important information about incidents or potential liabilities, such as lawsuits, in the notes section of the statements. This information reveals how much money may be paid out. If your organization is facing any pending litigation, and it appears that the charges are true or that the defendant will win the suit, then you should disclose a contingent liability in the notes to the financial statements. A *contingent liability* is a potential liability pending a certain action, such as a court matter to be decided by a settlement, a judge, and/or jury.

With this information, internal and external users get a better picture of your true financial status and any potential liabilities. Check out the nearby sidebar about how insurance can safeguard your nonprofit from lawsuits.

Identifying the Financial Statements

In order to show an accurate picture of your nonprofit's bottom line, you prepare financial statements. These statements show how much revenue has come in, what your expenses are, and whether you're in the red or black. The following sections give a quick outline of the different financial statements your nonprofit needs to compile and prepare at the end of your accounting period.

Reading the statement of activities

The *statement of activities* (also known as the *income statement;* the *statement of revenue, expenses, and changes in fund balances;* or the *profit and loss statement*) reveals where the nonprofit money came from, where it went, and how a nonprofit has operated during a given period. It reveals whether your organization was profitable for the year. Figure 3-1 shows a sample.

All grants, contributions, interest income, and gains on the sale of marketable securities or sale of stock — basically, any money you bring in — are *revenue* line items on the statement of activities, followed by all *expenses* — any money you spend, whether it's for salaries, new programs, or events to raise more money.

The first item to pay attention to when reading a statement of activities appears at the end of the statement. After you add all the revenues and subtract all the expenses, you'll either have a surplus (net profit) or deficit (net loss). A *net profit* is when revenues are more than expenses, while a *net loss* is when expenses are more than revenues. You want to know whether the bottom line is a positive number or a negative number.

OASIS, Inc.
Statement of Activities
For Year Ended December 31, 20XX

	Unrestricted	Temporarily Restricted	Total
Revenue			
Contributions	$150,743	12,500	$163,243
Event income:			
Annual Conference	47,818		47,818
Mentoring Symposium	64,790		64,790
Special events	23,333		23,333
Christmas Gala	45,833		45,833
Total Event Income	181,774		181,774
Other Programs:	6806		6,806
Interest Income	550		550
Miscellaneous Income	36		36
Total Revenue	339,909	12,500	352,409
Expenses			
Program			
Mentoring Program	155,275		155,275
Tutoring Program	93,535		93,535
Total Program	248,810		248,810
Management and general	57,055		57,055
Fundraising	14,536		14,536
Total Expenses	320,401		320,401
Change in Net Assets	19,508	12,500	32,008
Net assets, beginning	102,992		102,992
Net Assets, End	$ 122,500	$ 12,500	$135,000

Figure 3-1:
A statement
of activities.

Protecting your nonprofit with liability insurance

If your nonprofit has direct contact with vulnerable people, such as children, the elderly, or individuals with developmental disabilities, you probably should protect yourself from potential lawsuits. To protect your nonprofit from potential disaster, consider speaking with your board about liability insurance. Liability insurance is important because it protects your assets.

Insurance can protect against lawsuits for any of the following:

- ✔ Alleged violations
- ✔ Breach of contract
- ✔ Discrimination

- ✔ Fraudulent conduct, reports, or financial statements
- ✔ Improper self-dealing
- ✔ Misuse of restricted funds
- ✔ Personal injury
- ✔ Sexual harassment
- ✔ Violation of state and federal laws
- ✔ Wrongful termination

If your organization has any of the preceding charges pending litigation, you should consult with an attorney.

At the very bottom of the statement of activities you find net income (or net assets). *Net income* is the difference between revenues and expenses. This figure is transferred to the statement of financial position as an asset (see the "Working with the statement of financial position" section for more on these statements).

Anytime you see the word *net* in relation to financial statements, it means whatever remains after subtracting deductions, expenses, or losses. A good way to think of net is to think of a paystub. You have gross pay less deductions, and the employee takes home the net pay.

Although the statement of activities may be the first statement that comes to mind when you think of financial statements, the information is useful, but limited. The statement of activities doesn't give the full financial position. You also need to rely on the other financial statements I explain in this chapter. This section gives you a starting point to help you grasp the statement of activities better. I cover this statement in more detail in Chapter 15.

Figuring out FASB

The Financial Accounting Standards Board (FASB) sets standards for nonprofit organizations concerning financial matters. To understand what it is and what it does, think of the agency as the financial rule maker. The Securities and Exchange Commission (SEC) authorized FASB to establish financial accounting and reporting standards for publicly held companies. When you have to compile or read a statement of activities, statement of financial position, or another page filled with accounting numbers, you have the FASB to thank.

Working with the statement of financial position

The *statement of financial position* (also referred to as the *balance sheet* or the *statement of changes in fund balance*) reports the amounts of a nonprofit's assets, liabilities, and net assets as of a specified date (see Chapter 2 for explanations of these terms). The statement of financial position (see Figure 3-2 for an example) is a true indicator of financial health as of a given date for a specified period.

A quick glance at the statement of financial position reveals the organization's solvency. *Solvency* indicates whether an organization can meet its obligations on time. If current assets are less than current liabilities, then you need to sell some investments, borrow some money, or hold a fundraiser to stay financially healthy. (*Current* means now or within one year.) Flip to Chapter 16 for more nitty gritty on this statement.

Developing the cash flow statement

The *cash flow statement* (also referred to as the *statement of changes in financial position* or the *cash flow of fund statement*) records cash coming in and cash going out. This report (refer to Figure 3-3) isn't done just at the end of the year; most nonprofits like to keep a close eye on the timing of donations to ensure they have enough money on hand to pay their debts, whether it's an employee's salary or a bank loan. This report is done monthly, quarterly, and annually.

The most crucial internal statement needed on a monthly basis, particularly for your executive director and board members, is the cash flow statement because it determines whether the lights stay on. Face it: Your nonprofit isn't operating on a fixed income. Its livelihood depends on donations from others.

OASIS, Inc.
Statement of Financial Position
December 31, 20XX

Assets

Current assets		
Cash:		
Checking Account	$	69,000
Mentoring Checking	$	22,193
Tutoring Checking	$	7,794
Money Market Account	$	13
Total Cash	$	99,000
Certificates of Deposit	$	66,500
Accounts Receivables	$	5,500
Total Current Assets:	$	171,000
Fixed Assets:		
Office Equipment	$	25,000
Less Accumulated Depreciation	$	(21,000)
Net Fixed Assets	$	4,000
Total Assets	**$**	**175,000**

Liabilities and Net Assets

Liabilities:		
Accounts Payable	$	2,900
Deferred Revenue	$	37,100
Total Current Liabilities	$	40,000
Net Assets:		
Temporary Restricted	$	12,500
Unrestricted:		
Designated for Scholarships	$	45,000
Undesignated	$	77,500
Total Unrestricted	$	122,500
Total Net Assets	$	135,000
Total Liabilities and Net Assets	**$**	**175,000**

Figure 3-2:
An example
statement
of financial
position.

Donations can fluctuate, so your cash flow will go up and down within any given month. If you make a sudden move while driving your car on the interstate at 70 mph, you're subject to crash. The same is true of your nonprofit; if sudden changes in giving trends take place, the walls may tumble down. Keeping a close eye on cash can prevent potential disaster.

The cash flow statement resembles a monthly household budget. When you subtract your expenses from your income, you get either a surplus or a deficit. A *surplus* is a positive number, which means your income is more than your expenses. A *deficit* is a negative number, which means your expenses are more than your income.

OASIS, Inc. Cash Flow Statement For Year Ended December 31, 20XX	
Cash flow from operating activities	
Receipts:	
Contributions	157,148
Events Receipts	214,820
Other Receipts	7,475
Total Receipts	379,443
Cash Disbursements	–313,020
Net cash provided by operating activities	**66,423**
Cash flow from investing activities	
Purchases of Fixed Assets	–2,363
Purchases of Certificates of Deposits	–8,716
Net cash used by investing activities	**–11,079**
Net increase in cash	55,344
Cash and cash equivalents, beginning of year	41,739
Cash and cash equivalents, end of year	$ **97,083**

Figure 3-3: A sample cash flow statement.

In a nutshell, the cash flow statement reveals how liquid your organization is. *Liquid* refers to your ability to easily convert your current assets into cash without losing your socks. Liquid assets have the following characteristics:

✔ The sale of a liquid asset doesn't result in significant loss.

✔ A liquid asset usually can be converted into cash within 24 hours.

Chapter 17 provides more in-depth coverage on the cash flow statement.

TIP

Grasping the statement of functional expense

The *statement of functional expense* presents expenses listed on the statement of activities based on their use. The statement of functional expense separates expenses based on how much time was spent doing something. At the end of the day, everyone wants to know how you spent your time and money. Allocating expenses provides an accurate gauge when analyzing expenses. For example, you can take the total fundraising expenses and divide it by total expenses and get a better handle on how much was spent on fundraising costs. Without adequate accounts for time, it's virtually impossible to know how much your organization actually spent.

Generally, functional expenses are classified as

- ✔ Program
- ✔ Management and general
- ✔ Fundraising expenses

Figure 3-4 shows a sample statement of functional expense. This breakdown shows exactly how much was spent on what. I talk more about the analysis of these expenses in Chapter 18.

Documenting the notes to the financial statements

You can find the most pertinent information about your nonprofit's financial situation in the *notes to the financial statements,* commonly referred to as *footnotes.* Accurately reporting your organization's financial statement is a matter of ethics. As a nonprofit manager, executive director, or board member, you have a responsibility to stay on top of the organization's financial situation.

OASIS, Inc.
Statements of Functional Expense
For Year Ended December 31, 20XX

	Program		Management & General	Fundraising	Total
	Mentoring	**Tutoring**			
Advertising			1,140		1,140
Awards	11,275				11,275
Bank Service Charges			203		203
Board Meeting			3,287		3,287
Speaking Contest	5,800				5,800
Mentor's Sports Day	13,000				13,000
Conference Registration	694	694	596	298	2,282
Credit Card Fee			1,451		1,451
Depreciation	360	360	667	154	1,541
Dues and Subscriptions	681	681	1,265	292	2,919
Equipment	54	54	31	16	155
Interest				158	158
Liability Insurance			933		933
Marketing			4,055		11,055
Miscellaneous			616		616
Payroll Taxes	4,569	4,569	1,632	816	11,586
Postage and delivery	715	715	441	221	2,092
Mentorship Training	17,500				17,500
Mentor's Retreat	12,500				12,500
Printing and Publication	5,091	5,091	625	312	11,119
Rent	2,378	2,378	787	394	5,937
Mentoring Project	8,703				8,703
Tutoring Project		9,708			9,708
Salaries	57,109	57,109	21,726	10,656	146,600
Sponsorship	4,100				4,100
Supplies	311		327		638
Professional Services			1,706		1,706
Telecommunications	1,626	1,626	929	485	4,666
Travel	8,809	10,550	11,325	734	31,418
Web Site			3,313		3,313
Totals	**$ 155,275**	**$ 93,535**	**$ 57,055**	**$ 14,536**	**$ 320,401**

Figure 3-4:
An example statement of functional expense.

Reading the notes can provide to the internal and external users additional information that may greatly influence their judgment about the future livelihood of your organization. In the notes, you can find the following:

- ✔ **Summary of accounting policies:** This section discloses choices made from different accounting methods, such as cash or accrual basis of recording transactions. The difference between cash and accrual basis is in the timing of when you record transactions (see Chapter 2 for a full explanation).

- ✔ **Detailed information about all the statements:** This section includes info about all financial statements, such as property, equipment, and debts.

- ✔ **Contingencies:** These are future events that may occur but whose occurrence is not certain.

For example, if you notice drastic changes or fluctuations in net assets, one quick way to detect what has happened is to look at the notes. All changes in accounting procedures and methods must be disclosed in the notes. The following sections point out what information you need to include in your nonprofit's notes to the financial statements. (For more info about the notes and a sample document, see Chapter 19.)

Explain changes in accounting methods

If you modify your accounting methods, the notes to the financial statements is the place to explain the whys and wherefores of what you did. Changes in accounting methods directly affect an organization's finances. Tinkering with the accounting methods can make your organization look profitable or unfavorable. In the wake of the accounting scandals over the last decades, tougher laws and a call for accountability are inevitable for nonprofits. As a result, when executive directors, board members, and accountants decide to make a change, it should be disclosed in the notes.

A general rule for accountants is to choose a method and stick with it, thus referred to as the *consistency principle.* Changing your method of depreciation and accounting method from *cash* to *accrual* have a profound effect on accounts on your statement of financial position. (Check out Chapter 2 for clarification on these two accounting methods.)

Disclose relevant information

One of the most important bits of information you need to have in the notes to the financial statements is an accurate representation of your nonprofit's overall financial position. All organizations are required to disclose this information. Furthermore, the *disclosure principle* requires that any pertinent information that affects the representation of your nonprofit's financial position — positively or negatively — be disclosed in the notes.

According to the generally accepted accounting principles (GAAP) Full Disclosure Principle, all important information should be explained to users to help them better understand your nonprofit's financial status. Anything that can change your financial position must be shared with internal and external users in the notes.

For example, information about pending lawsuits should be disclosed in the notes to the financial statements. Refer to the previous section, "Indicate lawsuits: Contingent liabilities," for more information.

Your accounting system fulfills the reporting requirements for all internal and external users. Your internal accounting records may reflect more detail than your published records. This is not to suggest that something is being withheld, but merely that your reports address the needs of the group viewing them. For planning and strategizing, you may need more detailed reports about expenses and revenues than are required in the statement of activities.

Chapter 4

Keeping Good Records: Using a Manual System or Computer System

To keep good records, you need a central location where you keep all of your transactions. Having quick access to reports about your financial position is your objective. Record keeping involves tracking your accounts and keeping the documents that support the transactions and leave a paper trail. This way you always know how much money you have, how much you've spent, and what you've spent it on.

Choosing the method by which you'll track your income and expenses is up to you. You have two choices: You can set up a manual system or use a store-bought computer system. It doesn't matter which method you choose as long as you get the job done. So where to start? This chapter looks at your two options and helps you choose which one is best for you and your nonprofit. I also show you how a manual accounting system works, how to convert a manual system into a computerized system, and the benefits of doing so. I also introduce you to some software and share with you how to protect your computer from dangerous viruses.

Going the Manual or Computer Route?

Even with all of the modern technology and computers, many bookkeepers and accountants still start with a pencil, pad, and calculator (preferably a 10-key adding machine) in hand. Many prefer this method because it allows them to understand how the numbers come together. Computers sometimes break down, freeze up, or just outright stop working. Being able to do your books on paper can save you when a computer glitch sneaks up on you or the system fails.

However, some bookkeepers and accountants do rely heavily on computers because they provide updates automatically to all files when changes are made. For example, computer software can be set up to recalculate totals when you make one change to a number or add another one. Using a computer to keep track of your books saves time and energy.

The choice of which system to use is personal. You may need to consider how much activity is going on in your nonprofit. Does keeping track of your accounting records by using a manual system leave you feeling overwhelmed? If the answer is yes, then you should consider a computerized accounting system to ease your burden. Make sure you understand how your accounts are set up. I like to take a pen and pad and write things down first, and then I use the computer to verify my math.

In the beginning, I suggest you incorporate both systems into your nonprofit's bookkeeping and accounting systems. The best way to do so is to create a paper file with hard copies of your *working papers* (the numbers added on paper). Then transfer the numbers from your working papers into your computer files for safekeeping. Press the Print button on your computer at least once a month and put the printout with your manual set of accounting reports to keep them up-to-date.

One advantage to using both systems is that you have documentation to support your activities. This will prove helpful when you close out your books at the end of the year (see Chapter 19 for more on this). You'll have a clear paper trail to support your activities.

Computer systems aren't foolproof

As wonderful as computers are at making life easier, they're not immune to problems. Occasionally, things get lost, or users make mistakes. One day our system analyst did an overnight backup and deleted or misplaced some important accounting information.

I told the person that my files were missing and I needed them within the next week to do a quarterly report. The analyst was out of town during the week I needed the data, so he wasn't able to get me the missing info. What saved me were the hard copies I had printed out and filed. I had to resort to a pen, pad, and calculator to do my reports. My manual backup system saved my hide.

Choosing a Manual System

A manual bookkeeping system is great if you're a hands-on type of person. With this system, you can easily monitor all transactions because you have hard copies of all records. Furthermore, writing down numbers and transactions helps the brain to remember them. A manual system entails much more than just keeping a check register or organizing all of your receipts and canceled checks in an orderly fashion. The following sections take a closer look at the pros and cons of using a manual system and the characteristics of this type of system.

Knowing the pros and cons

Before you can maintain a manual bookkeeping system, you need to have a firm grasp of the advantages and disadvantages of using such a system. Being aware of these important considerations can help you more fully understand what your manual bookkeeping system can and can't do for you and your nonprofit.

The following are some pros of using a manual system:

- It's less prone to errors because you're writing things down.

- You have hard copies of your records available at your fingertips.

- You gain a greater understanding of your accounting system because every step is processed by hand.

Meanwhile here are some important cons for you to consider as you maintain your manual system:

- Using this system can be time consuming because you have to move numbers from one report to another manually. If you make an error, you can't correct it without redoing everything or ending up with sloppy reports.

- Paper files take up space, and if you need something, it can take some time to go through your files to find it.

- Paper discolors and deteriorates, and paper mites find their way to old files. Older paper tends to smell funny and turns a brownish color. To handle these potential problems, you can scan your documents into your computer and then store the hard copies in airtight containers.

Scanning your paper documents and saving the electronic copies on a CD is an excellent way to preserve them for long-term storage. After I've calculated something on paper, I transfer it to a spreadsheet, and then I print out the spreadsheet and attach the handwritten paper. Then I place the two in a file. As time permits, I create CDs. I destroy the original documents after about three years.

Eyeing the parts of a manual system

To use a manual bookkeeping system, you need to understand the tools you need: a checkbook register, an adding machine with a tape, and a filing system. This section focuses on the three main components you use when maintaining your nonprofit's books manually. *Remember:* The name of the game is to account for and track all transactions with solid documentation to back you up.

Using a check register: Documenting checkbook transactions

Inside every new box of checks, you find a checkbook register where you can document each transaction affecting your account. This register is an essential part of your manual bookkeeping system. Logging every transaction as soon as you know a deposit has been made or a check has been written is good financial management. You use this register to record your written checks, deposits, checking fees, and debit card transactions. Maintaining the register takes a little time and effort, but it's important to balancing your finances. Check out Chapter 7 for more information on how to use the register.

Punching a 10-key adding machine: Calculating your income

A 10-key adding machine that runs tape is another important component of your manual bookkeeping system. Using this machine is a good way to calculate income. When working with numbers, it's easy to make transposition errors and write numerals down differently than how they appear. The tape that the 10-key adding machine spits out is an excellent tool to verify your numbers after you've calculated them. (You can use a calculator that doesn't print out a tape, but then it's harder to check for mistakes when the numbers don't add up correctly.)

Attach your adding machine tape to the documents you took the numbers from and file everything together.

Keeping track of everything: Organizing hard copies

The third component of a manual bookkeeping system is good organization. You have to keep track of all the merchant receipts, written checks, and so forth. Doing so helps you prove purchases, and it also proves that a transaction took place on a certain date at a given time and in a given place. Mistakes happen (that's human nature), and you need to protect your assets and guard your money. You can correct errors faster and easier by having the necessary papers organized and accessible.

You'll also want to keep your donors list on file for auditing purposes. It's important to keep records of all the income your nonprofit receives and the sources of that income. This information is needed when your books are audited. (For more about donor information, see Chapter 7.)

If you decide to track the day-to-day operations manually and then deliver the necessary documents to your accountant to prepare your financial statements, the first thing your accountant will want to see is proof of purchases and transactions. If you're not organized and don't have everything in order, you're in for a frustrating experience.

To keep your paperwork organized, I suggest you do the following:

- ✔ Make a hard copy of all records.

- ✔ Place all important documents in clearly labeled and easily accessible file folders. Some nonprofits label files by the month and create a cross-reference system if they do a lot of transactions with a large vendor. This system makes it easier to do monthly and quarterly financial reports.

- ✔ Store all records for at least three years for auditing purposes.

Trying Excel: The Easy Computer Route

If you want to use a computer bookkeeping system for your nonprofit, you don't have to start off with an expensive, intricate system that requires a PhD and CPA to master. Even if you're not computer savvy, you can still incorporate Excel into your bookkeeping system. The program is popular with many bookkeepers and accountants today.

Excel is an electronic worksheet program that sorts, stores, and calculates data. Using the software, you can create spreadsheets, which consist of rows and columns. After you enter information into the spreadsheet, you can calculate totals, create tables and graphs, and analyze financial data. The program is also useful for making lists of donors and charts of accounts.

The following are some pros to using Excel:

- ✔ You can use the software to compare information from one period with current information.

- ✔ You can store your accounting information on your desktop or a CD.

- ✔ With a little practice you can put together some professional-looking reports using Excel spreadsheets. You can include some pretty impressive pie charts and graphs in your financial reports.

Working with Excel isn't all efficiency and automatic calculations, though. Here are some important cons to consider:

- ✔ Excel offers so many options in the toolbar that you may feel you have too many choices until you get familiar with the program.

- ✔ You may become too dependent on the computer doing all the work. If the software or your computer fails, you'll need to remember how to keep your books manually.

In the following sections, I show you how you can take baby steps and use Excel in your bookkeeping. You can see how a simple spreadsheet can make your life easier. For more detailed information about how to use Excel and all of its bells and whistles, check out *Excel 2007 For Dummies* by Greg Harvey (Wiley) or *Excel 2003 For Dummies* by Greg Harvey (if you're using an older version).

Breaking down the spreadsheet

Spreadsheets are the centerpiece of Excel. They're where you enter your data; after you've completed that task, you can crunch the numbers, sort data, track spending and income, and perform countless other functions. This section gives you a quick overview of the all-important spreadsheet.

A spreadsheet is commonly referred to as a *worksheet*. Every Excel spreadsheet has the following components:

- **Columns:** Columns run up and down (vertically), and they're identified alphabetically on the top of the spreadsheet.

- **Rows:** Rows run from side to side (horizontally). Each row is numbered on the left side.

- **Cells:** The place where a column and row intersect is called a *cell,* and it looks like a rectangle. A cell is labeled by a letter and number (so a cell two columns in and three rows down would be labeled B3). You enter the data into the cells.

You can use spreadsheets to make your job easier, no matter your position with your nonprofit. Spreadsheets store the following three basic types of data:

- **Labels** are written text with no numerical value and are used to identify information. Labels consist of data that begins with a letter, like a list of names. They are typically found in the first cell of a column or row. For example, you can create a list of the donors who gave to a fundraiser by entering names of individuals.

- **Numbers** are digits or entries that have a fixed value. For example, you can enter the amount given by each donor in the cell next to the person's name.

- **Formulas** are mathematical equations used to make calculations. On the toolbar at the top of the spreadsheet is a button used to do mathematical computations. For example, if you want to know how much a donor has contributed over the year, you can use the Add Sum button to get the total.

Converting your manual system into a spreadsheet

If you've been using a manual bookkeeping system and want to move to a computer system, an Excel spreadsheet is a good place to start. You can use Excel to verify your totals in your manual bookkeeping system until you become more comfortable with Excel. To make this conversion, complete the following steps:

1. **To open a new spreadsheet, click the Office button. Then scroll down and click New on the Office menu to open a blank spreadsheet.**

2. **To set up the spreadsheet, enter labels in the first cell of each column and row.**

   Creating these labels allows you to identify the data. For example, you can enter donor names in the first column, one name per cell, and various fundraising events in the first row, one event per cell.

3. **Enter your data into the appropriate cells.**

   The cell where a column and row intersects is where you enter the data specific to those two situations. So if Mr. Smith donated money at Fundraisers A, C, and D, you'd enter a number in the appropriate cells, skipping the one for Fundraiser B (or entering a zero).

   To quickly move from one cell to another, use the arrow keys on your computer keyboard. Another way to navigate through an Excel spreadsheet is by using your tab key.

4. **After you enter your information, click the SUM button to tabulate your totals.**

   When you're ready to calculate totals on your spreadsheet, you'll use formulas. You can use the SUM button to have the computer do the math and make your job easier. The SUM function button (it looks like a very angular capital E) is located at the top of the toolbar underneath the Help button on the upper-right-hand corner. Clicking it calculates values in a range of cells faster than you can even imagine. It can add, subtract, divide, multiply, and compute averages and means in a range of cells. All you have to do is enter data into the cells and use the SUM button to do the math.

   All math equations or formulas must begin with an equal sign. The computer automatically inserts an equal sign when you use the SUM button, but if you decide to write your own equations, make sure you start with an equal sign. Otherwise, the computer won't compute anything for that cell. (I don't cover equation writing in this book. If you're ambitious enough to tackle that, check out one of the *Excel For Dummies* books mentioned earlier in the chapter.)

Here's how to use the SUM function:

1. **Click the cell where you want your total to appear on your spreadsheet.**

2. **Click the SUM function button on your toolbar.**

3. **Drag your mouse over the cells that you want to add and press the Enter button on your keyboard. The total should appear in the cell you clicked in Step 1.**

You can use the SUM button to do more than add numbers. You can click inside a formula and change the colon to

- ✔ A minus sign (–) to subtract numbers
- ✔ A asterisk (*) to multiply numbers
- ✔ A backslash (/) to divide numbers

For example, if you want to know how much money you've got left at the end of the month, you need to subtract your expenses from your income. First add all your income in one column, and then add all expenses in another column. After you have those totals, you can select those two cells and tell the computer to subtract the expenses from the income just by changing the colon to a minus sign. (If you get a negative answer, you probably need to reverse the order of the cells in the formula.)

If you need more help getting started with Excel, just click the Help button (the question mark) on the toolbar to go to the tutorial. This easy-to-follow information can help you navigate your way around a spreadsheet.

The best way to get comfortable with using Excel is to play with a spreadsheet by entering information and clicking different icons on the toolbar. Do this on simple numbers when you've got some time before trying to use the software to meet a deadline.

Naming Other Available Software

If you're a tad bit more computer savvy and want to elevate your nonprofit's bookkeeping and accounting, you may consider using more advanced computer software. Several programs are available to make bookkeeping and accounting much easier for your organization.

Although these programs can greatly help your organization, they do require you to invest some time in reading up on the software and spend some money for it. Check out some of the more common ones available to help you with your nonprofit's bookkeeping and accounting.

QuickBooks

QuickBooks is widely used by smaller organizations because of its price and ease of use. You can purchase QuickBooks Premier, which includes a version for nonprofit organizations, for $400 to $1,000, depending on the number of people who'll be using it. QuickBooks can help you

- Track bank account balances
- Calculate payroll and sales taxes
- Prepare payroll
- Prepare and print financial reports
- Track credit cards
- Write and print checks

QuickBooks isn't a bad investment because it can help your organization with quite a few tasks. However, before you drop coin for this software, make sure you're aware of its limitations. QuickBooks isn't for an organization with more than five users online at the same time. So if you have managers, board members, and office staff who share your computer files, no more than five people can use the software at the same time because of the terms of the license agreement. For a free download of QuickBooks, go to www.quickbooks.com. If you're interested in checking out how it can help your organization, check out the latest version of *QuickBooks For Dummies* by Stephen L. Nelson, CPA, MBA, MS (Wiley).

Microsoft Office Accounting

You may want to consider Microsoft Office Accounting for your accounting needs. The price starts at $200. The program offers the following features:

- A payroll center that allows you to run payroll, print checks, print reports, file taxes, and so on
- Journal entries for recording transactions, and if you attempt to enter account information that throws your system out of balance, a warning message is displayed
- System accounts including accounts receivable, accounts payable, payroll liabilities, bank charges, and so on
- Report generation for budgets, financial statements, and so on
- The ability to work with Microsoft Excel and export data to Microsoft Office Accounting

Even though Office Accounting is ideally suited for small businesses, it's not specifically designed for nonprofit organizations. However, it is affordable. Another drawback is that you may be forced to upgrade other Microsoft programs to keep all the programs (such as Excel and Word) compatible. Office Accounting Express is offered as a free download at `http://office.microsoft.com`.

Peachtree Accounting

Peachtree Accounting software has been around for more than 30 years. As your financial needs expand, Peachtree allows you to upgrade your software package. Peachtree is for larger, more advanced nonprofits with large operating budgets that can't keep up with their bookkeeping without automated help. This program costs a bit more at $550. Unlike Office Accounting, Peachtree is specifically designed for nonprofits. Some of the functions performed by Peachtree include

- An advanced internal accounting review system that checks for common accounting mistakes. It also tracks unusual transactions and flags them for review.

- An online bank reconciliation system that reconciles your records with your bank statement. This feature saves lots of time when everything balances.

- The ability to export data to Excel keeping formulas intact. This allows you to work from a different worksheet and convert your information with ease.

- Easy conversion from QuickBooks. If you started out small with QuickBooks and you've grown, Peachtree allows you to convert your QuickBooks accounts into its system.

- Creation of sophisticated reports that allow you to compare finances from the current periods with other accounting periods. For example, if you want to see how your donations came in during a certain month in the last three years, this system can easily retrieve that information.

The pros of using Peachtree may also be cons, depending on the size of your organization. This software allows you to do extensive analysis of your accounting records and allows you to compare your numbers to other nonprofits. However, you may not need the advanced reports and analysis tools that Peachtree offers. If you're a small nonprofit and only a couple of people need access to your books, Peachtree may be too much system for you. To try Peachtree Accounting for 60 days, go to the following Web site: `http://offer.peachtree.com/ppc`.

Ensuring Your System Is Secure

Your nonprofit's financial records contain important and confidential information that you can't risk losing, damaging, or having fall into the wrong hands. Security is especially important when your bookkeeping and accounting records are on a computer system. If your system becomes contaminated with a virus, you may lose your files and never be able to recover them. In the worst-case scenario, if you store bank account information on your computer, someone may hack into your computer and steal the information he needs to liquidate your nonprofit's (or even your donors') bank accounts.

That's why ensuring that your computer system is secure is essential. Although nothing is 100 percent secure, you can take the measures I outline in the following sections to give you peace of mind.

You can choose from all sorts of programs to protect your computer system. Some of the software is free online, and some can be purchased for a hefty fee. Because I don't know the particulars of your situation, I give you the basics of what you need to know to protect your information, but I don't recommend specific software. Instead, talk to someone at your local computer store for help.

Firewalls and virus scanners

In securing your computer system, two of the first lines of defense are a firewall and virus scanner. A *firewall* is a barrier that prevents outside users from accessing protected areas of your computer system and tampering with or peering into sensitive materials. A firewall allows you to control who has access to materials you deem for public or private use. Firewalls come in two types:

- A *software firewall* is a program usually installed on a single computer that protects a computer against unauthorized users to and from the Internet.

- *Hardware firewalls* are called routers. *Routers* direct information to and from the Internet through a network. (A *network* is a group of computers that can transmit information between themselves.)

To figure out which type of firewall you need, talk to the person in charge of maintaining your computer system.

Meanwhile, a *virus scanner* is a program that checks for the presence of viruses by examining all the files that are located on your computer. A *virus* is technology's version of the common cold. It causes your computer to sniffle, cough, and spit out garbage. Many programs allow you to scan specific files and folders. They also monitor and scan the information that comes into your computer from outside your firewall, as well as stored information within your network. When the virus scanner finds a virus, its job is to stop it before the virus spreads to your computer and network.

Viruses may lurk in harmless e-mails and files. When delivered to your e-mail, they can do the following:

- ✔ Slow down your computer
- ✔ Make your computer unable to perform its normal tasks
- ✔ Cripple your system enough that soon it stops working altogether

Viruses are evil because they can wreak havoc wherever they strike. Viruses come in two forms:

- ✔ **Worms** replicate themselves and are usually found in e-mails. Their primary job is to slow down a computer or network's processes. They eat up computer memory and spread themselves from computer to computer.
- ✔ **Trojan horses** come hidden in programs and files. They don't replicate themselves, but they can mess up systems and sometimes even destroy and make them inoperable.

As a protective measure, don't open e-mails from people you don't know. And when you send e-mails to some people, their e-mail system is set up to ask you questions before the program will accept your message.

User privileges and file sharing

In ensuring your computer system's safety, another line of security is user privileges and file sharing. *User privileges* and *file sharing* mean allowing users in your nonprofit to access only the files they need. User privileges determine who can view, read, write, copy, modify, and print files, and which files may be shared by and with whom.

Usually only one person has control and access to everything, but your non-profit may require that more than one person has access to all files. This person, called the *administrator,* sets up the user privileges and file sharing protocols. The IT (information tech) manager is usually the administrator. Other users are given certain rights and privileges for accessing and sharing files. These users can be in your network, as well as those who are outside your firewall but have been granted access to information.

Most computer systems use password protection and identification to allow users the right to access certain files. It's a good idea to have your administrator set up your computer system so users have to change their passwords every 90 days. This security measure can keep intruders from accessing your computer files.

Miscellaneous security programs

Other security measures are available for your nonprofit's use, depending on how sophisticated of a system you want. To determine whether you need advanced security measures, you must first look at the data you have. Consider whether the information could be damaging to your nonprofit or others if it were to be viewed by the public. Third-party companies offer the necessary software online or at most retail stores that sell office software. Your IT or administrator can check into some of the other available programs.

Backing Up Your System

Backing up your system is an essential and vital part of securing your computer system. When you *back up* files, you save and archive important documents for potential future use. You should back up essential files that are used to run and maintain your nonprofit. This way, you have duplicate copies of files in the event of a system failure due to a power outage, equipment failure, inadvertently deleting files and folders, user errors, natural disaster, and malicious activities from within and outside your firewall. System backup is usually done by one of the following two methods:

✔ **Automatic backup:** The automatic backup can be set to perform backups at a specific time every day. The automatic backup uses a software program to search for and find system files and folders to save for you. Most computer operating systems come with automatic backup programs to restore your computer to a state before it became corrupt or inoperable.

You can back up your info to different media as long as your system can access these modes. Some options for automatic backup include

- **CDs:** Files are copied onto media and stored in a safe place. You need to have the correct equipment and software to read and write to CDs.

- **Your computer's hard drive:** The hard drive comes as an external and internal piece of equipment. The hard drive is the ideal storage place for multiple files because it has a large storage capacity and provides easy access to files.

- **Third-party software:** This type of backup duplicates your computer storage system as a mirror image of computer files and folders. Internet sites can provide free online storage for a certain amount of time. This option is a good choice if you live in an area prone to natural disasters because you can access the storage from another computer if yours is destroyed or inaccessible.

- **USB drive:** Also referred to as a *jump drive* or *thumb drive,* these storage tools are about the size of a lipstick tube. They don't hold as much data as a hard drive, but they hold a lot and can be transported conveniently.

✔ **Manual backup:** Manually backing up your system uses software also. In this process, you choose to save only certain files and folders or certain aspects or elements of your files and folders. This process can be tedious and time consuming. If you want to manually back up files, I suggest you ask your IT person to help.

Part II
Balancing Your Nonprofit Books

"I think I'd make a great company bookkeeper.
I'm good with details..."

In this part . . .

Keeping your books in balance can feel like a juggling act. Before starting your first act, though, you need to set a few things in action. This part helps you jump into everything related to keeping your nonprofit's books balanced.

I explain the importance of setting up a chart or list of accounts that you will use during the accounting cycle. Then, you can begin to record transactions in your journals.

You can find the center of your balancing act in your non-profit checkbook. Basically, you record donations coming in and expenses going out. Doing so keeps your eyes focused on cash inflows and outflows.

Before you can completely balance all the books, though, you have to have a financial plan in place. Your financial plan is the budget that supports your programs. Developing and operating from a budget is good financial management.

Throughout your entire balancing act — when you're setting up your books, recording your monetary activity, itemizing your checkbook register, and operating on a budget — you have to stay in compliance with state and federal nonprofit guidelines.

Chapter 5

Setting up the Chart of Accounts for Nonprofits

In This Chapter

▶ Organizing a chart of accounts

▶ Setting up accounting codes

▶ Sorting all types of accounts

*I*n order for you to easily keep track of where money is coming from and going to in your nonprofit, you use a chart of accounts. The *chart of accounts* is a list of each account that the accounting system tracks; it captures the information you need to keep track of and use to make good financial decisions.

The chart of accounts is like a big reference card that contains numbers, or codes, and names of accounts; no transactions or specific financial information is recorded on the chart of accounts. An account code from the chart of accounts is recorded into the financial records, and from there into financial reports. So, for example, when you receive a donation, you code it with one account number. When you owe a vendor, you code it with another account number.

This chapter runs down the different accounts in a typical chart, how you can personalize your nonprofit's chart of accounts, and what you need to do to code funds coming in and going out of your nonprofit.

Identifying and Naming Your Nonprofit's Main Types of Accounts

When I talk about naming accounts, I don't mean choosing monikers like Sally, Sam, or Susie, so you can put away the book of baby names. Choosing names for your nonprofit accounts depends on the type of products or services you provide. Your chart of accounts consists of accounts found on your financial statements. Knowing which accounts go with which statements helps you to indentify the main types of accounts. For instance, the statement of financial position has assets, liabilities, and net assets (see Chapter 16 for more on this statement). The statement of activities has revenues, expenses, and increases or decreases in net assets (see Chapter 15 for more on this statement).

A typical chart of accounts (see Figure 5-1) is divided into five categories: assets, liabilities, net assets or fund balances, revenues, and expenses. Each account is assigned an identifying number for use within your accounting system. I explain these five categories in the following sections. Most nonprofit organizations have most of the following accounts. Name your accounts based on their function. For example, if an account is a revenue account, then give it a name to identify the source of revenue. In Figure 5-1, you see all revenue accounts start with the number 4. All federal grant revenue accounts begin with the number 4, and the second digit is a 1.

Assets
Current assets:
   1110 Cash
        1111 Cash in checking account
        1112 Cash in savings account
        1113 Cash on hand (petty cash)
   1120 Notes receivable
   1130 Grants receivable
   1140 Accounts receivable
   1150 Inventory
   1160 Prepaid rent
   1170 Prepaid insurance

Long-Term Assets
   1210 Land
   1220 Building
   1221 Accumulated depreciation: building
   1230 Equipment
   1231 Accumulated depreciation: equipment

Liabilities
Current liabilities
   2110 Notes payable
   2120 Accounts payable
   2130 Salaries payable

Long-Term Liabilities
   2210 Mortgage payable
   2220 Bonds payable

Nonprofit Equity
   3110 Net assets

Revenue
   4110 Federal grants
   4200 Corporate grants
   4300 State grants
   4400 Program fees
   4500 Interest income
   4600 Fundraising
   4700 Individual donors

Expenses
   5110 Fundraising
   5200 Salaries expense
   5300 Depreciation expense
   5400 Rent expense
   5500 Interest expense
   5600 Office supplies

Figure 5-1:
A typical chart of accounts.

Aside from certain conventions regarding numbering and the order in which information is presented, you can tailor your chart of accounts to your organization's specific needs. Your chart of accounts belongs to you. It's an internal system used by you to keep track of where things go. It classifies accounts by giving them a name and number, and it's the first thing any bookkeeper needs to keep your books in order. It arranges all similar accounts in order to give clarity to what's what. If you run out of numbers, you can assign new numbers. My example chart of accounts in Figure 5-1 is merely a suggestion of how you can set up your chart. You must decide what's best for you.

Accounting for assets

The first grouping of accounts in a chart of accounts is the assets. Assets are the tangible items an organization has as resources, including cash, accounts receivable, equipment, and property. Basically, assets provide economic benefit to your organization. The following are the main types of assets:

- ✔ **Current assets:** An asset that will be sold or depleted in the near future (within one year) or a business cycle. An example of a current asset is cash.

- ✔ **Fixed assets:** A fixed asset is a long-term tangible asset that your non-profit uses, and there is no intent to sell the asset. It shouldn't be sold within the current year or business cycle. An example of a fixed asset is real estate or furniture.

- ✔ **Other assets:** Statement of financial position classification that covers miscellaneous assets. These are usually valued at less than 5 percent of total assets. An example is scrapped equipment held for sale.

Assets are usually listed in descending order of liquidity. This means that cash and other assets that are easily converted to cash are listed first, and fixed assets are listed last. Notice that all asset accounts begin with the number 1 on the chart of accounts (see Figure 5-1). (Check out the "Coding the Charges: Assigning Numbers to the Accounts" section later in this chapter for more info about numbering.)

The following are asset accounts:

- ✔ **Checking account:** Here's where you record cash on deposit in a checking account with a bank.

- ✔ **Petty cash, change funds, undeposited receipts, cash on hand:** This account includes cash used by the nonprofit organization for revolving funds, *change funds* (cash used to supply change to customers and others; can also be used to cash payroll checks), petty cash funds, and undeposited receipts at year-end.

- ✔ **Savings accounts, money market accounts, certificates of deposit:** This category records funds on deposit with banks and other financial institutions in the form of savings accounts, money market accounts, certificates of deposit, and other interest-bearing deposits.

- ✔ **Contributions receivable:** When people give you pledges, you record them here, even if the donor restricts the pledged contribution to use in a future period. However, if the pledge won't be paid until a future period, it should be classified as a non-current asset.

- ✔ **Land:** This account records the amount paid for the land itself, costs incidental to the acquisition of land, and expenditures incurred in preparing the land for use.

- ✔ **Buildings and improvements:** This account records the cost of relatively permanent structures used to house people or property. It also includes fixtures that are permanently attached to buildings and can't be removed without cutting into walls, ceilings, or floors, or without in some way damaging the building.

- ✔ **Furniture and equipment:** This account records the cost of furniture and equipment such as, office desks, chairs, computer tables, copy machines, large printers, and the like.

- ✔ **Data processing equipment:** Here's where you record the cost of data processing equipment used by your nonprofit, such as flat-screen monitors, desktop computers, hard drives, and such.

- ✔ **Leasehold improvements:** These costs usually include improvements made to facilities or property leased by your organization.

- ✔ **Accumulated depreciation:** This account records depreciation that has accumulated over time by periodic adjustments for annual depreciation. When an asset is sold or a lease is terminated, depreciation recorded for the item is removed from the records.

Labeling liabilities

Liabilities are obligations due to creditors; in other words, they're bills your nonprofit owes. Liabilities are payable in money, or in goods or services. Liabilities tell readers how much debt the nonprofit is in. Liabilities can be classified as current or long-term:

- ✔ **Current liabilities:** These are obligations that are due within one year or within the business cycle. An example is accounts payable.

- ✔ **Long-term liabilities:** These are liabilities that aren't due within one year or within the current business cycle. Long-term notes payable is an example of a long-term liability.

You list current liabilities first followed by long-term liabilities because you want to show what's due in the current business cycle first. All liabilities start with the number 2 in the chart of accounts (refer to Figure 5-1). The current liabilities second digit is a 1. The long-term liabilities second digit is a 2. (Check out the "Coding the Charges: Assigning Numbers to the Accounts" section later in this chapter for more info about numbering.)

See the following list of liabilities and an explanation of each.

- ✔ **Accounts payable:** This account records current liabilities, which represent debts that must be paid within a relatively short period, usually no longer than a year.

- ✔ **Salary and wages payable:** Here's where you record the liabilities for salaries and wages and employee benefits.

- ✔ **Accrued payroll:** This account records the liability for payrolls accrued at year end. The accrual should include all salaries and wages earned by employees; thus, this entry would include all time worked by employees up to the end of the year.

- ✔ **Payroll taxes payable:** These accounts record liabilities for various payroll taxes payable to governments arising from salaries and wages and payroll withholdings.

Deferred

- ✔ **Unearned revenue:** This account records amounts that have been received by your nonprofit, but the earning process hasn't been completed. For example, if your nonprofit offers subscriptions for one year to your inside newsletter and people pay for them annually, you have revenue that has been received but not yet earned.

- ✔ **Notes payable:** You use this account to record the outstanding principle due within the next year on notes owed by your organization.

- ✔ **Mortgage payable:** This is just what it sounds like. You record the outstanding principle due within the next year on mortgages.

- ✔ **Accrued interest payable:** This account records interest due on notes, capital leases, and mortgages at the end of the accounting period.

- ✔ **Grants payable:** If you owe outstanding grant awards to outside organizations, you record it here. The figure represents amounts earned but not paid at year end.

- ✔ **Long-term debt:** This account records non-current liabilities, which represent debts that must be paid in a future period that is at least one year or more after the current fiscal period.

Net assets: What you're worth

Net assets (your nonprofit's equity) show the financial worth of the organization. They represent the balance remaining after liabilities are subtracted from an organization's assets. (Accounting software designed with for-profits in mind may report net assets under the heading *equity*.) Net asset accounts often begin with the number 3. (Check out the "Coding the Charges: Assigning Numbers to the Accounts" section later in this chapter for more info about numbering.) They are classified as:

✔ **Unrestricted net assets:** This account records the balance of *unrestricted net assets* (unrestricted assets less liabilities that will be paid with unrestricted assets). Unrestricted net assets generally result from revenues that were derived from providing services, producing and delivering goods, receiving unrestricted contributions, and receiving dividends or interest from investing in income-producing assets, less expenses incurred in fulfilling any of those tasks.

✔ **Temporarily restricted net assets:** This account records the balance of temporarily restricted net assets. *Temporarily restricted assets* are for

- Support of particular operating activities

- Investment for a specified term

- Use in a specified future period

- Acquisition of long-lived assets

Donors' temporary restrictions may require that resources be used in a later period or after a specified date (time restrictions), or that resources be used for a specified purpose (use of purpose restrictions), or both.

✔ **Permanently restricted net assets:** This account records the balance of permanently restricted net assets. *Permanently restricted assets* have donor-imposed restrictions that don't expire with time or with the completion of activities that fulfill a purpose.

Only people and organizations outside your nonprofit can place restrictions on grants and gifts. Your board of directors may designate a gift for a specific use, but it can turn around and undesignate it. Your nonprofit can't place restrictions on gifts. Restrictions are only enforceable when imposed by outside entities.

Revenue: What you earn

Revenue accounts measure gross increases in assets, gross decreases in liabilities, or a combination of both when your nonprofit delivers or produces goods, renders services, or earns income in other ways during an accounting period. Keeping your revenue (donations and income) separate is important because you may have to account for what you did with the income. For example, you need to account separately for government grant revenue, which can be kept separately by using your chart of accounts. You may have to account for gifts received with restrictions on them. So assign account numbers that clearly identify all revenue sources because this will serve as documentation for you during an audit.

Your chart of accounts helps you keep track of revenue sources. Notice how revenue accounts are identified by the second digit (see Figure 5-1). Revenue accounts often start with the number 4. (Check out the "Coding the Charges: Assigning Numbers to the Accounts" section later in this chapter for more info about numbering.) See the following list of accounts:

- **State grants:** Generally, state grants and revenues are earned from operating grants by incurring qualifying expenses, and they go in this account. In this context, *qualifying expenses* refers to expenses that are allowed by the grant award or regulations, are allocable to the grant, and are reasonable and necessary to meet the program's objectives. Establish a subaccount for each state grant.

- **Federal grants:** This account records revenues earned for grants from federal agencies. Generally, revenues are earned for operating grant programs and by incurring qualifying expenses. Establish a subaccount for each federal grant.

- **Private gifts and grants (contributions):** Here's where you record revenues from private gifts and grants, including corporate gifts, grants from private foundations, and contributions from individuals. This account can also be used for pledges that aren't contingent upon future events. Set up a subaccount for each corporation, unless anonymity is requested.

- **Noncash contributions:** The value of contributions from individuals or organizations not made from cash go in this account. A *noncash contribution* is a transfer of an asset or cancellation of a liability without consideration.

- **Donated materials — facilities and equipment:** This account is used to record the value of donated materials, facilities, and equipment. Generally, value is based on the fair value of materials or equipment at the time of the donations. Value should be based on a reasonable objective basis. For example, when the use of a facility is donated, value should be based on the rental value of similar facilities in the area.

- **Donated services:** This account is used to record the value of donated services. They are divided into two categories:

    - **Donated services — specialized skills:** These meet the requirements of FASB Statement No. 116 for financial reporting purposes.

    - **Donated services — other:** These don't meet the requirements of FASB Statement No. 116.

See Chapter 9 for more about FASB Statement No. 116, Accounting for Contributions Received and Made

✓ **Fees from special events:** When you collect membership fees and funds raised through special events, you record them in this account. Subaccounts should be established for each type of fee collected.

✓ **Special events (net revenue):** This account records the *net proceeds* (gross collections less expenses) from special events. Establish subaccounts to record receipts and expenses.

✓ **Investment income:** This account records income from investments. The balance of these accounts should include investment income received during the year, as well as accrued investment income earned but not received by year end.

Nonprofit expense: What you spend

You can't make money without spending money. That's the informal definition of a *nonprofit expense. Expenses* are expired costs, the using up of assets, or incurrence of liabilities from operations. Examples include personnel costs, costs of supplies, or current obligations, such as accounts payables. Also, losses resulting from the sale of assets such as investments are included in this category.

Expenses should be recognized when they are incurred, and revenues should be recognized in your accounting books when they are earned. Expense accounts often start with the number 5. (Check out "Coding the Charges: Assigning Numbers to the Accounts" later in this chapter for more info about numbering.)

See the following list of expense accounts:

✓ **Personnel:** This account records personnel costs, payroll taxes, employee benefits, professional services (consultants and so on), and stipends paid to board members. The objective of this group of accounts is to provide information on total personnel costs.

✓ **Salary and wages:** Here's where you record the cost of salary and wages paid to employees of your nonprofit. This account includes both full- and part-time personnel costs.

✓ **Social Security and Medicare contribution:** This account records the employee's share of Social Security and Medicare taxes applied to salary and wages paid to employees.

✓ **Retirement contribution:** This account records the employee's contribution toward her retirement.

✓ **Disability insurance contribution:** This account is used to record the employee's contribution toward her disability insurance program.

- **Unemployment insurance contribution:** This account records the employer's contribution for employees' costs of the state unemployment insurance program.

- **Workers compensation:** Here's where you record the cost of workers compensation insurance premiums for your nonprofit.

- **Board member compensation/stipends:** When you pay stipends to board members, you record them here. Reimbursements for board members expenses' aren't recorded in this account; they go in the current obligations account.

- **Donated services:** This account is used to record the value of services donated to the nonprofit and expensed as program services.

- **Contracted services:** This account is used to record transactions to obtain outside services typically provided by employees of the organization.

- **Accounting and tax services:** This account records accounting and tax services for bookkeeping services, payroll, and preparation of tax returns.

- **Legal services:** This account is used to record legal services either for specific services or retainers.

- **Temporary services:** If you use temporary services (like temporary clerical or secretarial) from manpower agencies, you record the expense in this account.

- **Management services:** This account records the costs of management services acquired by the organization. For example, these can be consulting services.

- **Honorariums:** When you pay *honorariums* (a sum paid to a professional for speaking engagements or other services for which no fee is set), you record the amount in this category.

- **Supplies and materials:** This account records the cost of supplies and materials used in the daily operations of your organization.

- **Current obligations:** This account records the ongoing cost of operations other than personnel, supplies and materials, and fixed charges.

- **Travel:** Here's where you record the costs of employee travel, including food, lodging, and transportation.

- **Communication (telephone, postage, and so on):** This account records the costs of telephone (both local service and long-distance charges) and postage.

- **Utilities:** This account records just what you'd expect: costs for things such as electricity, water and sewer, and gas.

- **Printing and binding:** This account records the cost of printing, binding, and copying.

- ✔ **Repair and maintenance:** Can you guess what this account covers? Yep, the costs of routine repairs and maintenance, including service contracts.

- ✔ **Computer services (accounting, payroll, and so on):** This account records the cost of purchased computer services, such as accounting and payroll processing.

- ✔ **Employee training:** Here, you record the cost of employee training, including tuition, conference registration, and training materials.

- ✔ **Advertising and promotion:** This account records the cost of advertising program services, solicitation of bids, obtaining qualified applicants, or advertising fundraising events.

- ✔ **Board member expense:** Here's where you record the cost of board member travel and per diem expenses.

- ✔ **Fixed charges and other expenses:** This account records reoccurring expenses related to your nonprofit's operations. For example, these are costs that occur monthly, quarterly, semi-annually, or annually. They include things such as property taxes and interest on bonded debts.

- ✔ **Office rent:** This is what it is: the cost of office rent. No more, no less.

- ✔ **Furniture rental:** This account records the cost of furniture rental. Lease-purchase agreements that meet the criteria of a *financing lease* (a lease recorded as an asset accompanied by borrowing of funds) should be recorded as *capital outlays* (a liability intended to benefit future periods).

- ✔ **Equipment rental:** This account is used to record the cost of equipment rental. Lease-purchase agreements that meet the criteria of a capital lease should be recorded as capital outlays.

- ✔ **Vehicle rental:** You record the cost of vehicle rental in this account. Lease-purchase agreements that meet the criteria of a capital lease should be recorded as capital outlays.

- ✔ **Dues and subscriptions:** Here's another straightforward account. It records the costs of dues and subscriptions.

- ✔ **Insurance and bonding:** This account records the costs of insurance on facilities and liability insurance.

- ✔ **Books:** When you purchase reference materials for the use of employees and program participants, you record the cost here.

- ✔ **Depreciation:** This account records the estimated periodic charge against asset values for use, deterioration, or obsolescence.

- ✔ **Contracts, grants, and stipends:** This account is used to record contracts, grants, or stipends with outside organizations or individuals.

- ✔ **Other expense:** This account records any other expenses not classified above.

Net income/increase – decrease in net assets

The statement of activities subtracts all expenses from revenues to get net income or an increase or decrease in net assets. To calculate your net assets results, take the change in net assets and add it to your beginning net assets to get your net assets, ending balance. For example, after you subtract your expenses from your revenues, you get the difference, which is referred to as a *change in net assets* or *net income* or *loss.* Take the beginning balance you started the period with and add it to your change in net assets. This amount equals your net assets ending balance.

Consider the statement of activities; you have revenues, expenses, and a change in net assets. This change in net assets is considered net income or net loss. Consider the statement of financial position, where you have assets, liabilities, and net assets. The difference between your total assets and total liabilities equals your total net assets. These total net assets are your nonprofit's equity.

Coding the Charges: Assigning Numbers to the Accounts

Your chart of accounts is a list of all accounts used in the five categories I discuss in the previous section. The chart of accounts assigns specific account names and numbers to each account found on your statement of activities and statement of financial position.

You recognize account types by looking at the first digit or leading number. To number your accounts, remember this basic numbering system:

- ✔ Asset accounts begin with the number 1, so 1110 to 1999 are assigned to asset accounts.

- ✔ Liability accounts begin with the number 2, so 2110 to 2999 are assigned to liability accounts.

- ✔ Equity accounts begin with the number 3, so 3110 to 3999 are assigned to equity accounts.

- ✔ Revenue accounts begin with the number 4, so 4110 to 4999 are assigned to revenue accounts.

- ✔ Expense accounts begin with the number 5, so 5110 to 5999 are assigned to expense accounts.

Within each category of accounts, the second digit identifies the subclassification. For example,

✔ Within 1110 to 1231 of asset accounts, you have

- 1111 to 1170 as current assets.
- 1210 to 1231 as long-term assets.

✔ Within 2110 to 2220 of liability accounts, you have

- 2110 to 2130 as current liabilities.
- 2210 to 2220 as long-term liabilities.

You use your chart of accounts to code accounting transactions. This chart can help you locate accounts in your ledger. Furthermore, you need to follow a systematic approach of assigning numbers to your accounts. Having a systematic method to identify your accounts helps when errors are made while preparing your trial balance. For more about your ledger and trial balance, see Chapter 6.

Chapter 6

Recording Transactions and Journal Entries

*J*ust like a coin has two sides (a head and a tail), an account has two sides (a debit and a credit). When your nonprofit makes a transaction, you have to record in two or more accounts the *debit* (the left side of an account) and *credit* (the right side of an account). When you record the transaction in your accounting books, you're making a *journal entry*.

This chapter touches on the basics, including the different types of accounting and an overview of the accounting process. With this information you can make journal entries, prepare a worksheet, make adjusting entries, and find errors in your books.

Choosing Your Basis of Accounting

Most organizations use two methods of accounting to track their transactions. Your nonprofit's *basis of accounting* basically is the method by which you account for things. You can account for things when they happen or you can wait until later. The method you choose affects when you make journal entries about transactions. They're centered on how and when you recognize revenues and expenses.

You need to choose between the two following methods:

- **Cash-basis accounting:** The cash-basis method is simple to use because you recognize that a transaction has taken place only when you receive or distribute cash.

- **Accrual-basis accounting:** The accrual-based system recognizes revenues when a promise or pledge is given and when revenues are earned, while expenses are recognized when they're incurred and not when they're paid.

Your donors aren't concerned with which method you use to account for your finances. They're more concerned that you effectively manage the funding and use it for its intended purpose. Check out Chapter 2 for more on the ins and outs of these two types of accounting methods.

Using the accrual method of accounting is your best choice. All financial statements must be prepared according to generally accepted accounting principles (GAAP) using the accrual method. To keep things simple, go with the accrual basis to stay in compliance with GAAP.

If you're running a small nonprofit and you're keeping your own books or you have a part-time bookkeeper doing the work, you may want to account for your transactions on the cash basis and pass the books on to your accountant or CPA firm at the end of the year to compile your financial statements. Your CPA can convert your cash-basis books to accrual basis.

Going through the Accounting Process

Although accounting can be quite maddening at times, it does follow a clear logic. As you try to get a firm grasp of the accounting process, start with the end in mind first. In the end you provide financial statements. Your donors care that your financial statements fairly represent your true financial position for a given time period as of a certain date. So your goal is to keep adequate records that enable you to account for every transaction. The following sections highlight the nuts and bolts of the accounting process and what the general recording process looks like.

Eyeing the specifics of the process

To fully understand how to record and track your nonprofit's financial transactions, you need to understand the ins and outs of the process. You also need to know what the different accounts are and how putting them together creates your nonprofit's bottom line.

So how does the process work? It starts when your organization receives a donation. You enter the donation into a journal and post it to the general ledger (check out the later sections in this chapter for the specific how-to). Once a month or when the accounting period is over, you (or your book-keeping and accounting staff) prepare a trial balance. A *trial balance* is a listing of all accounts and their balances. If the total of the accounts debit balances equals the total of the accounts credit balances, then your accounts are in balance (refer to the "Reaching the Trial Balance" section later in this chapter for more specific direction).

At the end of the month or year, you take your *unadjusted trial balance* (a trial balance prepared before adjustments; it's the account balances from your ledger) and make adjusting entries. *Adjusting entries* are made to your accounts to bring them to their actual balance. For example, adjustments are made for prepaid accounts and for expenses incurred but not yet paid. You make adjustments to

- Accrued revenue (earned revenue that hasn't been recorded because payment hasn't been received)
- Accrued salaries that are unpaid and unrecorded
- Depreciation (allocating the cost and usage of assets as expense)
- Prepaid expenses, such as insurance
- Office supplies used
- *deferred* Unearned revenue (payments received in advance)

After you finish adjusting the entries and everything balances, you're ready to do an *adjusted trial balance.* Your adjusted trial balance verifies that things are in balance. If your entries are out of balance, then you must find your errors. I help you with this in the "Correcting errors" section later in this chapter. Figure 6-1 provides a snapshot of the accounting process.

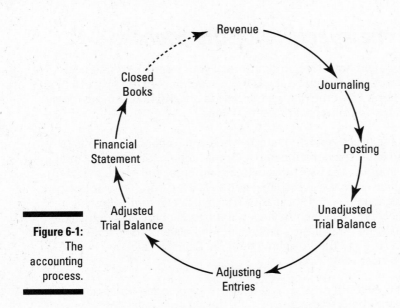

Figure 6-1:
The
accounting
process.

Looking at the two sides of an account

Before you begin recording transactions and making journal entries, you need to understand debits and credits. You even need to record purchases made with cash in your books. Why? When you disburse cash, it reduces the amount you have available. You make a journal entry to decrease cash, or a credit. And if the purchase adds something of value, such as an asset, you increase what you have, so you debit. When you fully understand debits and credits, you'll be able to do journal entries like a pro. Knowing this information is important because it's the building blocks for your record-keeping transactions. If you make a mistake at the beginning of the accounting cycle, finding it later is more difficult and can throw your books out of balance.

For example, you purchase $100 of office supplies. You have to credit your cash, which means your cash decreases by $100. You enter this transaction on the right. You also debit your office supplies, which increases your assets. You enter this transaction on the left.

To understand journal entries, you need to know the mechanics of accounting. You should remember the following.

- ✔ Revenue, liability, and equity accounts are increased by credits.
- ✔ Asset and expense accounts are increased by debits.

Think of accounts as having two sides. The debit side is on the left, and the credit side is on the right. And because credits increase revenue, liability, and equity accounts, debits decrease them. Think of your journal page like a capital "T." Any transaction you enter on the left is a debit; anything you enter on the right is a credit. If you hear someone talk about "T" accounts, this is what they mean.

Consider the debit and credit outline in Table 6-1. This table shows you how normal balances affect accounts on the statement of financial position and statement of activities. *Normal balances* indicate what you do to increase the accounts. To decrease the accounts, you do the opposite. For example, because a debit increases an expense account, to decrease an expense, you credit the account.

Table 6-1	Understanding Normal Balances of Accounts
Balance Sheet Accounts	*Normal Balance*
Assets	Debit
Liabilities	Credit
Equity	Credit
Income Statement Accounts	*Normal Balance*
Revenue	Credit
Expense	Debit

Recording Journal Entries

I try to write in my personal journal every day to reflect on the events of the day. In accounting you use a *journal* to record transactions in the order that they occur. A journal is often referred to as the *book of original entry* because it's the first place where you record transactions in the accounts.

Your journal doesn't have to be a physical book. Calling it a book doesn't mean you need to purchase a notebook to write down your transaction. You can do it on your computer. Or if you choose, you can use columnar paper and three-ring binders.

Journaling is recording transactions in a journal. Each account has a title or name, such as "cash," and you record monetary increases and decreases for each one. Your journal entries indicate the transaction date, the names of the accounts involved, the amount of each debit and credit, and an explanation of the transaction. At the time you record journal entries, you don't need to make any specific reference; just make sure you get the info recorded. See Chapter 5 for more about making the entries in the right accounts.

Every transaction is recorded in at least two accounts with equal debits and credits to keep your accounting books in balance. For example, if you purchase supplies for $75 on October 8, 2009, you need to record the transaction in two accounts. First you need to debit supplies for $75 and then credit cash for $75. You make the first entry in your journal.

Figure 6-2 shows a sample journal entry. (Flip to Chapter 2 for explanations of double-entry bookkeeping.) The following sections dive in to recording the actual journal entries in three easy steps.

	General Journal		Page 1
Date	**Account Titles and Explanation**	**Debit**	**Credit**
20XX			
Dec.	2 Advertising Expense	300	
	Cash		300
	To pay for monthly radio ads		
	3 Computer Repair Expense	75	
	Cash		75
	To pay computer technician		
	5 Cash	500	
	Donation Revenue		500
	To record donation from United Way		
	6 Salaries Expense	400	
	Cash		400
	To pay receptionist salary		

Figure 6-2:
A sample journal entry.

Step one: Write the transaction date

The first step you take when making journal entries is to record the transaction date. This information includes the year in small figures, the month on the first line, and the day. You need to know the dates that transactions took place to help keep your books current and up-to-date. You record journal entries in the order of their occurrence.

So, for example, you receive a check for $1,000 from a donor on Oct. 8, 2010. Besides putting a smile on your face for receiving the money, you also need to deposit the check. You create the following journal entry:

Date	Debit	Credit
20XX		
Oct. 8		

In this journal entry, you increase your cash by $1,000 by debiting cash. And you increase your donations by $1,000 by crediting donations. Cash is an asset account. Donations are revenue accounts.

When recording journal entries and ledger postings, don't use dollar signs because the only thing you can debit and credit to accounts is money. Everyone knows you're talking about money.

Step two: Write the account names

The second step of recording your journal entries includes writing the names of the accounts to be debited and credited. You write the name of the account to be debited first, and write the name of the account to be credited indented about 1 inch. Doing so helps readers identify quickly which accounts have been debited and which have been credited. Placing the account to be debited first is important so other bookkeepers can follow your flow.

For example, to record the $1,000 donation you received, you may write the account names as such:

Date	Debit	Credit
20XX		
Oct. 8 Cash		
Donation Revenue		

Step three: Write the amount of each debit and credit

In the third step, you write the debit amount in the debit column opposite the name of the account to be debited, and write the credit amount in the credit column opposite the account to be credited. So, if doing one thing to one side of an account increases the account, then the opposite happens when you record the entry on the opposite side. Asset and expense accounts are increased by debits; to decrease them, you credit them.

For example, for the $1,000 donation, record the amount as such:

Date		Debit	Credit
20XX			
Oct. 8	Cash	1,000	
	Donation Revenue		1,000

Step four: Write an explanation or reason for transaction

Each transaction has an explanation. The final step to recording a journal entry is to state the reason for the transaction. Write the explanation on the next line, indented about ½ inch. Keep this explanation short and to the point, but be sure to include enough info to explain the transaction.

For example, in the case of the $1,000 donation, you record the following:

Date		Debit	Credit
20XX			
Oct. 8	Cash	1,000	
	Donation Revenue		1,000

To record $1,000 individual donation from Jasmine Bentham, check #1299.

Leave some space between journal entries to set them apart. This space keeps entries from running together and makes it easier for you or someone else to read later.

When you're making journal entries, usually no posting references or numbers are listed, but when you get ready to post to your general ledger, you'll enter account numbers of the ledger accounts to which the debits and credit are copied. See the next section on posting to your general ledger.

Posting to the General Ledger

With bookkeeping and accounting, you want to keep track of how many assets you have in the different accounts in the chart of accounts (see Chapter 5). You keep track of this information by posting it or recording it in your *general ledger,* which is basically a group of accounts. Inside your general ledger are all the accounts that appear on your financial statements. Assets, liabilities, and net assets (statement of financial position accounts) are placed first, followed by revenues and expenses (statement of activities accounts).

Your journal is the book of original entry. Depending on the magnitude of your accounting transactions, posting journal entries information from the journal to the ledger is usually done near the end of the day. Everything entered in your journal for that day should be posted to your ledger.

Accounts in the general ledger are arranged in the following order:

- ✔ **Cash:** This includes coins, currency, checks, money orders, checking and savings accounts, and short-term CDs.
- ✔ **Donation receivables:** They are promises and pledges to give.
- ✔ **Inventory:** This account records the price paid for any product sitting on your shelves that you plan to sell.
- ✔ **Prepaid insurance:** Here is what you've paid in advance for insurance coverage that expires as the days go by.
- ✔ **Land:** This account includes land purchased or owned by your organization. Although a valuable asset, land should not be depreciated (see Chapter 2 for more on depreciation).
- ✔ **Buildings:** This includes your office building if you're buying or already own it. Buildings usually have a depreciable span of 39 to 40 years.
- ✔ **Equipment:** This account records the purchase of copy machines, vehicles, office furniture, file cabinets, and similar items. Equipment usually has a useful life span of three to seven years.
- ✔ **Notes payable:** These are liabilities or promises to pay a certain amount on a certain date.
- ✔ **Accounts payable:** These are short-term liabilities usually paid within a month or two. They're considered a current liability.
- ✔ **Salaries payable:** These are usually recorded on the statement of financial position because employees have earned salaries but haven't been paid yet.
- ✔ **Mortgage payable:** This is a long-term liability to a creditor for a large purchase of land or buildings.
- ✔ **Bonds payable:** This is a long-term liability between the issuer and lender. Some organizations borrow large sums of money to finance large purchases, equipment, and other assets. The money is obtained by issuing bonds. Bonds are paid back, and usually you have a bonds payable and interest payable account to account for bonds payable.
- ✔ **Revenue:** These accounts are established for all sources of income: donations, grant, fees from services rendered, and interest income. For

most nonprofits, donations from individuals, corporations, foundations, and state and federal grants each are recorded in a separate account.

✔ **Expenses:** These are usually the last group of general ledger accounts. You name your expense accounts according to their purpose. Some typical expenses are rent expense, supplies expense, insurance expense, salaries expense, and so on.

Keep in mind the accounts in the general ledger vary from one organization to another. Which accounts you set up depend on

✔ The nature of your organization

✔ The way you operate

✔ The size of your nonprofit

✔ The amount of detail required by your board

✔ State and local laws

✔ Requirements by federal programs

Before you can post to your general ledger, you need to know which accounts are applicable to your nonprofit. Your ledger is like a master file or group of accounts that you record your accounting activities. To determine how to classify accounts, see Chapter 5.

When transferring your debit info from your journals to your general ledger, you post information following these steps:

1. **Find the account name in your ledger.**

2. **Copy the date of the transaction as written in the journal to your ledger.**

3. **Write the debit amount as shown in the journal in your ledger.**

4. **Enter the letter G (general journal) and the journal page number in your ledger.**

5. **Enter the new balance after making the entry in your ledger.**

6. **Enter the account number of the account to which the amount was posted in your journal.**

   This account number is a cross-reference to trace your steps. One other benefit to writing the account number last is it indicates that the posting process is complete.

For entering the credit entry, you perform the same steps in your ledger, just write the credit amount as shown in your journal.

Check out Figure 6-3 for an example of what a general ledger page looks like after you've posted your transaction from your journal.

Cash **No. 1110**

Date	Debit	Credit	Balance		Date	Debit	Credit	Balance
20XX				continued...	22		100	2,200
1-Oct	2,000		2,000		22		100	2,100
5	200		2,200		27		100	2,000
6		500	1,700		29	300		2,300
10		200	1,500		29	500		2,800
13	300		1,800		3-Dec	200		3,000
14		100	1,700		3	300		3,300
19	200		1,900		3		100	3,200
22		400	1,500		5	300		3,500
29	500		2,000		6		500	3,000
1-Nov	300		2,300		9		400	2,600
1		200	2,100		13		100	2,500
2		100	2,000		17	450		2,950
3	100		2,100		19		200	2,750
7		500	1,600		20	250		3,000
8	250		1,850		21	125		3,125
14	2,000		3,850		22		225	2,900
16		1,500	2,350		28	3000		5,900
17		350	2,000		29	1000		6,900
20	500		2,500		30		1,900	5,000
21		200	2,300		31		4,675	325

Figure 6-3:
A sample general ledger page.

Reaching the Trial Balance

After you post the last entries to your general ledger, it's time to prepare a trial balance. Your *trial balance* lists all the balances of the general ledger accounts and totals all accounts having a debit balance and all accounts having a credit balance. The total debit and credit balances of each account in the general ledger are transferred to the trial balance. The sum of the debits in the trial balance must equal the sum of the credits.

The following sections walk you through creating a trial balance, help you make adjustments as needed to come up with the final balance, and address what to do when you find errors.

Preparing the trial balance: The how-to

Your trial balance is a test to see if your debits equal your credits and to provide evidence of accuracy in the accounts. This allows you to verify that your numbers are correct before you prepare your financial statements. Most organizations prepare a trial balance at the end of the month. Most accounting software on the market today doesn't allow you to enter accounts that are out of balance. They'll send a warning message when debits and credits don't balance.

To prepare a trial balance, you write down all your account titles from your ledger and the debit or credit balances in each. Each time you've posted to your ledger, you've balanced it, so now all you need is to make a list by writing down those account titles and their balances. That's it!

Understanding which accounts require adjustments

Two accounting principles dictate making adjustments. *Adjustments* are journal entries of changes in accounts. For example, adjustments are made to correct, to depreciate, and to make any changes required by an auditor.

Generally accepted accounting principles (GAAP) require you to assign revenues to the period in which they're earned (the *realization principle*). And expenses are reported in the same period as the revenues earned as a result of them when it is practical to do so, thereby matching revenues and expenses (the *matching principle*). For example, if it's time to close your month or year and you have salaries that have been earned but not paid, you need to make adjusting entries to record that salary expense.

For example, adjusting entries are as follows:

Date		Debit	Credit
20XX			
Dec. 31	Salaries Expense	105	
	Salaries Payable		105
	To record the accrued wages.		
20XX			
Dec. 31	Unearned Daycare Fees	125	
	Day Care Fees Earned		125
	Earned day care fees that were received in advance.		

In other words, revenues should be reflected on the financial statements in the period in which they're earned. And expenses should be charged to the accounting period in which they're incurred. Sometimes this requires making adjustments.

Adjusting entries affects accounts on the statement of activities. Revenue and expenses accounts may require adjustments. You probably need to prepare adjustments for the following accounts:

- ✔ **Prepaid expenses** include payments in advance of use. A prepaid expense is considered an asset until it's consumed in the operation of your business. An example of a prepaid expense is paying an insurance premium for a year.

- ✔ **Accrued expenses** are expenses incurred but not yet paid. For example, at the close of your accounting period, but prior to your year-end close, some things remain unrecorded because payment isn't due. Examples of accrued expenses are utilities, telephone bills, and unpaid wages.

- ✔ **Unearned revenues** include payments prior to delivery of the product or service. This can be the sale of tickets for a benefit dinner or golf tournament. You may collect money weeks in advance of the event.

- ✔ **Depreciation** is an allocation of the purchase price of an asset based on its useful life. Assets are expensed over their useful life through depreciation. As they lose their value, a portion is written off as an expense.

Check out the "Correcting errors" section later in this chapter to see how adjustments are made to these accounts.

Finding errors

No matter how careful or meticulous you are with this accounting stuff, you're going to make mistakes. There's no way to avoid it. If you find an error in your trial balance, don't despair. It happens to everyone. You know you have an error when your figures don't add up when you total all debits and all credits that were adjusted.

If you know you have an error because the figures don't add up, I suggest you organize all of your records (see Chapter 4 for more on the importance of record keeping) and then take a short break before coming back to the problem. Walking away from the numbers for a few minutes can give you a fresh outlook and help you solve the problem faster. Count to ten, take a restroom break, grab something to eat, and then come back to the problem.

What if you've re-added the numbers, pored over your paperwork, and checked the figures, but you still aren't sure where the error is occurring? Spend some time looking over the following areas.

Ferreting out basic errors

Your general ledger is only as accurate as your journal. If you entered incorrect data while journaling, you probably transferred the same wrong information to the ledger. Go back to the beginning and compare journal entries to general ledger entries. If you still can't find the error, go back over each transaction and look at receipts, invoices, checks, and bills. Carefully review each item to ensure that you recorded the correct information in your journal and in your ledger.

If you find that your trial balance is still out of balance and the difference is evenly divisible by 9, you've made a transposition error. A *transposition error* occurs when you switch the order of the digits. You write 428 instead of 482, for example (see Chapter 7 for more on detecting these mistakes).

Even if your accounting system is computerized, you or one of your staff members has to enter the numbers. Every once in a while, the person entering the information makes a mistake that throws things off. One of the objectives of an audit is to find or detect errors that have a material effect on an organization's financial statements. Do the following to locate errors:

- ✔ Refer back to your journal and check the posting and totals
- ✔ Check the posting and balances in your general ledger accounts
- ✔ Check all balances in the trial balance

Being aware of hidden errors

Keep in mind that some errors can't be detected. For example, if you forget to record a transaction, or if you copy the incorrect debit amount and credit amount in accounts, it's highly unlikely these would be found.

Some errors cancel each other out. If you make a $1,000 error twice, the two may cancel each other out. Or you may make an error by debiting the wrong account within the same account group. For example, if you charge something to Vehicle Expense that should have been charged to Office Supplies, you probably wouldn't detect this error. However, your auditor probably will detect material amounts. He'll also define for you what's considered material for your nonprofit.

One way to reduce the chance of errors like these is to create a monthly trial balance. Tracking your accounts by creating a monthly trial balance can save you lots of time and energy. If you keep everything in balance month by month, you'll breeze through the final process at the end of the year. (See Chapter 19 for more on closing the year-end books.)

Correcting errors

So after hunting through your transactions, you find your error. Although some errors are easier to find than others, most are easily correctible. Errors made in calculations and balancing, posting to the wrong side of an account, entering the wrong amounts, or simply forgetting to enter a transaction can be easily corrected. The trial balance shows these errors pretty quickly. How you correct the error depends on whether it's in the journal and the general ledger or in your journal only.

Making a journal correction

Depending on where and when you find an error in the journal affects how you correct it. Usually you can correct it by drawing a line through the error and writing the correct amount or title above the error. If the data has been journalized and not posted to the general ledger, that's all you have to do.

For example, say you see the following entry in your journal:

Date		Debit	Credit
20XX			
Oct. 8	Office Furniture and Fixtures	75	
	Cash		75

To record the purchase of office supplies.

If you made the previous entry when you purchased office supplies on Oct 8, then the following entry is needed to correct the error.

Date		Debit	Credit
20XX			
Oct. 8	Office Supplies	75	
	Office Furniture and Fixtures		75

To correct entry of Oct 8 when the Office Furniture and Fixtures account was debited in error instead of Office Supplies.

The debit to Office Supplies records the purchase in the right account and the credit to Office Furniture and Fixtures cancels out the error of the first entry. There's no need to bother with cash, because it was handled properly.

If the incorrect information from the journal has already been recorded in the ledger, you have to take a few more steps to make everything right. I explain how in the next section.

Making a ledger correction

If you find a mistake after it's been posted to the ledger, you need to correct the journal and ledger entry to fix the problem. For example, if you purchased something for cash and you accidently recorded it as an Accounts Payable, by making the following entry

Date		Debit	Credit
20XX			
Aug. 14	Office Supplies	50	
	Accounts Payable		50

To record the purchase of office supplies.

To correct this error the following entry is required:

Date		Debit	Credit
20XX			
Aug. 31	Accounts Payable	50	
	Cash		50

To correct an error in the entry of Aug. 14 in which office supplies purchased for cash was recorded to Accounts Payable.

After you record adjusting journal entries in the journal, you have to post to the accounts in the general ledger, just like the earlier journal entries. It's the same process — journal first and then post to the ledger.

Chapter 7

Balancing the Checkbook: Donations and Expenses

The center of every transaction in nonprofit organizations starts and ends in the checkbook register. In fact, you can find the keys that unlock your nonprofit's financial position in the checkbook register and bank statements. Having more money than you thought you had in your checking account is okay, but having less money can cost you if a check bounces.

The bank records every donation deposited and expense paid out of your checking account and sends you a monthly statement showing this activity. All deposits are considered *credits* (additions) to your account, and all withdrawals are considered *debits* (subtractions). The difference between credits and debits equals your checking account *balance*.

Having a checking account saves you time and energy. For example, driving to each utility to pay your bill in cash would take a lot of time away from bigger duties — serving your community. It makes it easier for bookkeeping and record keeping if you pay bills out of a checking account instead of using cash. That's why organization is a must. Having a plan to track all donations and expenses is essential; if you don't have a plan, you'll inevitably run into major problems because you won't know whether you have enough money to cover your expenses and pay your bills.

Writing a check creates a paper trail between your checkbook, the bank, and the vendor or bill you're paying. It's easier to trace your steps when you have a bank that provides a bank statement. This paper trail comes in handy during your nonprofit's audit.

This chapter focuses on how to use the checkbook register to balance your nonprofit's checking account and shows you how to record and log transactions when they occur.

If you just opened a checking account, balancing the account in your head may seem like a practical approach when only a few transactions are taking place. Don't rely on this system as an adequate method. You'll regret it later. Not balancing your checkbook can cost you returned check fees and overdraft fees, and cause you to lose your credibility.

Getting the Lowdown on Your Checkbook Register

Before you can balance your nonprofit's checkbook register, you first need to know what the register is. You're probably familiar with your personal checking account register. In fact, you've probably been annoyed at the supermarket while you waited in line as someone writes in her checkbook register. However annoying she may be, she's recording the check amount to keep track of her money. With your nonprofit's checking account, the checkbook register holds valuable information.

You use a *checkbook register* to record the following:

- ✔ Each check when written
- ✔ Each deposit when made
- ✔ Each withdrawal either from an ATM or at a teller window
- ✔ All bank service charges

Figure 7-1 shows you an example of a checkbook register for a fictional nonprofit organization. In this figure you can see entries for the transactions that take place in the checking account. The rest of this chapter discusses how you record information in your register to balance your nonprofit's checkbook.

Duplicate checks can be a lifesaver when it comes to recording information in your checkbook register. *Duplicate checks* create a copy of a check as you fill it out so you have all the details of the check after you hand it over to pay for something. These nifty copies help you stay on top of your account balance because you can look at the copies and transfer the transaction information to your register.

Date	#	Payee/Description of Transaction	Withdrawal, Payment (−)	Deposit, Credit (+)	Balance
Beg Bal					$ 1,000.00
10/1/09		Donations deposit		500	$ 1,500.00
10/5/09		ATM - Machine Withdrawal	50.00		$ 1,450.00
10/8/09	255	George Rembert/to purchase supplies	100.00		$ 1,350.00
10/8/09		Bank service fees	8.00		$ 1,342.00
10/9/09		Fundraiser/Deposit		750.00	$ 2,092.00
10/9/09	256	Web Designer	25.00		$ 2,067.00
10/10/09	257	Salaries Payable	925.00		$ 1,142.00
10/13/09		Donations Deposit		300.00	$ 1,442.00
Balances			1,108.00	1,550.00	$ 1,442.00

Figure 7-1: A nonprofit's checkbook register.

Another lifesaver to keeping your register balanced is online banking. You can see an updated and current balance in your account when you access your account online. Online banking gives you a heads-up. But even with online banking, you still need a paper trail because one day you may be audited, and you'll need to have all deposits and withdrawals from your checking account recorded in the check register. Even if you're not a number cruncher, you still need to keep a checkbook register because you need to stay on top of your finances.

Adding and Tracking Nonprofit Donations

To have a complete picture of how much money your nonprofit has on hand, you want to keep an accurate picture of the money coming in. Most of what comes in is in the form of *donations* (charitable contributions that individuals as well as organizations give to your nonprofit). Your nonprofit may have other sources of income (check out the nearby sidebar "Identifying other potential income sources" for more info). However, you mainly deposit cash donations into your checking account.

Most of your donations may come in the form of checks written by donors, foundations, and corporations. Keeping track of those donations and depositing them into your checking account is important because you want to make deposits in a timely fashion so the money is available to support your organization. If you don't deposit a donor's check right away, it may bounce. It's best to deposit all checks right away so they can clear the donor's account, allowing your nonprofit to avoid unnecessary bank fees.

Identifying other potential income sources

Your nonprofit can collect revenue from more than a dozen sources. The most common include contributions, corporate and foundation grants, government grants, government contracts, membership dues, interest on savings and temporary cash investments, dividends and interest from marketable securities, rental income, gains or losses on the sale of investments, special events, and so on. Although you have many potential income sources and you can't operate without income, you have to be careful how you generate income to sustain yourself.

I know you have to have income to keep your nonprofit operating, and I know you may be tempted to come up with a money-making venture to keep your nonprofit operating at maximum capacity. But be careful not to earn too much money by doing things outside the scope of your purpose. When you step outside your scope and purpose by generating income unrelated to your purpose, you may have to pay income taxes.

Income unrelated to your purpose is called *unrelated business income (UBI)*, and there's a tax form to go with it — Form 990-T. For more about unrelated business income, see Chapter 14.

The following sections focus on how to log monetary donations into your checking account, the different types of donations you may encounter, and why you need to differentiate between them.

Logging donations in your register

As your nonprofit receives donations, you need to make sure you write them down (or *log* them) in your checkbook register as soon as you deposit them. Keeping your checkbook register current is necessary to avoid *overdraft fees* (fees the bank charges you when you write a check for more money than you have in your account) and to stay on top of your organization's income and expenses.

For example, if you don't record a deposit, you may put off making an important purchase because you think you don't have the money (when in fact you do). Or if you incorrectly record a deposit, such as writing $2,850 when the deposit was actually $285, you may end up being charged an overdraft fee if you write a check for more money than you have in your account.

To record your deposits in your checkbook register, you enter the date, the source of the deposit, and the amount of the transaction in the corresponding columns. In the checkbook register in Figure 7-1, you have three deposits. The first deposit of $500 was made on October 1, 2009; the second deposit for $750 was made on October 8; and the third deposit for $300 was made on October 13. The total of your deposits is $1,550.

Raking in the cash, checks, and other donations

People can write checks, hand you cash, or pay by credit card when they donate money to your organization. Larger groups may give you a grant to finance your mission. No matter what form the donations take, you need to know the type of donation they are before you can record them in your checkbook register. This section takes a closer look at the different types of donations that you need to record as deposits.

In addition to tracking donations, you need to keep a list of donors. The donors list should include donors' names and addresses, and amount donated. You'll need this list for information purposes and to track your donations. Your auditor will use your donors list to randomly verify donations received (see Chapter 20).

Cash donations

Although cash donations are probably the most common type of donation your nonprofit receives, cash is also one of the hardest types of donations to track. Cash, a problem? Cash can present a problem because it's so easily transferable without leaving a paper trail.

Searching for the right bank

Shopping for and finding a bank that addresses your nonprofit's needs is especially important. You want a bank that will honor your status as a nonprofit organization by waiving checking account fees. In today's market, banks are competitive, so if you do your research, you can find one that will benefit your nonprofit the most.

So what should you look for in a bank? Ask yourself what's important for your nonprofit. One important factor to consider is how much activity you transact within a given month. Pay attention to banks that offer free services up to a minimum number of transactions, and then charge $1 per transaction thereafter. However, if you make lots of deposits and use your bank card daily, you may end up paying your bank too

much. The bank I use for my nonprofit's checking account doesn't charge me service fees or fees for online banking.

Many banks offer *overdraft protection* — where the bank will pay the check if you overdraw your account. This can save you some embarrassment and some money, not to mention overdraft fees from the merchant and the bank. Talk with your banker about overdraft protection.

Online banking is an excellent way to keep an eye on your bank account. You need to keep an eye on your checking account because banks make mistakes too. Find out if online banking is free before you sign up for it.

The best way to handle a cash donation is to give the donor a receipt if the donation is made in your office. If you receive cash in the mail, you should send the donor a receipt. You don't want to turn down cash just because it's hard to track, but your nonprofit should have some checks and balances in place to properly account for cash donations. (See Chapter 2 for more on setting up checks and balances.)

For example, what if someone walks into your organization and gives a $1,000 cash donation to your receptionist? What procedures do you have in place to ensure the money is reported? Although you hope everyone in your office is honest, you also know people face hardships in life, and sometimes the temptation to pocket the money is too great. If the receptionist is in the office alone, what happens if she decides to borrow it until payday? When payday comes, the receptionist decides to wait until next payday. What started out as a mere loan has turned into a pile of debt, and no one knows about it but the receptionist.

Donations made by check

A big chunk of your donations probably come in the form of a check. Although these are more secure than cash donations, they can be tedious to process. (See the "Handling and recording the donations" section for more about depositing donations.)

Watch out for bad checks. Be prepared because donors will write you checks that they don't have enough funds in their checking accounts to cover. The best way to stay on top of knowing whether you've received a bad check is to review your account online. Even then it may take a few days before you know whether a check has cleared. It may appear that you have a good working balance in your checkbook register because people have been giving and you've recorded the donations as deposits. But don't count your chicks before they hatch. Until those checks clear your bank, don't count them as available cash.

Protecting your cash

While working for a doctor a few years ago, I noticed that patients were paying their bills with cash. I knew the doctor couldn't watch the cash and take care of the patients, so I put a control system in place.

First, I bought a duplicate cash receipt book. Second, I placed a sign on the wall by the cash drawer that stated, "If you don't get a receipt, then your services are free." You know the patients were watching and waiting to not get a receipt. So the patients took care of this one.

In addition, I wrote down the beginning-of-the-day and end-of-the-day cash balances. Then I subtracted the beginning-of-the-day balance from the end-of-the-day balance. The difference was how much we had taken in during the day. The copies of the receipts should add up to this amount. This simple procedure can help you track your cash.

If you can afford it, purchase a *check-swiping system,* such as TeleCheck, to speed up the checking-clearing process. These systems are connected directly to banks and reject a check if the money isn't in the account. This is the best way to avoid delays in waiting for checks to clear your bank account. This is the same system used by some of the large retail stores. You've probably written a check at a store and handed it to the clerk, who swipes the check through a machine and gives it back to you. You can do the same for checks written to your agency. The cost of the terminal and printer runs between $399 and $999. Plus, you'll pay transaction fees and monthly customer service fees. For more about quick check-clearing processing, visit the following Web site: www.instamerchant.com/check-guarantee.html.

Credit card donations

Credit card donations are another popular way you receive donations. However, when reporting these donations, you need to know that when someone donates $1,000 on his credit card, you don't receive $1,000. So you can't record credit card donations for the total amount donated. The major credit card companies — American Express, Discover Card, MasterCard, and Visa — all charge a user fee or percentage for processing the payment. When a donor contributes to your organization by swiping his credit card, you're not going to get the total amount.

For example, when you swipe a donor's credit card, the bank takes 1 to 5 percent of the amount donated as its processing fee. If a donor uses his credit card to give you a $100 donation and the bank charges a 2 percent fee, you only receive $98 in your bank account. The donor has given a $100 donation, but you have to pay a $2 bank fee.

Don't count credit card donations before they clear the bank. The credit card company may reject the payment and cause you to overdraw your checking account. The amount of time it takes for the transaction to clear your bank depends on your bank, the credit card company, and the day of the week. Some transactions are transmitted, posted, and delivered to your account within minutes, while others take a bit longer. You can always call your bank to check the status of credit card donations.

Direct bank draft donations

Direct bank draft donations allow people to donate a large sum of money broken into smaller amounts over a longer period of time. Each month the employer takes the designated amount out of an employee's paycheck as a payroll deduction and sends the money to the nonprofit. These types of donations are a win-win; the donor can make small donations that add up over time without feeling a big difference in take-home pay, and the nonprofit receives a donation that's often larger than a one-time donation would be. Some of the larger nonprofits, like United Way, do direct bank drafts from employees' pay.

This method results in the deposit going directly into your bank account around the same day of each month. You need to pay attention to the timing of these deposits so you can record them in your checkbook register on the right day.

Banks don't record deposits on weekends or holidays. Keeping this in mind can help you with the timing differences and help to keep everything in balance. When the deposit date falls on a nonbusiness day, the bank will make the deposit according to its policy, which usually is the next business day.

Grants

A *grant* affords your organization large sums of money that you don't have to pay back. Some foundations and corporations donate grant money in the form of a check, while some government grants reimburse you by direct deposit after the money is spent. No matter how you receive the grant money, remember that a good steward manages grant money by tracking and monitoring how the money is used. For more information about managing grants, see Chapter 11.

All contributions received from the grant should be deposited into your bank account and recorded in your checkbook register. Make a copy of the check before you deposit it; don't just cash it. Some people open a new account just to manage the grant, but this is up to you. Whether to open a separate account depends on how much money the grant is for and how likely it is that you'll have problems keeping transactions separate.

Handling and recording the donations

When you receive donations, you need to properly track and record them. You want to ensure you create a paper trail that leads back to the donors list for auditing purposes. You want to get those donations in your bank account and write your donor a thank-you letter. Make sure you do the following:

1. **At the end of the day, add all the donations you received during the day. Record the amounts on a bank deposit slip.**

   If the money came from a new donor, add the person to your donors list. If the donation came from an established donor, open the donor's account and record the new donation.

2. **Make copies of the checks and deposit slip before you deposit the checks.**

   Because banks make mistakes every day, it's important for you to keep track of every deposit made to your account. Keep copies of the deposited checks and deposit slips in a safe place so when the bank sends the monthly bank statement, you have proof of deposit. This is very important if you make deposits after banking hours through night depositories.

3. **Write down the deposit in your checkbook register.**

   Not writing down a deposit can throw your checking account out of whack. Forgetting to write down a deposit is not as bad as forgetting to write down a written check.

4. **Take the checks and the deposit slip to the bank and make the deposit.**

   If you have a high volume of checks coming in for large amounts, you don't want to keep them at your office any longer than necessary. Your bank has a night deposit box that you can use to make your deposits after hours. This requires a trip the next day to pick up the deposit slip and bank bag, but it may be worth the trouble. Plus, keeping checks at your location for extended periods of time isn't a good idea. You open yourself up for possible robbery or some other unforeseen event.

At the end of the month, you can compare your records against the bank's records. You'll receive a *bank statement* that lists all the transactions made on your account. This statement makes it easier for bookkeepers to track the transactions that the bank received and serves as a checkpoint. Just eyeballing this statement isn't enough; you should use the statement to balance your checkbook register (see the "Tie It Together: Balancing the Checkbook" section).

Subtracting Your Expenses

To balance your checkbook, not only do you need to record and add all donations (as the previous section explains), but you also need to record and subtract all expenses. Every check you write to pay a bill is an expense; if you don't carefully record all these expenses, your checking account balance won't be accurate, and you may end up overdrawing your account.

The following sections take a closer look at the types of expenses you need to subtract from your checkbook register and how to record the transactions in your register. By paying close attention to this information, you can get a clearer picture of how much money is in your checking account.

Making the necessary deductions in your checkbook register

Receiving bills each month is like death and taxes. They're inevitable. When you receive them, you can't ignore them. You have to pay them and record them in your checkbook register right away. If you forget to record just one transaction, you can throw your account out of balance and end up paying unnecessary bank fees.

For example, you have $1,840 in your checking account, and you have to write checks to cover your utilities for $300, your rent for $1,000, and your insurance for $300. You subtract each check from your total; now you know you have $240 in your account. If you don't write down one of these expenses, such as the insurance bill, you'll think you have $540 in your account, which may cause you to write a check for $500 to cover your car payment. Doing so results in an overdraft and potential costly overdraft fees.

After you pay the expenses, make sure you log them in your checkbook register. Doing so keeps your checkbook register current.

To record your expenses in your checkbook register, you simply log them in as you write the checks. For example, Figure 7-1 shows that check 255 was written for $100 to George Rembert to purchase supplies; check 256 was for $25 to pay the web designer; and check 257 was for $925 for salaries payable. You list each piece of information for the transaction in its own column: date, check number, payee, and withdrawal/payment. For each amount, you subtract it from the running balance in the last column labeled "Balance."

Now, suppose you had to pay your $1,500 insurance bill, but you forgot to log in the $100 check written to George Rembert. Your account balance would show $1,542, and you'd think you had just enough money to pay your insurance. As you can see from the account balance, you only have $1,442 in your account. If you forget to log in a check for even $100, it can put your account into overdraft.

In addition to keeping track of checks you've written, you also need to keep track of expenses associated with the use of a check or debit card. Most of the time when you open a checking account, the bank sends you a check card. Because they look like credit cards, these cards can cause you to forget to track expenses associated with their use. The bank card can be used as a credit card or a debit card. A fee is usually charged to your account for using it as a debit card, so you need to know the fees associated with each type of use. Don't forget to write down these fees to keep your balance current.

Identifying common expenses

As much as you may want to, you can't avoid the dreaded cycle of paying your nonprofit's bills. In fact, it may seem like every time you open your mailbox, you have at least one rearing its ugly head.

You need to have a clear grasp of the types of bills your nonprofit may receive so you know what needs to be deducted from your check register. Some common expenses paid out of your checkbook are:

✔ **Rent:** This is an expense for your office space or building that you're leasing.

✔ **Utilities:** These include telephone, fax, electricity, water, garbage, and so on.

✔ **Payroll/wages:** These are expenses in paying those who provide a service.

✔ **Payroll taxes (federal, state, Medicare, Social Security taxes):** These are expenses that are reported, deducted, and must be paid, if applicable, to federal and state governments.

✔ **Contract labor:** This expense is used when additional help is needed and a contract is issued and signed for a specific time to complete the task at hand.

✔ **Travel expenses:** These expenses occur from going to and from different destinations. They include transportation and lodging, as well as meals.

✔ **Licenses and permits:** These are expenses for your nonprofit licenses and permits that allow you to operate and be recognized as a nonprofit organization in your state, county, and city municipalities.

✔ **Insurance:** This expense is a necessary component to protect you, your clients, your board, and your organization from potential hazards that could be disastrous to your nonprofit.

✔ **Office expenses and supplies:** These include paper, pens, and other small-ticket items, including postage and printing-related supplies.

✔ **Office furniture:** This is usually for desks, chairs, and tables.

✔ **Computer hardware and software:** The category includes computers and software used to help you in run your nonprofit.

✔ **Internet Web site expenses:** This expense may include Web page design, domain name fee, the maintenance and updates of your Web page, and the storing and processing of Web page data.

✔ **Bank service fees:** Banks are competitive, and most allow you to have a free checking account because you're a nonprofit organization. This doesn't mean you get your checks for free, but you won't be charged a fee for the account. Pay attention to the hidden banking fees. Other types of bank fees include the following:

  • **Credit card processing:** These fees may be charged by your banking institute for handling monies deposited and withdrawn with credit cards.

  • **Transaction fees:** These are fees for using a check card or debit card rather than writing checks to make purchases.

- **Non-sufficient funds (NSF) fees:** Your bank charges these fees for processing a check or credit card transaction when the money wasn't available in your account. This is commonly referred to as a *bounced check.*

- **Fee per transaction:** These fees may be charged if you go over the amount of transactions designated by your bank. Some banks offer free checking with a maximum of 25 transactions. With the 26th transaction, you may be charged $1 per transaction thereafter.

- **ATM user fees:** If you use an ATM owned by a different bank, you may be charged. These expenses can range from $1 to $3 per transaction.

✔ **Electronic payment fees:** Receiving and paying bills electronically is part of the going-green concept. It not only offers convenience, but it saves the environment when you receive your bills in your e-mail account versus in the mailbox. Electronic billing is faster than traditional mail and saves time and energy.

To avoid these fees, I steer away from companies that charge to do online payments. For those companies, I use the old-fashioned, albeit slower, method — the mailman.

If you do choose to pay your bills electronically, either directly through the utility or through your bank, watch out for utility bills that go up and down during the year. Not knowing how much will be drafted from your checking account is tricky business.

As a general rule, most people don't keep a lot of extra money in their checking account. If your utility costs are up and down, then you must keep an adequate amount in your account to cover the differences.

✔ **Building security expenses:** This expense may include security cameras and security guards, as well as security alarm system installation and monthly access fees.

✔ **Miscellaneous expenses:** Any fee not listed in the preceding categories that only occurs occasionally or is incidental may be classified as a miscellaneous expense. For example, this may be the tip you give for prompt delivery of your new computer system or some other small, non-essential expense.

Be careful with bills that aren't a fixed amount each month. For example, because the price of natural gas is up, I opted for the budget plan for the gas bill. The *budget plan* means I pay the same amount for gas year round, eliminating really high or really low bills throughout the year.

Relying on direct or automatic bank drafts

To prevent potential errors, you can set up automatic or direct bank drafts with your checking account. *Automatic* or *direct bank drafts* are bills that are paid directly out of your checking account on the same date every month. You should consider direct drafts for bills that are the same amount each month, because bills that fluctuate in balance can do a number on your checking account.

For example, a few years ago I had direct bank draft for my gas bill. Before the price of oil went sky high, my gas bill was averaging $40 a month. In December 2005, my gas bill went up to $289.41. That's nearly a $250 difference. The gas company took $289.41 out of my account when I was expecting a debit of about $40.

Using automatic bank drafts has a few advantages and disadvantages. Some of the advantages are:

- ✔ You save time by not having to write a check.
- ✔ You save money by not having to buy stamps.
- ✔ You save time and money by not going to the post office.
- ✔ You save time by not having to remember to pay the bill.

Because direct drafts are automatic, they pose the following disadvantages:

- ✔ You may forget to record and deduct the draft in your checkbook register.
- ✔ You may forget to make sure you have enough money in your account to cover the payment.
- ✔ If you don't have enough money to cover the draft, you may be hit with an overdraft fee on your account.

I wouldn't advise doing a direct draft for bills that may fluctuate considerably. For example, it's probably safer to have a landline phone bill come directly out of your checking account than a cellphone bill.

It's a good idea to subtract direct drafts on your check register at the beginning of the month. If you're really organized, you can make a note to record the draft when the payment is scheduled to be made directly from your account. Forgetting to log in these expenses can put your organization's finances in a whirlwind.

Tie It Together: Balancing the Checkbook

Most nonprofits hire a bookkeeper to handle the day-to-day finances of the organization and a part-time accountant to tie it all together. Bookkeepers and accountants perform different duties. A good bookkeeper captures everything needed for the accountant to put together your financial reports (see Chapter 2 for more on bookkeeper and accountant duties).

No matter whether you're doing the bookkeeping yourself or you have someone else do it, this section gives you two ways you can ensure your books are balanced and your nonprofit is tracking and recording donations the right way. The bottom line: You need to know what's going on financially with your nonprofit's checking account. You do so by tracking donations and expenses carefully. Doing so can save you time later when filing reports to the IRS, your nonprofit's board of directors, and auditors.

Don't allow a lot of time to pass without reconciling your checkbook register to your bank statement. Banks have a set amount of time to make good on their mistakes. Waiting too long can cause you to lose money.

To help you reconcile your account, I suggest ordering duplicate checks or choosing a bank that sends copies of each check. The more records you have as documentation, the easier it is to get everything to balance.

Using the bank statement

At the end of the month, your bank sends you a bank statement. The bank statement contains a list of deposits and withdrawals (whether cash you've taken out or checks you've written) that have been made to your account. The statement also has a handy-dandy worksheet on the back to help you reconcile the differences between what the bank shows in its records versus what's in your checkbook register. You want to compare the balance you have in your checkbook register with the balance on the bank statement.

Unfortunately these two figures probably aren't going to be the same. You need to make sure you know how much money is in your nonprofit's account. To do so, you reconcile. To *reconcile* your checking account means to account for the differences between the bank statement and your checkbook register. Follow these steps to reconcile:

1. **Compare your bank statement to your checkbook register to figure out which checks have cleared your account and which haven't. Put a checkmark next to the checks that have cleared.**

   A check has *cleared* when the money has been moved from your account to the payee's account.

2. **Repeat Step 1 for your deposits.**

3. **Repeat Step 1 for withdrawals and debit card purchases.**

   If the bank shows something that isn't listed in your checkbook register, check your records to make sure you made the transaction. If you did make the purchase and forgot to record it, write it in now. If you didn't make the transaction, call your bank and ask for more information about it.

4. **Repeat Step 1 for any bank fees or interest the account may have paid or earned.**

5. **List the outstanding checks on a separate piece of paper. Also list any outstanding withdrawals and debit card purchases. Add the numbers.**

   When a check or other transaction is *outstanding,* it hasn't cleared the bank yet. You know which transactions are outstanding because they are the ones you didn't put a checkmark by in Steps 1, 2, and 3.

6. **List any outstanding deposits. Add the numbers.**

7. **Write down the ending balance shown on your bank statement.**

8. **Subtract the amount of outstanding checks and withdrawals that you came up with in Step 5 from the ending balance you wrote down in Step 7.**

9. **Add the amount of outstanding deposits you came up with in Step 6.**

   After completing Steps 8 and 9, your total should match the balance in your checkbook register.

10. **If the number you came up with in Step 9 doesn't match the number in your checkbook register, you have some sleuthing to do.**

    Double-check your math in your checkbook register; make sure you've accounted for all checks, deposits, withdrawals, and fees in your checkbook register; go through Steps 1 through 9 again to make sure you didn't leave anything out or do the math incorrectly.

If your bank statement comes in the mail, you can use the handy worksheet on the back of the statement to balance your checkbook. It has a grid and instructions (similar to the ones I present here) that walk you through the process.

When reconciling your account, you should rely more heavily on your own records than the bank's. The bank statement only covers a set time period; your records are current and up-to-date because you have been tracking every transaction. The following transactions can make it difficult to balance your checkbook:

✔ Checks written but not yet cleared (see the "Considering outstanding checks" section later in this chapter).

✔ Online bill-pay transaction fees. Sometimes utility companies charge a fee to process online payments. It's easy to forget to record these in your register.

> ✔ ATM/debit card transactions and fees. You may have recent transactions that occurred between the time the statement was printed and now.
>
> ✔ Deposits made or recorded after the statement date.
>
> ✔ Bank fees and earned interest not recorded in the checkbook.

Entering the information into QuickBooks

If you're a techie kind of person, consider using the software program QuickBooks for Nonprofit Organizations for help with your nonprofit bookkeeping and accounting needs. QuickBooks can help you with payroll, check writing, accepting credit card payments, and accurately completing and demonstrating financial accountability. It also can help you balance your nonprofit's checkbook.

With QuickBooks you skip all the manual steps taken to track and manage your nonprofit finances. For more information about QuickBooks, see Chapter 4 or go to www.qbalance.com.

You can buy QuickBooks software to download on your computer for under $200. The same company that developed QuickBooks also developed Turbo Tax. This means it's easy to convert your day-to-day bookkeeping and accounting records to financial statements and IRS reports.

Smoothing Out and Avoiding Errors

As careful as you are when recording your donations and expenses, and reconciling your checkbook to bank statements, sometimes errors will happen. A few simple tricks can help you lower the chances of having errors. The following sections explain what to do if you encounter an error and offer some suggestions about how to lower the odds of errors.

Finding and addressing errors

Errors made when writing down numbers are called *transposition errors.* These errors can drive you crazy because it looks like the numbers are adding up correctly, but they aren't. You add the numbers once and get one amount ($859.89), but when you add them again to double-check the math, you get a different amount ($859.98). See how tricky those two numbers are? Somewhere along the line you may have written down the digits you're adding in the wrong order (or entered them in the wrong order if you're using a calculator or adding machine).

To figure out whether an error is caused by transposing digits and not incorrect math, find the difference of the two sums. If it's evenly divisible by 9, you know you have a transposition error. So when you subtract $859.98 and $859.89, you get $0.09. Because that amount is evenly divisible by 9, you know you've got a transposition error within the numbers you added to reach the total.

To avoid these kinds of errors, take your time when writing down and adding numbers. A 10-key adding machine can be useful when checking your math. It gives you a tape of what you keyed in. You can also use a computer spreadsheet to check figures. The old pencil-and-paper method is still a good one to use.

If you've checked and can't find the difference, consider the following suggestions:

- **Ask someone else to look at the numbers.** A fresh set of eyes may be able to find the problem.

- **Call your bank and ask for help.** Because the management values you as a customer, someone will help you.

Considering outstanding checks

You can also prevent errors in your nonprofit's check register by being aware of outstanding checks. *Outstanding checks* are checks you've written that haven't cleared the bank yet. Your bank only records the checks that have been paid out of your account. Your bank doesn't know about the checks you've written but it hasn't received yet. These checks haven't made it to your bank, so they aren't reflected in the bank's balance of your account.

To avoid outstanding checks from being a problem, make sure you keep up with your own balance and check your records against the bank's every month. It's your responsibility to manage your money and account for all expenses as accurately as possible. Staying on top of outstanding checks is important to accurately account for all transactions.

Some organizations hold on to checks for long periods of time before depositing them. If you're not keeping track of your own account, when these checks hit your account, checks could start bouncing.

Some banks have time restraints on how long a check can be held before cashing. Some are only good for 90 days, but you should find out from your bank how long it will honor payments on checks. You may want to consider printing "Void after 6 months" on your checks to avoid problems with old outstanding checks.

Some banks cash checks without even looking at the date. Regardless of when the check is cashed, you owed someone something, and that's the reason the check was written. Overlooking outstanding checks can put you in a financial bind. Talk with your banker about overdraft protection to alleviate the fees associated with a bounced check.

When considering outstanding checks, you also need to account for the timing difference in available funds. For example, when you deposit money, it may not be available for a day or two, but when you write a check, the money is gone within a day, if not instantly. So you have to make sure that when you pay bills you have enough money to cover them. Make a note of when you expect the check to clear and pay close attention to see when it clears.

Chapter 8

Balancing Cash Flow: Creating an Operating Budget

Your organization needs to know where it's going, whether you put it in writing or not. However, to spend money without thinking or planning indicates a lack of control and responsibility. A budget helps you manage your money and prioritize your spending, and also serves as a checkpoint to impulsive buying. It shows revenues and the amount set aside for planned expenses. To keep track of your money, you need a budget to keep cash flow in balance.

Basically your budget is your organization's financial plan. Without a detailed budget, your nonprofit's risk of failure increases significantly. Not to worry though. This chapter explains why your nonprofit needs a budget, what you need to do to create a budget, and how to create, track, manage, and evaluate your financial plan.

Eyeing the Importance of Having a Budget in the Nonprofit World

For your nonprofit to survive and thrive financially, you must create and follow a budget. In fact, it really can be life or death for your organization. A *budget* is an itemized list of what income you have and expect to receive and what you expect to pay out during a given time period, whether a month, quarter, or year. It expresses in monetary terms what your objectives are. It's almost impossible to know when you've reached your target goal if you don't know what you need.

Without a budget, you're on a cross-country road trip without a map. If you start out on a trip with no planned destination, who knows where you'll end up. Your nonprofit is too important to allow things to just happen to it. You need to control as much about your finances as you can. A budget can tell you

- ✔ How much cash you need now and in the future to meet payroll and other expenses
- ✔ How much cash you have readily available in your bank accounts
- ✔ How much money you're expecting to receive from fundraisers and grants
- ✔ How much money you need to borrow
- ✔ How much in stocks or bonds to sell
- ✔ How much you need every month, quarter, and year for operating expenses

Operating on a budget is important at all times, not just when money is tight. Following your budget means you're planning for income and expenses and controlling your money. Your budget is a prediction or forecast (not the kind you get from a crystal ball) based on prior events and expected future events. Not only does a budget include projections, but after time expires, you have the reality of what actually happened.

You can use your budget to cut costs and run your organization more efficiently. It's smart management to look at your income and expenses and how you can reduce your overhead expenses. For example, if a program grant is discontinued, you need to know the impact on your organization. Without a budget, you won't know what hit you and how much it's gonna hurt you. And without a budget you won't have a clue about the steps you need to take to deal with the effects of the unanticipated grant closure.

Many people feel that having a budget limits their spending ability. But contrary to popular belief, a budget means you're aware of and in control of your money.

Large corporations monitor and control their spending. They're always assessing and re-assessing how they manufacture products and how they can reduce expenses to keep profits up. Although you're not in your field for the money, your organization can't be successful without money. Therefore, it's important that you have a financial plan or budget.

Innovative short-term ways to reduce expenses

As a nonprofit, you're always looking for ways to reduce expenses. If you need to reduce your expenses, you may want to consider some short-term approaches. For example, you may cut overtime and pay increases, freeze hiring, stop all travel, and downsize your expense accounts. You can also focus on reducing your electricity bill by setting the thermostat to around 72 degrees during the summer and 68 degrees during the winter. You may even have the thermostat set to come on one hour after arriving to work and to shut down automatically one hour before closing.

Getting Off to a Good Start: Preparing to Create an Operating Budget

Before you can put together your nonprofit's operating budget, you have to make the necessary preparations. If you were planning a month-long trip to Europe, you wouldn't wake up on the morning of your flight and run to the airport with only a carry-on bag and no planning. Weeks in advance you have to book your flight and hotels, pack accordingly, and have a general idea of where you're going.

Your budget is your resource allocation instrument. Creating an operating budget for your nonprofit follows the same lines. You have to prepare by determining guidelines, setting your priorities and goals, and keeping everything organized. By creating your operating budget, you'll know how much money you have, how much you plan to receive, how much you need, and what you can plan to achieve. You can use your operating budget to plan for future purchases. You can also use your budget to determine how much you need to secure in contributions to sustain your nonprofit.

Your financial statements indicate what has already happened (check out the chapters in Part IV for putting together your nonprofit's financial statements). You prepare these statements after the fiscal year ends. You can use your financial statements as a tool to help you predict your budget for the upcoming fiscal year. Use your financial statements to figure out why things happened and then analyze the figures to come up with your new operating budget to offset some of the occurrences that occurred (and may occur again). Creating an operating budget gives you another chance to plan and control what happens in the upcoming year.

Start your budget process by forming a team that includes your executive director, chief financial officer, and finance committee or budget task group (see "Establishing a budget task group" later in the chapter for more on this topic). Then make sure to have a copy of your mission statement handy. The team assigned to draft your budget will use your mission statement to come up with the guidelines, priorities, and goals needed for the budgeting process.

The following sections walk you through the different steps your organization needs to take before creating your nonprofit's budget.

Setting clear guidelines

Start your budgeting process by looking at your organization's vision and purpose, as defined in your mission statement. Your *budget guidelines* are centered on your mission and what it takes to accomplish your organization's goals. They guide your nonprofit in developing a budget that shows how your funding priorities support your strategic plan. Most strategic plans cover three to five years, defining steps to achieve goals with charts that direct the process. Your strategic plan should be in writing so you can look at it and see whether you're on track. (For help in establishing your strategic plan, check out *Strategic Planning For Dummies* by Erica Olsen [Wiley].)

Budget guidelines allow you to review and evaluate budget requests and submit recommendations to your board of directors. These guidelines help you make measurable progress toward your goals. All budget items should be tied to performance indicators so you can measure their outcomes.

Your guidelines define how you plan to improve the effectiveness of your current system. Some of the items included in budget guidelines are

- ✔ Guidelines for salary increases
- ✔ Budget for operations
- ✔ Line item transfers
- ✔ Guidelines for adjustments
- ✔ Annual fundraising goals and priorities

Remember that these budget guidelines are just that — guidelines — and they're not written in stone! You may have to make adjustments as your fiscal year progresses.

Having clear guidelines helps you recognize the importance of budget maintenance for your organization. Your budget allows you to focus on items and issues that are relevant to your board's fiscal priorities.

Identifying your nonprofit's objectives

As you're creating your budget and setting and following your guidelines, it's important for you to establish and know the importance of your objectives. These objectives are what your organization wants to achieve — in other words your organization's *priorities*. You need to identify your objectives and put them on paper so you can track your progress and see what needs your immediate attention.

With so much to do every day and so many distractions, having clear goals and objectives for your organization and for each program is important. What may be a priority for you may not be for the next person. Knowing your priorities makes day-to-day decisions easier. Planning and strategizing aren't just for the for-profit industry. As a nonprofit, you need a plan for your future. A five-year plan with set priorities is an excellent road map.

Commonly stated budget priorities include all of the following:

- Maintain financial stability of the organization
- Maintain commitment to target population
- Assess and ensure quality of program delivery
- Improve and expand capital campaign

To identify your priorities, do the following:

1. **Write down the activities that are most important and rank them in order.**

   Ask yourself what your organization's most important activities are.

2. **Make a list of current and future activities that you plan to achieve.**

   Ask yourself what the benefits of the activities are. Determine the purpose and goals and rank your list according to the greatest benefit to the groups that will be helped.

   Many organizations assign a score for priorities within each program. For example, you can assign a number to each priority on your list indicating its importance.

Eyeing goals

Without a vision, organizations perish. Your nonprofit's *goals* are visionary statements that motivate you and others to do something. Goals are end results that you desire to obtain. Before you can put together your operating budget, you need to know what your organization's goals are.

Defining clear goals and having a plan in place to reach them can save you from going into financial crisis mode. You're in financial crisis mode when you operate day to day with no definite plan for sustainability. To avoid operating in crisis mode, set clear, concise goals for your organization as a whole, as well as for each of your programs.

To obtain your goals, you have to have objectives that are tied to the goals. Activity makes goals happen. But if you do nothing but think about it and take no action, nothing is going to happen. For example, I've had a personal goal to lose 10 pounds for the last three years. It's not a priority, but it's something I desire. Because it's not a priority, nothing is happening. Actually, I believe I've gained 5 more pounds while thinking about losing 10. If I cut back on my eating and implement an exercise routine, the weight would fall off.

Ideally your goal statement starts broadly by first identifying the overall goals for the organization and then indicating on a program-by-program basis what the major actions should be for the upcoming budget year. Start with goals for the entire organization and then look at goals for each program.

The organization's goals

Your nonprofit's goals are the big picture of success for your organization. They may include growth in personnel, effectiveness in the sphere of influence, the ability to partner with other organizations, and so on.

You, as the director of your nonprofit, and your board need to set your organization's goals. To do so, take the following steps:

1. **Decide what you want the end results to be.**

2. **Set a measurable way to indicate performance.**

3. **Assign a number by which you can gauge whether you've met your goals.**

   This number serves sort of like a checkpoint. You need to decide and set realistic measurable performance numbers, such as 10 percent more people will be served in the upcoming year.

After you set your organization's goals, you then have to prioritize them. Some people assign numbers to their goals based on priority. To prioritize, you need to rank in order the steps needed to accomplish your goals. Whatever the first step is to reaching your goal can be assigned number one. Your top priority is the first step toward reaching your goals. Just work your list by moving on to step two and so on.

Setting goals alone doesn't yield results. You have to do something to bring your goals to reality.

You can't accomplish your organization's goals without a clear funding plan. Your *funding plan* defines how much money you need to raise from all sources to operate. You need the following to organize a funding plan:

- ✔ Mission statement defining your purpose or vision
- ✔ Funding goals
- ✔ Funding objectives
- ✔ List of potential funders
- ✔ Action plan

To create a funding plan, simply write down the five preceding items on a sheet of paper or on your computer. Your funding plan contains information about where you plan to get the money (list of potential funders) to fund your programs. I suggest you do your budget first, so you can identify what your goals, objectives, and needs are and then do your funding plan.

Individual program goals

You also need individual program goals to keep you and your staff motivated. These *program goals* are performance levels of what you see as the end result of a particular program. The only difference between organizational goals and programs goals is organizational goals include program goals, whereas program goals are only for one particular program. For example, if your program is a mentoring project, then your goal may be that 5 percent more children will be mentored this year than last year.

Program goals require much of the same thought process as setting organization goals. You need to have clearly defined goals, a well-written plan in place to keep programs up and running, and innovative ideas to attract funders. You can then use these goals to help you establish a program budget.

Creating a separate budget for each program shows good fiscal management. Separate program budgets allow you to see what programs are sustaining themselves and which ones are experiencing cash shortages. Tailored budgets also help when a program needs to be cut or budget items have to be reduced. You create a budget for a program the same way you create a budget for your organization, except you may have different categories. (Check out the "Coming Up with an Operating Budget" section later in this chapter for how to develop your program budgets.)

After you set a goal, begin working toward achieving it right away. Every activity you do should lead to accomplishing your goal. A good way to reach your goals is to break them down into smaller steps. So if you have a fundraising goal for the year of $15,000, you may want to see how much you've raised after each quarter. When you get to each quarter, you can check to see whether you've achieved one-quarter, half, and three-quarters of what you plan to achieve. If you haven't, then you can make adjustments to the budget or look for ways to increase funding.

As you reach your goals, cross them off the list. If you reached your goal of raising $15,000 at the midway point, you can cross that goal off the list, because you've achieved it.

And your program goals don't have to stay the same year after year. As your organization changes, you have to re-evaluate your goals and priorities.

Staying organized

In order to achieve your goals for your organization and programs, you can't let important details slip through the cracks. Staying organized is key to meeting your goals (and staying on budget). Planning and getting organized not only helps with your goals and budget, but also with your stress levels. Being organized allows you to find things, so it saves you money. Remember the old saying, "Time equals money, and money equals time." So if you spend less time looking for things, you'll be more productive and focused on operating your organization.

Staying organized requires paying attention to details, timeframes, and deadlines. It's a process that takes time, energy, and motivation. To stay organized, I suggest these tips.

Use a detailed calendar with timeframes and deadlines

For staying organized, calendars on which you note timeframes and deadlines are essential. You handle many tasks within your organization that have beginnings and endings. Knowing these dates allows you to schedule time to work on them so you don't miss important deadlines.

Your budget and work plan should be scheduled so everyone involved is on the same page. Developing a budget calendar with a timeline can help your board, finance committee, budget task group, and treasurer stay on track. You can use helpful tools such as planners, phone and address books, PDAs, and client databases to keep calendars updated.

You want to schedule the timeline for creating next year's budget based on your fiscal year. Most people allow at least three months from preliminary to approval. So if your fiscal year starts in May, you'd start working on the new budget no later than February 1. Some larger tasks can be broken down into smaller tasks, and the due dates for those incremental steps should be noted and shared with everyone.

File all paperwork in a timely manner

You evaluate your budget and monitor your progress throughout the year. Therefore, you need to create a set of files to keep up with the changes so you can easily access the information. Organizing your papers helps organize your thoughts. You can purchase a file cabinet, a file box, and some hanging file folders and manila folders to sort the papers. You can label files by month. Filing the paperwork month by month saves time and reduces your stress levels. Make sure you keep up with receipts for major purchases and supplies, as well as documents related to payroll taxes.

Throw away what you don't need

As your board meets to discuss changes needed to the budget and new programs that need to be implemented, you may find yourself swimming in paperwork. It may not be a good idea to hold on to the paperwork from the first budget meeting 15 years ago. At some point, you need to clear out the old and make room for the new. Throw away anything more than 5 years old. De-clutter your storage files and cabinets. Consider dumping or donating items you don't need. Manage your mail. Pick up a magazine rack and throw away magazines older than a month.

Outline your tasks

When you outline tasks, you create a systematic way to know when to start and complete something. You can make a to-do list and prioritize which tasks need to be done and when. For example, I create a to-do list every day to organize my work and time. Even if I don't finish everything on my list, at least my priorities are already organized for the next day. When you complete a task, you can cross it off your list and then manage the remaining tasks to know which ones you can realistically expect to complete.

As you set your goals, you establish an outline of tasks to ensure that you reach the goal. As you accomplish a goal, cross it off the list and start on another one.

To complete your tasks, you use a bit of time and money. If you know how much of each is needed, assign that portion so you can get an overall idea about what is needed financially to accomplish each task and ultimately reach your goals.

Your spending plan is your budget. To outline your spending plans for the coming year, you want to review the following tasks:

- ✔ Developing new programs
- ✔ Expanding existing programs
- ✔ Creating fundraising recommendations
- ✔ Securing funding for new projects through grants
- ✔ Developing a dedicated Web site for donations
- ✔ Locating in-kind funding to match grants

Some people like to group tasks into phases. Phase one is usually the planning phase. Phase two may be securing funding for a project. Phase three is implementation of a project.

Coming Up with an Operating Budget

After you make the necessary preparations by establishing guidelines, identifying your priorities, and setting goals, you're ready to put everything down on paper in the form of a budget. You want to look at what your expenses are and how much money it takes to cover them. Also, consider new programs that are needed and think about how you might fund them. With these points in mind, you're ready to create your organization's operating budget (see Figure 8-1).

The following sections take you on the budgeting journey by explaining the simple steps of how to put together an operating budget, including the ins and outs of what to include.

You may wonder how your budget differs from the financial statements you're required to prepare. Your budget shows what you expect to happen financially; it's based on predictions. Your statement of activities shows how much you collected and how much you spent; it's based on the reality of what happened.

20XX Mentoring Program Budget

Revenues	Actual	Budget	Difference
Private donations	50,000	45,000	5,000
Public donations	150,000	140,000	10,000
Collected Fees	25,000	28,000	-3,000
Total Income	*225,000*	*213,000*	*12,000*
Expenses			
Rent	12,000	12,000	0
Utilities	2,700	3,000	-300
Telephone	600	750	-150
Legal & Accounting	2,400	2,400	0
Salaries	87,750	87,750	0
Payroll Taxes	7,500	7,500	0
Office Supplies	500	650	-150
Insurance	1,200	1,200	0
Miscellaneous	350	500	-150
Total Expenses	*115,000*	*115,750*	*-750*
Increase (Decrease) Net Assets	*110,000*	*97,250*	*12,750*

Figure 8-1:
A draft budget for a mentoring program.

Walking through the steps to the budget: The how-to

Creating a budget isn't complicated. Start with a blank piece of paper in hand and follow the steps in this section.

Step 1: Prioritize and determine the need

Look at last year's budget and compare it to every new item to be added to this year's budget and ask yourself the following questions:

- Is there a need for this activity?
- How important is it that we do it?
- Are there ways we can reduce the cost of running a program?
- How much does it really cost us?

This process is time consuming and one of the reasons many organizations don't create a budget. However, by not taking this step, you miss things that need attention, like how you fund your activities and if there's a less costly way to provide more services for the same or less amount of money. You then refer to the results of these questions as you start talking numbers.

Step 2: Make a list of everything coming in and going out

Take a blank sheet of paper and write down your actual revenue amounts and their sources — the grants and donations you already have — followed by your actual expenses and their amounts. Refer to Figure 8-1 for an example.

You have two types of expenses to consider:

- **Variable expenses:** These are amounts you pay that change from month to month. An example is the cost of utilities.

- **Fixed expenses:** The cost of these expenses is the same from month to month. A rent payment is generally considered a fixed expense.

To make more expenses fixed, such as utilities, see if the provider offers a budget plan. The *budget plan* takes an average of a year's worth of utility costs and charges you the average amount each month. It stops fluctuations in bills. Going on a budget plan can help you stay in balance with your expense projections.

If you're not sure exactly how much to budget for, take a look at last year's budget and receipts from last month, last quarter, and last year. Use these documents to make realistic predictions about what will happen next month, next quarter, and next year.

Step 3: Separate actual income vs. projected income

Your budget is an estimate of your expected cash flow. Based on prior periods, you can gauge what will happen in the future. When creating a budget, you focus on these two items:

- **Actual amounts:** Your actual amount is what you have already received or a fixed amount. (*Fixed amounts* are those things that are preset and not subject to change, such as money you already have on reserve, and existing grants and contracts.)

- **Projected amounts:** Your projected amount is what you expect to receive, such as a large donation. Your projected income includes your actual income plus your expected income.

One of three things is going to happen: You'll get what you expect (project), or you'll get more or less. Yet, forecasting your expectations is crucial to your organization's budgetary process.

So when separating actual and projected income, do the following:

1. **Take realistic projections.**

   Begin with amounts you feel somewhat sure about, like grants and contracts you've received in the last year. Make sure these amounts are realistic projections, not merely a wish list, because what you plan to purchase and how you plan to pay your employees are contingent on you being realistic.

2. **After the time period expires, list what actually happened.**

   You can do so at the end of the month, quarter, or year. Just make sure you compare what you projected with what you received. Then keep a close eye on your budget as time passes, so you can be prepared to make adjustments as needed. You want to know how well you've planned things to help you plan better the next time.

3. **Evaluate the difference between what you projected and what actually took place.**

   All you do here is subtract what happened from what you expected to happen and look at the results. Sometimes you may get more than you expect, which is good. Other times you may have less. So plan an alternative way to raise the money, which may be another fundraiser or loan. It's a decision that you and your board need to discuss.

Step 4: Compare income to expenses and make adjustments as necessary

After you know what your expenses are likely to be and how much money you expect to bring in, you can figure out your projected bottom line for the period. In other words, you can subtract your projected expenses from your projected revenues and see whether you'll have a net increase or decrease in assets (refer to Figure 8-1).

If your budget shows a positive number, you've got a net increase in assets, meaning you've got some money left over. You can increase your spending in one of the expense categories, or you can plan to save the additional revenue in case something unexpected happens — the economy takes a nosedive, you have to replace the heating and cooling system, you lose grant funding, or some other unfortunate event takes place.

If your budget shows a negative number, you've got a net decrease in assets, meaning your expenses are larger than your revenues. You can handle this a couple of ways:

- You can take a look at your expenses and see where you can cut some costs.
- You can look at your revenues and see if there's a way you can increase the amount of funding you're bringing in.

Getting your budget approved

Your organization's finance committee should have a budget timeline for preparing, reviewing, and getting board approval of your budget in an organized and timely fashion. Most nonprofits have a calendar with a time-line of budget meetings that covers a two- to eight-week period. As things happen or change, you can make adjustments to your budget. Your annual budget may require your board's approval, but you can evaluate your budget as new grant programs are funded, as old grant programs expire, and any other time something happens in your organization that directly affects your revenues and expenses.

If you're the executive director, you and the finance committee discuss and assess the organization's priorities and present the budget to your board of directors. Your board of directors reviews and evaluates your operating budget to assess how it aligns with your budget priorities, mission, and strategic plan. Your board of directors adopts your annual budget through recommendations and an approval process.

Now, your board and executive staff can compare the expected amounts to the actual results. Seldom do things go as planned, but nevertheless you must plan. Your board and management staff carefully evaluate the gap between actual and budget performance and use it as a tool for future endeavors.

Reviewing Budget Performance

As you proceed through the year, you simply can't set your budget aside and hope that all of your projections were accurate. You have to regularly review the budget to ensure you're on pace. Many organizations review the budget monthly. Usually at quarterly points or mid-year, organizations recast and revise their budgets if their estimates were off significantly.

Furthermore, after your accounting period ends, you need to evaluate the budget and look for ways to become more cost efficient before you start the new budget for the next year. The following sections address some ways you can review your budget and make the necessary revisions for future budgets.

Establishing a budget task group

Your finance committee keeps an eye on the progress of your budget and evaluates it at year-end. Your board may also want to set up a *budget task group* to help evaluate your organization's budget. A budget task group's primary role is to recommend innovative ideas for savings and income generation and to achieve a balanced budget by examining and questioning the need for every line item in your budget.

Some budget items place pressure on the budget. Things like salaries, pensions, reductions in grants, and increasing expenses place a strain on your overall organization. Your budget task group must examine ways to ease the pressure, and it may need to do some serious brainstorming to address the shortfall. The group members may suggest ways to generate income or stimulate giving. They may come up with creative ideas to stir something inside of your donors to increase their desire to invest in your organization. Or they may come up with innovative ways to streamline operations to cut costs the following year.

Making adjustments

Good things as well as bad things will happen to your organization. Equipment will break down, and employees will quit; but you'll also have unexpected revenues from donors. When good things happen, it makes things better. But when bad things happen, you need to be prepared.

After careful analysis of what has happened, you may be able to predict what will happen in the future. You can use the "Difference" column on your budget worksheet (see Figure 8-1) to help you determine what your next step should be.

For example, if your actual revenues were $250,000 rather than $225,000, you would be in a better financial position than you expected. But if you only collect $200,000, and you expected to bring in $213,000, what do you do? Now you have $13,000 less than you planned. (In this case because expenses are relatively low, you'll probably be okay. But if coming up short in revenue becomes a trend, eventually it will present cash flow problems.)

With the budget in front of them, your board members may make adjustments by revising tasks and schedules. Some programs may be canceled and budget line items reallocated. You may also consider scaling back on purchases or increasing the costs of services. Other places to look for additional funds are in your reserves and donor restricted gifts. If possible, you should ease the reserve policy.

If you have a budget *deficit* (a shortage of funds or when expenses outweigh revenues), devise a plan to manage down the deficit. Get rid of your deficit as fast as you can to avoid potential collapse of your entire outfit.

If you've received an unexpected windfall, some new programs may be implemented based on your organization's goals and the needs of your target population. Flexibility is needed to keep your organization operational.

When you've had a particularly good year financially, consider establishing a rainy day fund. This is something that is very important to have. Place some of the money in a savings account or marketable certificate of deposit (CD) that's easily accessible so you can withdraw the cash quickly in an emergency.

Chapter 9

Staying in Nonprofit Compliance

In This Chapter

▶ Obeying federal and state guidelines

▶ Conforming to GAAP, FASB, and SOX

▶ Ensuring the auditor's independence

▶ Keeping your activities on the up and up

K nowing the rules of engagement for your nonprofit is similar to following the laws to drive your car. If you understand and obey traffic laws, register your vehicle, and renew your license, you get to keep your driving privileges. The same is true for operating your nonprofit. As long as you perform according to federal and state laws, you get to keep your nonprofit status. You need to know exactly what the IRS expects of you and what your state officials require of you. The core standards of operations come from the IRS. Then you have to comply with the state laws regarding your nonprofit's operation.

Federal and state laws are full of references to accounting rules set by the Financial Accounting Standards Board (FASB). The FASB develops accounting standards, principles, and statements about how to prepare, present, and report financial information. Accounting standards aren't laws, but the IRS and state government tell you to follow them.

If you don't keep up with accounting standards and rules, complying with federal and state laws can cause you some grief. However, if you have a firm grasp of federal and state laws and the accounting standards, you can sort through the red tape and know what you need to do; then you're well on your way to staying in compliance. This chapter helps you determine how to comply with federal and state laws and accounting rules to keep your nonprofit in good standing.

Understanding Why Being Compliant Is Important for Your Nonprofit

The IRS has the authority to give and take away your nonprofit status. So, the bottom line is you want to keep the IRS happy and stay in compliance with the appropriate federal and state laws and accounting rules. You need to stay in compliance for two main reasons:

- ✔ **To keep your nonprofit status active.** Failure to comply with federal laws can cause you to lose your federal tax-free status. Because you're managing other people's money and you've been given a lifetime tax waiver from the IRS, you should follow the rules to keep your status active.

- ✔ **To keep your reputation of being a good steward.** Following the do's and don'ts keeps everything in good standing.

As long as you continue to provide the services you promised, stay within the purpose of organizing your nonprofit, and submit paperwork to the government in a timely fashion, you'll be okay. This chapter delves into these rules and explains in further detail what you should and shouldn't do. In addition to federal rules, you need to comply with your state laws. These laws vary from state to state. Check out the "Register with the proper state authority" section later in this chapter for what your state requires of you.

Staying in Compliance: The How-To

Knowing the state and federal laws governing your nonprofit isn't enough to stay in compliance. You and your staff have to take the necessary steps to make sure nothing slips between the cracks. Although keeping track and staying within those specifications can be stressful at times, your organization's nonprofit status depends on it. It may not be a fun job, but someone has to do it! The following sections address the four main components your nonprofit must adhere to in order to stay in good standing. I give you specific hands-on advice you can follow so your agency doesn't lose its nonprofit status.

Register with the proper state authority

The first step to ensure your nonprofit stays compliant is to register it with the appropriate state authority. Each state has its own guidelines about how you should account for nonprofit organizations. Some states require nonprofits to register with the secretary of state's office, state department of revenue, and/or state attorney general's office. Some states offer benefits similar to the IRS by granting a sales tax exemption. To find your state laws, visit the following Web site: www.irs.gov/charities/article/0,,id=129028,00.html. Or call your state attorney general's office to get more information about your state's requirements.

Account for nonprofit activities

For your nonprofit to be compliant, you also need to present your nonprofit's financial activities in accordance with the regulations established by the *Financial Accounting Standards Board (FASB)*. The FASB is the authoritative body for financial oversight for all organizations and businesses in the United States.

The Securities and Exchange Commission (SEC) has granted authority to the FASB to establish rules called *generally accepted accounting principles (GAAP)*. GAAP offer guidance and a list of rules about how to account for nonprofit activities. Federal and state laws, as well as the Internal Revenue Code, tell you to follow GAAP. Because presenting this how-to information is quite involved, I cover it in more detail in the "Following Accounting Standards" section later in this chapter.

Hire professional help

Once a year, you need an audit of your financial statements to stay compliant. As a result, you need to hire a *certified public accountant (CPA)* to perform this audit. The CPA evaluates your financial records to verify whether they comply with GAAP and properly reflect your activities. Based on the CPA's opinion, you either get a good report of being a worthy steward or a not-so-good report. (See Chapter 20 for more information about the auditing process.) Your CPA is qualified to offer an opinion as to whether your financial statements fairly represent your financial position.

You can hire a bookkeeper, accountant, or internal auditor for day-to-day bookkeeping and accounting, but only an external CPA or CPA firm can perform an independent audit of your financial statements. You can keep a CPA on retainer so you stay abreast of new rules governing your nonprofit. See the later "Selecting an audit committee to hire an independent CPA" section for more about choosing an auditor.

When hiring your nonprofit's CPA, you should try to adhere to the Sarbanes-Oxley (SOX) Act. Check out the "Sorting out the Sarbanes-Oxley Act (SOX)" section later in this chapter for the two specific points that SOX now regulates when hiring a CPA. Check out Chapter 2 for more specific information you can follow when hiring professional help.

Abide by IRS statutes

The last important process you need to do to ensure your nonprofit stays in compliance is to adhere to IRS statutes. To do so, you need to file an annual report to the IRS about your nonprofit's activities. Individuals and for-profit corporations pay income taxes by filing an annual income tax return, but nonprofits file an information tax-free form. Nonprofits file IRS Form 990, Return of Organization Exempt From Income Tax, which is informational only. (Chapter 14 has step-by-step instructions for filing Form 990.)

 The IRS requires financial information about all organizations given tax-exempt status to make sure they're complying with the agreement. Because your nonprofit isn't paying federal taxes, you're granted more lenience with filing your informational return to the IRS. However, if you file your annual return late, you may have to pay a penalty. And, if you forget to file your annual return for three years in a row, you can lose your nonprofit status. To reinstate your tax-exempt status with the IRS, you'll have to file the necessary paperwork and pay a fee. So make sure you don't make that mistake.

Following Accounting Standards

To keep your nonprofit operating according to federal and state laws, you need to follow some accounting standards. The federal and state laws that govern nonprofits include references to generally accepted accounting principles (GAAP), the Financial Accounting Standards Board (FASB), and the Sarbanes-Oxley Act (SOX). Did someone spill a can of alphabet soup?

So what do all these letters mean? GAAP covers the specific rules of conduct, while the FASB is the actual authoritative body of accounting standards (some of the standards are called *principles,* and some are called *statements*). If these regulations weren't enough, the SEC decided that new rules were needed to clarify the old ones, so the agency adopted SOX to keep management and accountants on track. The following sections take a closer look at these three sets of regulations and what you need to do to ensure your nonprofit is in compliance.

The fascinating FASB

The FASB governs and provides financial accounting and reporting oversight for your nonprofit. You don't deal directly with these folks, but you need to stay abreast of rules that they create. In most cases, your state or the IRS is your first point of contact, but the rules have a trickledown effect. This section focuses on the two statements you need to know about to stay in compliance.

FASB Statement No. 116: Accounting for Contributions Received and Made

Statement No. 116 dictates how you should recognize donated assets, contributions made, contributions received, the classification of contributed assets and services, and the disclosure of all of these. If you make or receive contributions, Statement No. 116 applies to you.

You should keep in mind four things when handling contributions according to Statement No. 116:

- **Contributions received are recognized as revenues in the period they're received and recorded at their fair market value.** *Contributions received* are the donations people make to your nonprofit. *Fair market value* is the price a buyer is willing to pay and a seller is willing to sell for.

- **Contributions made are recognized as expenses in the period made at their fair market value.** *Contributions made* are donations your nonprofit gives in support of someone else.

- **Unconditional promises to give should be recognized as revenues in the period received at their fair market values.** *Unconditional promises* are donations received that have no restrictions about how or when they can be used, and they're treated like contributions made.

- **Conditional promises to give, whether received or made, should be recognized when they become unconditional.** A *conditional promise* is a donation given based on a specific condition or the passage of time. When a conditional promise becomes unconditional, you should recognize it as revenue in the period it becomes unconditional at its fair market value. Assets received with a conditional promise to contribute them when certain conditions are met are recorded as a refundable advance (liability) until the conditions are met and the gift becomes unconditional.

In addition, FASB Statement No. 116 requires conditional promises to be classified based on whether donations received increased one of the following net asset classifications:

- Permanently restricted net assets

- Temporarily restricted net assets

- Unrestricted net assets

For definitions of these three types of net assets, check out Chapter 16.

You need to classify your contributions because you'll use this information to complete your financial statements. When you report your income and expenses on your statement of activities, you separately report the activity for each net asset class. Sometimes the class activities are shown in columns, other times in separate sections; it's your choice. The ending net asset balance for each classification on the statement of activities (think income statement) is transferred to the net asset section of the statement of financial position (think equity section of the balance sheet).

One final thing you need to keep in mind concerns volunteer time and services. I know you rely on volunteers to keep your nonprofit ticking, and many of the things your volunteers do aren't recorded on your books. According to FASB Statement No. 116, some volunteer time may need to be accounted for as contribution revenue from donated services.

I know these hours are a headache to keep track of. And I know you give your volunteers their props at social events, in your newsletter, and on your Web site. But you may be required to determine how much the services are worth (fair market value) and account for them on your financial statements as contributions made. You only have to account for volunteer services if

- **The services create or enhance nonfinancial assets.** This speaks to situations where an asset owned by your nonprofit is created or improved by volunteer efforts. A classic example of this is the construction or renovation of a facility with a volunteer workforce of skilled and unskilled labor. To calculate the value of such services, deduct the differences between the appraised market value of the finished asset and the out-of-pocket costs paid to do the project.

- **The services require specialized skills, are provided by individuals possessing those skills, and would typically need to be purchased if not provided by donation.** For example, an attorney who volunteers professional counsel for your organization is something you should account for as a contribution made. Determine the fair market value of the services and account for it.

Don't dread having to account for volunteers, because having these numbers comes in handy when preparing grant proposals. You can take the value of your volunteers' time and use it as a possible match in funds. For instance, if your potential funders ask you for a match in services, you may be able to use your volunteers' contributions as the match.

FASB Statement No. 117: Financial Statements of Not-for-Profit Organizations

FASB Statement No. 117 covers financial statements of nonprofits. It specifies information to be reported in financial statements and how to report assets, liabilities, net assets, revenues, expenses, gains, and losses.

According to FASB Statement No. 117, all nonprofit organizations should provide a complete set of financial statements, defined as the following (see the chapters in Part IV for more info):

- **Statement of financial position:** This statement sums up your organization's overall financial picture.

- **Statement of activities:** This document shows how your nonprofit's net assets have increased or decreased.

- **Cash flow statement:** This form shows how your nonprofit's cash position has changed.

- **Statement of functional expense:** This statement is required for voluntary health and welfare organizations, such as the American Cancer Society. This statement shows by line item and category how much you've spent for program costs, management and general expenses, and fundraising expenses. There are pending issues surrounding this document and talk about making it a required statement for all nonprofits.

    Your statement of functional expense can be its own financial statement (see Chapter 18), or you can include the information on your statement of activities or in the notes to the financial statements.

This statement requires a breakdown of your revenues (donations, program service fees, and so on), expenses, gains, and losses. In addition to clearly separating these items, you're required to classify them within classes of net assets — permanently restricted, temporarily restricted, or unrestricted on the statement of activities. (See Chapter 16 for more info.)

The world according to GAAP

GAAP lay the ground rules for accounting. All accountants use GAAP when accounting for, preparing, and presenting financial information. The principles allow you to fairly evaluate and compare numbers. Think of GAAP as a uniform way to examine and record financial activities. These guidelines create a level playing field, so all nonprofits play by the same rules. The way you present your financial position is the same way a nonprofit in another state evaluates its position, according to GAAP.

All GAAP-based financial statements are presented using the accrual basis of accounting, which deals with the recognition of transactions. For example, all transactions are recorded on the books when they occur, no matter when cash actually exchanges hands. (See Chapter 2 for more information about the accrual basis of accounting.)

To ensure that you stay in compliance and protect your nonprofit's status, make sure you adhere to the following GAAP principles:

✔ **Cost principle:** This principle requires assets to be recorded in the books at their cost. This is the price paid in exchange for the asset. This cost is commonly referred to as the *historical cost* because it doesn't change. It doesn't matter if the asset's current value goes up *(appreciates)* or goes down *(depreciates);* the value recorded on the statement of financial position remains the same, according to the cost principle.

✔ **Business entity concern:** This notion deals with the *separate legal entity concept,* which means that if you incorporate, your nonprofit is a separate legal entity from you and/or the owners. The biggest advantage to incorporating is to protect your board and staff from personal legal liabilities, such as lawsuits. If the nonprofit is separate from you, then it, not you, is responsible for its debts and any charges of misconduct.

Of course, being a separate business entity doesn't mean that you can't be sued. Anyone can file a lawsuit, so the ultimate protection is to acquire board of directors, management, and officers insurance.

✔ **Objective principle:** This principle states that you determine and verify the value of all donated items as objectively as possible. All donated items go on your financial statements as assets. To fairly represent your true financial condition, you have to give them an objective value.

When valuing assets donated to your organization, you should seek an objective opinion or outside help to evaluate the value. Asking a qualified independent third-party who has no interest in the outcome gives an objective view. To determine a donated asset's value, check the following sources:

- Sticker price or purchase invoice

- Sales invoice

- Property deeds

- Transfer of title

- Kelly Blue Book value

- Banker or creditor

Don't value the donated assets you receive by simply asking the donor and reporting the amount he says. You still need to verify the item's worth by asking an independent third-party who has no financial interest in the outcome to give you a value.

✔ **Matching principle:** This principle requires donations and revenues received and expenses incurred to be recorded in the same period you receive or incur them. In other words, you should recognize expenses in the period you incur the expense. For example, if you pay your employees in January for work done in December, when you complete your financial statements, you should record the liability in December.

You should match contributions received with expenses incurred in the same time period on the statement of activities. If someone makes a $50 donation to pay a volunteer, you should match that donation with the volunteer expense in the same time period, unless there are restrictions. (When I say time period, I'm talking about the accounting period, which is one year.)

✔ **Revenue-recognition principle:** When you receive donations, you must recognize them as revenue when they become unconditional. For more information about restricted and conditional contributions, see Chapter 16.

Conditional contributions and restricted contributions are often confused because restrictions can be conditions. But not all conditions are restrictions. A donor offers you a potential gift of say $10,000, but he won't give it to you unless your organization can raise X dollars or meet some criteria. If you meet the condition, you get the money with no strings attached; it's recognized as an *unrestricted contribution.* However, the donor may say you can have $10,000 for your capital campaign to be spent on bricks and mortar if you raise X dollars. Then if you raise the money, the gift becomes *unconditional,* but it's restricted, and so recorded as a restricted contribution. When spent on bricks and mortar, the restriction is met, and it becomes unrestricted.

✔ **Expense-recognition principle:** This principle deals with the timing of when expenses are recognized. Expenses are reported as decreases to unrestricted net assets on the statement of activities. A classic example of recognizing expenses occurs at the end of the year when employees have worked, but won't get paid until January. You need to account for this expense in the period you incur the expense. A lot of places pay you only after you've worked, and you may have a couple of weeks in the hole. When the paychecks are cut in January, they are for work completed in December. You should account for this on your statement of financial position and statement of activities ending December 31.

✔ **Full-disclosure principle:** This principle states that changes made to accounting methods, inventory valuation, and pending lawsuits must be disclosed in the notes to the financial statements. (Check out Chapter 19 for more information.) Anything that may have a big impact on your financial condition should be noted or disclosed in the financial statements.

✔ **Consistency principle:** You need to be consistent in your methods when accounting for revenues and expenses to fairly represent your financial statements. Accounting information is useful when you can compare it to prior years or to organizations of similar size. In making these comparisons, changes in accounting methods affect the numbers on your financial statements.

Using one accounting method for three months and then switching to a different method before the close of the accounting period probably isn't a good idea. You want to be consistent, and making the change can change your bottom line and could misrepresent your true financial position. Of course, any changes in accounting methods should be noted in the notes to the financial statements. Furthermore, flip-flopping your depreciation method can also adversely affect your net assets on your financial statements. The way you value your inventory and depreciate your assets affects your income or net assets. (To *depreciate* an asset means to write off the cost of an asset by charging it as an expense.)

For example, say you've been using the straight-line method to depreciate your assets, and you decide to switch to the double-declining balance depreciation method. The straight-line method writes off the cost of assets equally over the useful life of the asset. The double-declining balance method accelerates depreciation by writing off more of the cost of an asset in the early years. Because depreciation is an expense that's subtracted from revenue, if more expense is deducted, the result is less income. So changing methods can give you a more favorable outcome or a less favorable one. Check out Chapter 2 for a complete discussion of different depreciation methods and which one is best for your nonprofit.

The best time to switch accounting methods is when FASB deems it necessary. Of course, you must handle your records the best way to reflect your true financial position. It's probably best to wait until your current period ends before switching to a different method.

Although these principles don't have anything to do with actual math, you still need to follow them to keep your nonprofit out of financial trouble. In your nonprofit's accounting, you have to apply these GAAP rules consistently to evaluate the treatment of accounts. After accountants complete this evaluation, they then add, subtract, multiply, and/or divide.

Sorting out the Sarbanes-Oxley Act (SOX)

In response to public outcry after Enron and other public accounting scandals, Maryland Sen. Paul Sarbanes and Ohio Rep. Michael Oxley worked together on protective measures to stop the fraudulent practices of accounting firms and their clients across the nation. These protective measures resulted in the *Sarbanes-Oxley Act,* commonly referred to as *SOX*. The SOX Act is very complex, and it only applies to publicly traded companies — those registered with the SEC. However, many nonprofits have adopted provisions of SOX that help improve the management and financial reporting of their organization. You only need to concern yourself with the two important points I explain in the following sections.

Selecting an audit committee to hire an independent CPA

One of the many Sarbanes-Oxley Act initiatives deals with audit committees and auditors' independence. An *audit committee* is responsible for board financial and accounting oversight. The committee, which consists of at least three independent members of your board, with at least one being a financial expert, selects your auditing firm and ensures that the firm is independent. Individual board members aren't part of the organization's management team or paid management consultants; their only compensation is for being a board member. (See Chapter 20 for more information about forming an audit committee.)

The *general standards on auditor independence* outline what your audit committee should consider when choosing whether to enter into a relationship with or service provided by an auditor. To make sure an auditor's services are done independently, the auditor isn't allowed to perform certain non-auditing services and is prohibited from forming certain relationships. Your auditing committee should request a signed statement from the selected auditor verifying that none of the services in the upcoming list are being provided. These rules were created to make sure your auditor independently presents your financial statements according to GAAP.

The auditor is prohibited from providing the following non-audit services to an audit client, including its affiliates:

- Bookkeeping
- Designing and implementing financial information systems
- Appraisal or valuation services, fairness opinions, or contribution-in-kind reports
- Actuarial services
- Internal audit outsourcing services
- Management functions of human resources
- Broker-dealer, investment advisor, or investment banking services
- Legal services and expert services unrelated to the audit

The purpose for all of these guidelines is to make sure your financial statements fairly represent your financial position. To avoid a biased opinion, it's important that your auditor is totally independent and has no other deals with you that may possibly sway his professional opinion of your organization.

Prohibited relationships are also an important point to remember under SOX. They're relationships between you and/or your nonprofit and the firm, CPA, or auditor who will offer an opinion about your financial statements. The following are rules about prohibited relationships:

✔ **Employment relationships:** A one-year cooling-off period is required before you can hire certain individuals who were formerly employed by your auditor in a financial reporting oversight role. The audit committee should consider whether hiring someone who is or was employed by the audit firm will affect the audit firm's independence.

✔ **Contingent fees:** Audit committees shouldn't approve engagements that pay an independent auditor based on the outcome of the audit results. In other words, your auditor must give a professional opinion based on your records and reports, not on how much or how you pay him. Such compensation may color the auditor's independence.

✔ **Direct or material indirect business relationships:** Auditors and their firms can't form direct or material indirect relationships with the non-profit, its officers, directors, or major donors. *Direct business relationships* refer to relationships where something tangible or of value (such as an investment) is involved between you and the auditor. For example, a relationship where the auditor has an investment in your organization would not be good. *Material indirect business relationships* are ones where you may have some other business dealings with a family member or affiliate of the CPA firm or auditor, whereby ownership is more than 5 percent.

✔ **Certain financial relationships:** Your audit committee should be aware that certain financial relationships between your nonprofit and the independent auditor are prohibited. These include creditor/debtor relationships, banking, broker-dealer, insurance products, and interests in investment companies.

To avoid any potential problems, set up an audit committee, be cautious when using an auditing firm to provide non-auditing services except for tax preparation, and disclose all accounting policies and practices to your audit committee. Above all, make sure your auditor is independent. To maintain independence in the auditing of your financial statements, you should put your nonprofits audit out to bid every three to five years.

Requiring a signed financial statement

The Sarbanes-Oxley Act requires the chief executive officer (CEO) and the chief financial officer (CFO) to certify the appropriateness of financial statements and that the statements fairly represent the organization's financial condition and operations. The reason for this requirement is to shift the responsibility for the financial statements onto the CEO and CFO. Although signing off on a nonprofit's financial statements isn't legally required, doing so indicates management understands and takes responsibility for the statements. Having said this, you should take an active role in preparing and analyzing your financial statements.

A signature from an officer of the organization is required on the financial statements. Your signature indicates that the statements have been prepared according to accounting principles and that they reflect your true financial position.

Avoiding Activities that Can Call Your Compliance into Question

Certain acts by your executive director, employees, and board members may be misunderstood by the IRS and your constituents. Questionable activities usually involve deals with family members or friends, politics, and operating like a for-profit business. This section points out some actions that can potentially affect your compliance with GAAP, FASB, and SOX that you and people associated with your nonprofit should avoid.

Conflicts of interest

Participating in any activity that can potentially be considered a conflict of interest is something you and your staff want to avoid. A *conflict of interest* is a situation in which your service to the public is at odds with your own interests. Examples include lending money to executives, using nonprofit assets for your personal benefit, and giving benefits or services to someone in your family who doesn't qualify.

Having family members on your nonprofit's payroll may be considered a conflict of interest. Anytime nonprofit assets are used for personal gain, you tread very close to receiving excessive personal benefits. The IRS has penalties and sanctions for excess personal benefits. Selling, exchanging, or leasing property between executive directors and board members or key employees should not be done.

Lobbying or supporting candidates

Politics is sticky stuff, no matter what line of business you're in. To avoid any potential compliance problems and the possibility of losing your nonprofit status, the best advice I have is for you to steer clear of anything political. Trying to influence elections, votes, or legislation can cause the loss of your nonprofit status.

Every time you apply for federal or state grants, you're asked about your lobbying activities. Although you can encourage folks to register to vote, you're not supposed to influence how they vote. Only if you're a social welfare organization are you free to get heavily involved in political campaign activities. Furthermore, don't unduly influence politicians to promote your agenda or give you money.

As for politicking, supporting your favorite candidate by casting your one vote for them is okay. However, you threaten your nonprofit's status if you go any further. Don't use your organization's Web site to promote a candidate and don't distribute literature on behalf of a candidate. Unless you're a social welfare organization, such as the American Cancer Society, steer clear from lobbying and politics. For more information about politics, lobbying, and supporting candidates, visit the IRS's Web site at `www.irs.gov`.

Unrelated business income

Unrelated business income is money earned for purposes outside the scope or reason for your nonprofit establishment. For example, if you organized your nonprofit to provide meals to the elderly, and then you decide to start selling the meals to the general public for a profit, this could cause a problem with the IRS and seriously jeopardize your nonprofit status. Because you're helping people, the IRS has granted you tax-free status. If you start competing with businesses by selling your products for less, you disrupt the marketplace and present a problem for corporations and the IRS.

According to the IRS, you're not supposed to compete with for-profit companies. The name of the game in business is to earn a profit. The name of the game for nonprofits is to provide a service or product to the general public to make life better. If you earn $1,000 or more doing unrelated things, you owe the IRS taxes.

Part III

Accounting for Nonprofit Situations

The 5th Wave   By Rich Tennant

"Does anyone know anything about federal grants and bookkeeping? Bob, you spent some time in a federal prison, what are they looking for?"

In this part . . .

This part covers everything related to the feds. Grant money is an important source of revenue for your nonprofit, so you need to know how to access that money. When keeping your nonprofit's books, you need to pay special attention to the federal grant system if you receive any federal grant money. The feds have adopted their own rule book to keep up with grant dollars.

You need to make sure you comply with all the rules after you access grant money. Accountability needs to be at an all-time high for proper management, allocation, and handling of federal money. But don't think that no one will check up on you. You have to prepare for a grant audit, which makes sure you're spending Uncle Sam's money wisely.

And what would a part dealing with the feds be without a discussion on taxes? But you're a nonprofit, and you're exempt from paying taxes, right? Well, not exactly. You still have to pay employee payroll taxes and file Form 990. Paying payroll taxes doesn't have to be a burdensome task. As a matter of fact, you can do it yourself. You can also fill out your own Form 990 and save yourself some money.

Chapter 10

Introducing Federal Grants

Most nonprofit executives spend sleepless nights worrying about finances and wondering if donors will continue to support the organization's mission. Have you been one of those directors or managers who tossed and turned wondering where the money for your next project is coming from?

Well, you don't have to worry anymore. Why not consider other options to help fund your organization? What better way than with federal grants. Applying for and using federal grants are wise moves to secure more dependable sources of revenue. A federal grant is better than money in the bank. Although the check doesn't come in the mail nor will Ed McMahon ring the doorbell, the money is reserved for you at the U.S. Treasury.

Some nonprofit directors openly express a disinterest in federal money. One of the reasons is that they don't understand the process. Another reason is the stiff federal penalties and serious repercussion for abuse and mismanagement of federal grant funds. Nevertheless, I wouldn't attempt to operate a nonprofit without federal money. Why fight over the crumbs by begging the same foundations over and over for the same small pot of money? The federal government is holding our tax dollars, and it has set aside funding to fulfill the needs addressed by nonprofit charitable organizations like yours. You don't have to wait any longer to take advantage of this money to help your organization.

I'm sure you've heard the cliché, "No romance without finances." Well, receiving federal money does have strings attached. In this chapter, you discover how to romance the federal government and take advantage of the grant money available.

Grasping Why Federal Grant Money Is Important to Nonprofits

Finding money to fund your nonprofit's projects can be a time-consuming and stressful experience. However, a significant amount of federal grant money is available if you know where to turn and how to apply for it.

If a for-profit business wants money, all it has to do is sell a product or service. However, the current tax code is very specific about how nonprofits can obtain money. Federal grant money is particularly important for nonprofits for the following reasons:

- ✔ **Grant money has been set aside for nonprofit use.** Congress allocates our tax dollars to federal programs. Grant funds are allocated to states based on the following numbers:

    - Unemployment rate

    - Inmate population

    - Low-birth rates

    - Number of unwed mothers

    - Juvenile delinquency statistics

    - High school dropout rates

- ✔ **The government relies on nonprofits to address the needs in their respective communities.** Because of the nature of nonprofit organizations and their underlying purpose, the government looks to you to fill the gaps in society by addressing your community's needs.

- ✔ **Grant funds provide a stable, reliable cash flow for nonprofit organizations.** The funds allow nonprofits to focus on their missions and not worry about finances.

Every year, the federal government awards more than $450 billion in the form of grants that help to

- ✔ Further the common good by supporting nonprofit organizations so they can fulfill their intended purpose

- ✔ Expand social programs for educational and cultural enrichment

- ✔ Support human health and protect the environment

Unfortunately, grant dollars are susceptible to waste and abuse. Therefore, strict guidelines have been established to provide oversight of financial management of agencies' programs that are supported by federal grants. Even with all the strict guidelines and hoops to jump through, if your nonprofit isn't taking advantage of this money, you're losing out on funds that can make a real impact on your organization.

The 4-1-1 on Grants: Just the Basics

Right now people are sitting in federal offices writing and rewriting legislation, rules, and guidelines concerning federal grants for nonprofits. You may be overwhelmed by information overload and hate to read the fine print. You may be able to overlook some of it, but some of it is essential to knowing what your nonprofit needs to do to effectively account for federal money.

Federal grants are awarded for a specific project and require strict financial oversight. Because grants are closely monitored, you want to ensure you properly account for them. Not to worry: All you have to do is adhere to some basic guidelines. (Check out the "Managing Federal Grant Money: The Do's and Don'ts" section for more specific advice about managing grant money.) As long as you know and understand the ground rules, you can effectively account for grant funds.

This section gives you a clearer picture about federal grants and answers several questions, including what these grants are, who can take advantage of them, how to apply for these grants, and what you have to do if your nonprofit receives federal grant money.

Defining a federal grant

Before your nonprofit can take advantage of federal grant money, you first need to have a firm grasp on what federal grant money is. A federal *grant* is financial assistance in the form of money issued by the U.S. government to carry out a public purpose of support or stimulation authorized by law. Federal grants are available to nonprofits depending on their ability to implement, manage, and meet the obligation.

To be eligible for federal grants based on federal law, your organization must meet the federal government's definition of a nonprofit. A *nonprofit organization* means any corporation, trust, association, cooperative, or other organization that

- Is operated primarily for scientific, educational, service, charitable, or similar purposes in the public interest
- Is not organized primarily for profit
- Uses its net proceeds to maintain, improve, and/or expand its operations

Uncovering other (nongovernmental) stones for grant money

The government is the biggest grant maker in the nation, but there are some other large givers that I want you to consider. Many large corporations and foundations give grants too. For instance, the Bill & Melinda Gates Foundation gives money for health services and education. Some large corporations make so much money that they give it away. Why? The more you make, the more taxes you have to pay. I suggest you first look in your own community for grants to help your nonprofit. Identify any large corporations in your area and ask whether they have any sort of grant program for which your nonprofit may qualify.

Furthermore, some large corporations like Ford and Kellogg have sold so many cars (okay maybe not as many lately) and so much cereal that they owe the government lots of tax money. The companies have formed their own foundations to give the money to you and write it off as a tax deduction, rather than pay it to the government. Foundations like the Ford Foundation and W. K. Kellogg Foundation give millions of dollars away every year.

You can find information about all the foundations in the world by visiting the Foundation Center's Web site at www.foundation center.org or by visiting your local library.

If you're lucky enough to get a grant, then you're a *grant recipient*. A grant recipient is expected to

✔ Be a good steward of the grant money

✔ Use the grant money for intended purposes

✔ Keep copies of all bills and expenses paid for with the money

Finding and applying for federal grants for your nonprofit

If you're like me, you receive tons of spam e-mails about grants to pay your bills, buy a house, start a business, and so on. In addition, I get phone calls daily from people seeking advice after they've been misled by e-mails and infomercials. Federal grants aren't a joke or scam though. They're given to organizations that fulfill a need in society. The federal government knows it can't address people's needs by itself; therefore, it awards grants to nonprofit organizations that benefit society.

So where can your nonprofit locate these federal grant monies? Three primary places to find grant opportunities for your nonprofit are

- ✔ **Grants.gov:** Grants.gov is the one-stop shop designed to provide a level playing field for all organizations. Every funding opportunity offered by the 26 federal agencies can be found at `www.grants.gov`.

- ✔ **Catalog of Federal Domestic Assistance (CFDA):** The catalog identifies funding opportunities by assigning a program number. If you have the CFDA number, looking up the federal program is fairly easy. You can find a hard-copy of the CFDA at your local library or check it out online at `www.cfda.gov`.

- ✔ **The specific federal agency's Web site:** All 26 federal agencies have information on their respective Web sites about grant opportunities. A simple way to find any federal agency is to use an online search engine.

To position your organization to apply for federal loans, take a deep breath. Over the years, the U.S. government has made great strides in ensuring that the process is open to any nonprofit that qualifies by creating a one-stop shop. Unfortunately, accessing federal grant money isn't as easy as shopping at your local discount store. However, the good news is all organizations follow the same steps:

1. **Register with** `www.grants.gov`.

2. **Download a grant application package.**

3. **Submit your application online.**

The waiting period for finding out whether you've been awarded a grant is usually three to six months.

Documenting where the money goes

If your nonprofit receives federal grant money, you can't just throw a big party and start spending to your heart's content. Federal regulations require strict documentation of grant expenses. Uncle Sam wants to know how and where you're spending his money.

So why does Uncle Sam care how you're spending the grant money? You have to document costs for verification purposes, both for requesting payment for expenses and for audit purposes. As your nonprofit incurs program expenses related to the grant, you need to account for every transaction with supporting documentation to justify and verify expenditures. In the wake of government accountability, federal grants are under serious scrutiny. Although opening a separate bank account for grant funds isn't required, federal auditors and monitors require that nonprofits account for and keep track of every purchase, sale, and payment *separately*.

Tracking expenses separately can help you gather financial information for reports required by the federal government. These reports monitor your progress (see Chapter 11 for more about required reports), and all discrepancies will be documented in audit findings (see Chapter 12 for more about grant audits).

Nonprofits must do the following to account for federal grants:

- ✔ Report quarterly and annually on the use of grant funds.

- ✔ Use grant funds only for the purpose intended.

- ✔ Keep records showing use of grant funds.

- ✔ Have supporting documentation showing use of grant funds (bank statements, checks, invoices, paid bills, and receipts).

- ✔ Establish and maintain *internal controls,* which protect you from employee theft by segregating employees' duties. (For more about internal controls, see Chapter 2.)

In federal terminology, these accountability practices are called administrative requirements. *Administrative requirements* refer to matters common to grants in general, such as financial management, type and frequency of reports, and retention of reports.

It's very important to dot your i's and cross your t's by leaving a paper trail for every transaction that uses grant money. Federal program managers and auditors want to know that you're a good steward of federal monies. Believe it or not, the federal government wants to help you meet your organization's mission. For every grant awarded, a budget is attached that shows how the money is supposed to be spent. Receiving a federal grant award is a contractual agreement between your organization and the federal government. (Check out Chapter 8 for more on creating a budget.)

When you applied for the grant, you stated that you had a need; the government has signed a binding agreement with you to provide the necessary funds to address the need. Now your responsibility as the grant recipient is to properly account for every dollar by keeping backup documents that prove good stewardship.

Auditors and program managers will want to see the following documents:

- ✔ Grant receipts
- ✔ Grant-paid invoices

✔ Bid quotes and records of procurements

✔ Time and attendance reports for employees

✔ Payroll (salary and fringe benefits) expenses

✔ Leases for equipment

✔ Contractual agreements

 Being organized with these records helps when it comes time for audits and monitoring visits (see Chapter 12 for more on these). To help keep track of everything, organize all grant-related documents in a hard-copy file as well as in a computerized system (check out Chapter 4 for more about organizing your financial records).

Managing Federal Grant Money: The Do's and Don'ts

For years, federal agencies had in-house rules governing the administration of grants awarded. These rules were confusing to grant recipients because they made managing grants a burdensome task. To alleviate this confusion, all 26 federal agencies convened and came up with universal administrative procedures and rules that apply to organizations based on their *structural classification* (how you were formed at startup). The Office of Management and Budget (OMB), which evaluates the effectiveness of all federal programs, publishes and monitors these procedures.

The OMB has three *circulars* (government-speak for rule book) governing the accounting for, administering of, and auditing of grants. Circulars provide instruction and information, and are identified by the letter "A" and a number. The following sections take a closer look at these three circulars and their regulations; you can call them the do's and don'ts of accounting for grants.

 Don't get bogged down with the detailed information in these circulars or be intimidated by them. You only need to know a few ground rules, most of which will be included in your award letter. If you stick with your approved budget and talk with your program manager about anything that concerns you, you'll be okay.

 In addition, most federal agencies offer periodic training about how you should manage your grant. Talk with your program manager about grant management training.

2 CFR Part 215 for administrative requirements

The *2 CFR Part 215 circular* (formerly known as Circular A-110) addresses all nonprofit organizations, institutions of higher education, and hospitals, and lays out the specific rules for administrative requirement concerning federal grants. This Code of Federal Regulations Part 215 is important because it outlines the dance steps Uncle Sam wants you to follow if you want to keep the federal grant money flowing.

In an effort to ensure all nonprofits are treated the same, this circular sets standards outlining the administration of grants. It prohibits federal awarding agencies from imposing additional or inconsistent requirements on you. This circular also includes

- **Definitions of key terms** used throughout the circular.

- **Pre-award requirements** about different types of forms, public notice of grant opportunity, and whether there is a state single point of contact. (The *state single point of contact* is a designated person in your state who should be notified that you're applying to the federal government for funding.)

- **Post-award requirements** that explain financial and program management. (For more information about managing your grant, see Chapter 11.)

- **Closeout procedures** for reports and grant extensions.

Also, your nonprofit is expected to have written policies and procedures indicating that you don't discriminate against anyone based on race, sex, religion, or origin. Your auditor will want to see your organization's written Equal Employment Opportunity Plan. You can view a copy of 2 CFR 215 Uniform Administrative Requirements online at www.access.gpo.gov/nara/cfr/waisidx_06/2cfr215_06.html.

OMB Circular A-122 for cost principles

OMB Circular A-122 is used by all federal agencies to determine the cost of work performed by nonprofit organizations. This circular contains information about cost treatment and consistency of applying rules to determine whether costs should be charged to a grant. You can look here to read the detailed do's and don'ts concerning what to buy and not buy. Your auditor will check to see whether all of your costs are in compliance with generally accepted accounting principles (GAAP) and the cost principles outlined in OMB A-122.

Costs are classified as reasonable, allocable, and allowable.

- ✔ **Reasonable cost:** A reasonable cost isn't any higher than what an average person would pay under the same circumstances. In other words, just because Uncle Sam is paying, doesn't mean you buy the most expensive items. Treat the grant like your personal cash and exercise good judgment.

- ✔ **Allocable cost:** An allocable cost is chargeable to a grant because the expense is incurred specifically for the grant, benefits both the grant and other work, or is necessary to the nonprofit's operations.

- ✔ **Allowable cost:** A cost reimbursable by the federal government in accordance with the cost principles is an allowable cost. However, the cost must also pass other tests (for example, it must be allocable, reasonable, necessary, and consistently applied).

Just because your salary is paid out of the grant doesn't mean you can set it at any amount. Anyone paid out of a grant should be paid a reasonable salary based on the market and location. The Department of Labor has information on its Web site about how much positions pay, based on location. Before you accept a contract to hire someone or set your own salary, take a look at the following Web site to make sure the wages are reasonable for your area: www.dol.gov/dol/topic/wages.

Keep this circular on your bookshelf to use as a reference when you have burning questions about which costs are okay to charge against your grant. To print a copy of OMB A-122, go to www.whitehouse.gov/omb/assets/omb/circulars/a122/a122_2004.pdf.

OMB Circular A-133 for government audit requirements

I can't overstress the importance of accountability when spending Uncle Sam's money. A good practice is to dot every i and cross every t by following the rules. An audit of your grant files should prove that you're a good manager and can be trusted to do what's right. The *OMB Circular A-133* for audit requirements addresses these rules. You need to know about this circular so you know what to expect before, during, and after an audit. (You can also check out Chapter 12 for more on a grant audit.)

You're required to keep track of everything related to your grant by keeping copies of all grant documents. Your auditor and/or monitor will want to see what you bought and how much you paid for it. The audit will verify whether you followed administrative requirements and cost principles (see the preceding two sections for more on these).

You're spending federal money that comes out of the U.S. Treasury. The federal government wants to make sure you're spending it for the intended purpose and that you're following the rules and guidelines. For more information about OMB A-133 check out the following Web site: www.whitehouse.gov/omb/circulars/index.html.

If you don't follow the rules in this circular, you may face one of the following consequences:

- ✔ **Disallowance:** If your agency is disallowed, you lose your rights to get a grant.

- ✔ **Debarments:** If your organization is debarred, it loses its right to serve the community. It's like taking away a lawyer's right to practice law.

- ✔ **Sanctions:** If you fail to follow the rules, the government may charge you fines and penalties, and make you pay back the money you misspent. This is called imposing a sanction.

- ✔ **Restrictions:** If you face restrictions, the feds are going to watch closely how you spend every dime.

- ✔ **Federal prosecution:** The worse scenario for breaking the rules is to be prosecuted and sent to jail.

By the way, only a few nonprofits make the debarment list. The list is very short, but as a grant recipient, you shouldn't do business with anyone on the list. Ask your federal grant manger for a copy of the Excluded Parties List or go to the following Web site: www.epls.gov.

Not knowing the rules doesn't exempt nonprofit organizations from stiff penalties for abusing taxpayers' dollars. It's imperative that you keep adequate records (for three years after the grant) as to how each dollar was spent. Every invoice, bill, voucher, and check written should be copied to the grant files. All you have to do is spend the money for the reason you got it.

Working Through the Details of Your Grant Agreement

Grants are similar in many ways. They all have reporting requirements that can make your head spin. But after you understand the requirements, it's like learning to ride a bike. Your *Notice of Grant Award (NGA)* defines the grant agreement relationship between the federal government and your organization. The purpose of the relationship is to transfer money to you so you can accomplish the common good.

You may get a letter or an e-mail with a downloadable file about your grant award. In the letter you'll find important information about the terms of your grant award. Think of the terms as the rules of the grant game. You can't play the game if you don't know the rules.

The Notice of Grant Award discloses the terms of the grant agreement and guidelines for proper management of the grant by stating the

- ✔ Budget summary
- ✔ Due dates for financial status reports
- ✔ Special conditions of the award
- ✔ Award/project period
- ✔ Treatment of program income
- ✔ Indirect cost rate
- ✔ Federal share and nonprofit share (cost-sharing/match)

The following sections help you work through the details of your grant agreement. Following the rules is easy when you understand them.

Summarizing the grant budget

The *budget summary* helps you know how the government expects you to manage your grant. It indicates costs and revenues linked to grant activities and helps you monitor and control grant funds. The budget provides a clear indication of grant performance.

The budget summary indicates how much money has been allocated to each category. The typical budget summary includes the following accounts in the following order:

- ✔ Personnel
- ✔ Fringe benefits
- ✔ Travel
- ✔ Equipment
- ✔ Supplies
- ✔ Contractual
- ✔ Construction
- ✔ Other
- ✔ Indirect costs

Knowing the due dates for financial status reports

Unless otherwise noted in the special conditions (see the next section), financial status reports are due quarterly, annually, and at the end of the project period to close out the grant. The quarterly due dates are

Reporting Quarter	Due Date
January 1–March 31	May 15
April 1–June 30	August 14
July 1–September 30	November 14
October 1–December 31	February 14

To submit your financial status reports, use Standard Form 269 (SF-269), which is the most common financial report. It lists all expenditures from the grant money and the running grant balance. I cover this form in greater detail in Chapter 11.

Indicating special conditions

Pay attention to the Notice of Grant Award regarding any special conditions included in the agreement. *Special conditions* are rules that are usually numbered on the grant award notice. For example, I received an award letter stating that the agency had approved my grant request, but it imposed a special condition stating that I had to add another location to do training. After I satisfied the special condition, it was removed by the awarding agency.

Sometimes a grant applicant may have some issues that warrant special conditions placed on them by the awarding agency. A high-risk nonprofit may face special conditions. If a nonprofit has a history of poor performance, isn't financially stable, or lacks some responsibility in management systems, the federal agency may award the nonprofit a grant because the nonprofit is supporting a good cause, but impose special conditions because of the organization's problems.

A common condition of receiving a federal grant requires you to submit *progress reports.* The Performance Progress Report (SF-PPR) tells how many people you've helped with the federal dollars. These reports are used by Congress to determine whether the money is making a difference in the lives of the people it aims to help. Head to Chapter 11 for more about completing progress reports.

Keeping the award/project period in mind

Your grant has a beginning date and an ending date, which is called your *project period.* Your project period may range from one to three years. I always mark both my wall and electronic calendars to keep up with grant project periods. It's important to know how much time you have to spend your money.

If you forget to spend the money, it goes back to the federal government. Make sure you don't let a grant expire without using the funds.

Treatment of program income

Depending on how much grant money you get, holding the money in your organization's bank account can generate *program income* in the form of interest paid on the money. Some programs supported by grants receive additional money through donations or fees for services. Money earned that is directly generated by grant-supporting activity is also called program income.

Earning more than $250 of interest income can result in you having to pay the money back. The government allows you to keep the first $250 of interest earned on grant money. You report interest earned when you file your grant reports, and interest over $250 will be treated as a grant distribution to you. Always talk with your program manager if you're concerned about program income.

Figuring your indirect cost rate

While you're running your grant program, you're incurring costs of normal operations. A portion of the cost for telephone, lights, gas, rent, and other overhead expenses may be charged to the grant as an indirect cost. (An *indirect cost* is a necessity of doing business, and you incur them whether you run one or three programs.) To get an *indirect cost rate,* you have to submit a request for it to the federal government. Based on the information submitted about your overhead expenses, the government will give you an indirect cost rate, which is a percentage of all of your expenses to operate your nonprofit.

Federal and nonprofit shares

Unfortunately, sometimes not all of the costs to run a program are paid in full by the grant. Some grants require a match. A grant *match* is when your nonprofit pays a percentage of the total award. I like to think of it as sharing the expense. The Notice of Grant Award will indicate the amount the federal agency pays (called the *federal share*) and what, if any, the nonprofit must match (called the *nonprofit share*).

For example, if you submit a grant application stating it will cost you $100,000 to run your program, the granting agency may want you to pay 10 percent of that amount. Your 10 percent of the cost will be $10,000, and the 90 percent federal share will be $90,000.

Match requirements are listed in the grant announcement or notice of funding availability. Therefore, you'll know before applying for funding that a match is required. You can account for the nonprofit share of the match when you submit the budget with your application.

Sometimes your match can be contributed in ways other than cash. For instance, you may want to use the salary of one of your employees as a match. If a significant percentage of the person's time is spent working on the grant program, this is allowable.

The following can be used as a nonprofit share:

- ✔ Cash
- ✔ In-kind donations of supplies, services, or personnel costs
- ✔ Program income (gross revenue earned by a grant-supported program)
- ✔ Unrecovered indirect costs (the difference between the amount awarded and the amount which could have been awarded under the recipient's approved indirect cost rate; see the preceding section for more on indirect cost rates)
- ✔ A combination of these

Chapter 11

Tracking and Accounting for Federal Dollars

Go ahead and celebrate. You worked hard and you received the federal grant. You've been awarded grant funding to establish, develop, and implement a project for your organization. Now you have to manage your grant. Get ready for tons of paperwork, but don't worry; I walk you through the whole process in this chapter. After you find out what really matters, you'll be on your way to managing the fed's money in your sleep.

Your underlying responsibility is to understand your obligations to the federal government and your awarding agency. After you know what's expected of you, you can follow the directions your awarding agency gives you.

In this chapter, I give you some tips on how to stay on top of your federal grant game. This includes spending the money according to the grant budget; complying with the awarding agency's requirements by submitting all reports on time; and knowing how to close out the grant. If you're thinking that you'll be dealing with lots of paperwork, you're right. After all, you know that everything the government does involves lots of paper. (I focus on federal grants in this chapter; if you're curious about grants from sources other than the federal government, see the "Defining the difference between private and public grants" sidebar in this chapter.)

Defining the difference between private and public grants

You need to be aware of a few key differences between the application, review, and management processes of grants offered by private corporations and foundations (commonly referred to as *private grants*) versus those offered by the government (commonly referred to as *public grants*). How you track and manage your grants depend on the grant maker's terms. Everything that deals with the government, including its grant process, is very detailed and thorough, and information is easily accessible at www.grants.gov. On the other hand, corporate grant makers may not be as organized or open as the government in terms of grant details. Information about private grants may not be in one central location. Foundations and corporations may choose to advertise grant opportunities on their Web sites, but they may not.

Government grants are well defined and competitive, and you can request feedback if your grant application isn't funded. The grant process for public grants involves a peer review, in which a panel of at least three individuals reviews your application. This panel scores your application according to a predetermined numbering system that you receive before you turn in your application. This process is the same for every applicant, which ensures a certain level of consistency.

Private grants are a little different. Each awarding entity has the freedom to define its own grant process. Corporations usually have more leniency in the way they award, administer, and manage grants. Corporate funders set the rules and change them as they see fit. For example, a corporation may choose to give your nonprofit a check with no strings attached, or it may have a detailed process you have to follow throughout the duration of your grant.

Many community foundations are a bit more structured than corporations in terms of their grant processes. They often have grants that donors set up for specific purposes. These donors may even stipulate how the grant recipient should use the money. Some of the larger foundations, such as the Bill & Melinda Gates Foundation, Ford Foundation, W.K. Kellogg Foundation, and Mary Reynolds Babcock Foundation, use grant processes similar to those of the government.

Whether your grant has been awarded by a corporation, foundation, or government agency, make sure you find out all the rules you need to follow so you don't lose your grant.

Understanding Your Obligation

As *grant recipient,* you've agreed to fulfill a need in society, and the federal government has agreed to give you the money to do so. As a grant recipient, you're responsible for

✔ **Managing the money:** This can be a fun part of the job and includes

- Ensuring grant funds are spent according to the grant budget
- Monitoring grant activity and expenses
- Ensuring that grant funds aren't returned to the awarding agency

✔ **Handling the paperwork:** I know you don't want to be a paper pusher, but if you're going to spend the government's money, you have to keep track of every detail. Here's what you have to do:

- Prepare and file reports on time
- Maintain detailed documentations and records

✔ **Running the program according to your application:** This is likely the most rewarding part of managing the grant. You get to help people improve their lives, which is probably why you got into this field in the first place.

If you don't take care of these three aspects according to the grant guidelines, you can lose your funding. How you manage the money, fill out the paperwork, and run your program establish your organization's reputation with the federal government. If you poorly manage your grant, your awarding agency may give you additional reporting requirements that you have to meet for the duration of your grant. For instance, if you develop a history of poor performance and financial instability, your program manager may require you to present reports more often than quarterly or semiannually. (See Chapter 12 for more about special conditions and grants.)

I cover the money and paperwork aspects of grants in the rest of this chapter. I leave the managing of the grant program up to you. I know you can handle it.

Managing Grant Funds

Grant money is another form of income for your nonprofit, but you can't just throw it in the pot with all the other cash and do whatever you want to with it. You have to keep track of the grant funds so the awarding agency knows you did what you said you were going to do with the funds and didn't fritter the money away.

In the following sections, I explain how to manage your grant money separately from your other income and expenses, and how you go about getting the money that's been awarded to you.

If you need help setting up a system to help you manage your money, turn to Chapter 4. A good financial management system helps you record and track expenses, maintain records, and balance your grant budget.

Maintaining a separate budget for your grant dollars

When you received your Notice of Grant Award (see Chapter 10 for more on this), it included a grant budget. Your grant budget tells you how the federal government expects you to spend the money. You're expected to be a wise steward and to exercise good judgment when making decisions about what to buy and how much to pay.

Within your nonprofit, you need to keep a separate budget and set up separate accounts for your grant money. Your award letter comes with a grant budget that shows how much money you received and what you can and should do with it. This budget may be the same as or very similar to the budget you submitted with your grant application. You need to keep track of what you buy with the grant money so you can prove to your awarding agency and your auditor that you used the money according to the set budget. Keeping copies of *all* paperwork, especially receipts of purchase, pertaining to the grant is a good idea.

Pay attention to your grant period, because if you don't spend the money during the specified grant period on approved purchases, the awarding agency gets it back, and you lose everything you didn't spend.

Keeping separate accounts is important when you receive a federal grant because you need to avoid *commingling* funds, which means mixing grant money with your organization's other sources of income. Commingling of funds is one of the audit findings that can cause you to lose funding. (For more about grant audits, see Chapter 12.) Include your grant programs in your chart of accounts by assigning each program a different control number. Doing so solves the problem of mixing up the money. (For more information about setting up a chart of accounts for your nonprofit, see Chapter 5.)

If you're feeling a bit unsure about how to keep everything separate, you may want to set up a completely separate bank account for your grant money, which you can do at your local bank.

Someone has to oversee the project's progress and funding. Depending on how much money you received and your other responsibilities, you may want to consider hiring someone to manage the project's funding.

Making changes to your grant

Okay, nothing is written in stone. Things change, people move, prices go up and down; as a result, nothing in the budget is absolute. If you need to make budget changes, contact your program manager and ask for a *grant adjustment notice (GAN)*. A grant adjustment notice gives you written authorization to make changes to your grant agreement. These changes can be actual changes to your budget, extensions of the funding period, or changes in personnel, among others.

If you need to make a change to your budget that requires a grant adjustment notice, you need to call your program manager and request the form.

Following up this call with an e-mail to verify the request is always a good idea. After your program manager approves the changes, you receive a grant adjustment notice by mail; add the notice to your grant files.

Get all approved changes to your grant agreement in writing. Documentation is important for you to have so you can justify all of your actions pertaining to the grant.

Check with your program manager about the 10 percent rule for budgetary changes. The *10 percent rule* states that you can move up to 10 percent of your budget money (10 percent of the total grant amount) from one budget category to another without prior approval, as long as you don't create a new budget category.

Handling the responsibility of subgrantees

Subgrantees are the organizations that form a partnership with the lead agency, or *grantee,* to apply for the grant. If you're the lead agency, you're responsible for overseeing the financial management of yourself and the subgrantees. You establish this relationship through a subaward of your grant to your subgrantee.

The grantor is the federal agency that awards and establishes a grant agreement with the grantee through the Notice of Grant Award (see Chapter 10 for more on this document). The grantee may have partners that it included in the grant budget as subgrantees.

Subgrantees answer directly to the grantee and seldom have any direct contact with the grantor. The grantee establishes a grant agreement with the subgrantee similar to the agreement that the grantor has with the grantee. The grantee authorizes all payments submitted for reimbursement to the grantor and makes drawdowns from the grantor for both themselves and the subgrantees.

The grantee submits all reporting requirements to the grantor. The grantee places reporting requirements on the subgrantee. The grantee is responsible for overseeing not only the actions of its nonprofit but also the actions of the subgrantees.

For example, consider the following situation: United Way partners with the Red Cross on a $100,000 grant that the U.S. Department of Education awards United Way. The U.S. Department of Education is the grantor. United Way is the grantee and lead agency, and the Red Cross is the subgrantee. If a problem with how the money is managed comes up during the grant's duration, the responsibilities lie with United Way. If the Red Cross spends money carelessly, United Way is responsible for that careless spending because United Way had to approve and make all drawdowns for the Red Cross. If the Red Cross performs poorly, United Way has to carefully approve or disapprove its requests for payment.

Double trouble in Macon

The city of Macon, Georgia, has double trouble with managing its grants. Both the U.S. Department of Justice and the Federal Emergency Management Agency (FEMA) have disallowed questionable expenses and ordered the city to repay misappropriated funds. In addition, a U.S. attorney has threatened the city with a $1 million lawsuit.

In 2002, the Department of Justice awarded $900,000 to the city for a Safe Schools Initiative grant. In reality, the city kept only $170,000 of the total grant award because the city included several subgrantees in its grant budget. The city administered the remaining $730,000 among partners made up of faith-based organizations. The Department of Justice was the grantor, the city of Macon was the grantee, and the faith-based organizations were the subgrantees. The city of Macon was responsible for approving payments submitted by its partners. After an audit of the city's records, the Department of Justice found that the city lacked necessary documentation to support expenditures of $350,000. As a result, the city of Macon had to

pay back $350,000 for false claims it submitted to the Department of Justice.

The Department of Justice didn't go after the faith-based organizations because, as the grantee, the city was responsible for administering and managing the money — it had the right and responsibility to refuse false claims submitted by the faith-based organizations.

In addition to the debacle with the Department of Justice, the city of Macon found itself in trouble with another grantor, FEMA. FEMA awarded the city a grant to remove debris from severe flooding. In 2004, the Office of Inspector General (OIG) reported that $126,911 of the city's claims were excessive or duplicate charges against the grant. The problems that FEMA uncovered in Macon included double billing, overcharging for overtime, not having documentation to support expenses charged to the grant, and submitting false claims. The OIG disallowed the $126,911 of questioned costs, and the city had to come up with the money on its own.

Creating the grant agreement for subgrantees

Whether you call it an agreement or a contract, you need to have something in writing that states the terms of your agreement with the subgrantees — how much money you'll allocate, to whom you will allocate the money, what the money should be used for, and when you will allocate it.

The authorized representative of your organization should sign the agreement. Your authorized representative is the person responsible for the overall management of your grant, usually your organization's director. Keep in mind that your executive director doesn't have to administer or manage the program, but he is responsible for it. Also, the agreement should state when financial and progress reports are due from your subgrantees (see the "Reporting Requirements" section in this chapter for more about these reports).

Generally, grantees give subgrantees a deadline of two weeks before the reports are due to the grantor. As the lead agency or grantee, your financial reports are due 45 days after the end of the quarter. Therefore, if you're managing subgrantees, you should give them a deadline of 30 days to submit their financial reports to you. Your Performance Progress Report (SF-PPR) is due to the awarding agency 30 days after the end of the reporting period (see the "Reporting Requirements" section of this chapter for more about this report). Therefore, you should give your subgrantees 15 days to get their progress reports to you. Your subgrantees send information to you, and then you send it, along with your own reports, to the grantor or awarding agency.

Monitoring and verifying subgrantees' reports

As the lead agency, your responsibility is to monitor the reports that the subgrantees submit. Some questions to ask yourself when looking over these bills and documents include the following:

- ✔ Are the expenses the subgrantees submitted to you in the budget?
- ✔ Are the costs associated with the project?
- ✔ Do the subgrantees have an adequate accounting system?

Make sure you keep copies of all the paperwork your subgrantees send you. You may need it later to justify money paid to subgrantees. As the lead agency, you're responsible for managing both your own transactions and those of your subgrantees. You answer to the grantor if questions about your subgrantees' expenses arise.

When a subgrantee submits a claim for reimbursement to you, you need to review the expenses and check to see whether they're in the budget before you approve expenses. If the expenses aren't listed in the subgrantee's budget, you have to deny the claim. I've had claims submitted in which subgrantees try to use grant money to pay for something totally unrelated to the purpose of the project. Always compare the expenses to both the grant budget and the guidelines set in the grant award document.

Drawing Down Federal Dollars

The federal government doesn't send you a check for the total amount of your grant upfront. In fact, most federal agencies reimburse you rather than pay you in advance, so as a grant recipient, you have to request the money after you spend it.

This setup reminds me of the old saying "You have to have money to make money." When you're a grant recipient, you need to have some front money to spend before you can start receiving the grant dollars.

Before you can gain access to your grant money, you need to submit some information authorizing your bank to process the drawdown. The *drawdown* is the process by which you request your grant money from the awarding agency. You have to submit paperwork to the bank to authorize the transfer of funds into your bank account. After you submit this paperwork, you can begin moving money into your organization's bank account.

Inside your award package, you should find forms to set up electronic transfers from the U.S. Treasury to your bank account. You need to fill out these forms and send them to the awarding agency. You need to include your bank routing number, the name of your bank, your account number, the contact person — all the information you use when you authorize an electronic transfer.

After you set up your bank account to receive money from the government's account, you can start requesting drawdowns. You need the following information to request a drawdown:

- **Grant ID number:** Each grant awarded has a grant ID number, which the federal agency giving you the money assigns to you.

- **Employer identification number:** Your employer identification number (EIN) is the identifying number the IRS assigns to you for tax purposes.

- **Amount of money requested:** You need to know exactly how much money you're requesting. Keep invoices and bills to justify your requests.

- **Time period the money was used:** You need to know during which period your organization spent the money. For example, the period covered by this request can be a week, month, or quarter.

As you request drawdowns throughout the grant period, keep track in your own files of how much money has been drawn and how much money is left to be drawn (for more information on tracking your records, turn to the "Tracking the electronic transfer" section in this chapter). Make sure your records coincide with the numbers in your grant budget.

Transferring grant money

You can request or draw down your federal grant money either by telephone or over the Internet. Use whichever method you're more comfortable with:

- **Telephone method:** Requesting grant money over the telephone is a paperless method. You can find the number to call to request grant money inside your grant award package. After you dial this number, the system prompts you for the information I describe in the preceding section. Unfortunately, you don't speak to an actual person.

One disadvantage to the telephone method is that it can leave you wondering whether your request actually transmitted because you don't receive documentation verifying the transaction. But, you can create your own spreadsheet of the drawdown. See the "Tracking the electronic transfer" section for how to set up a spreadsheet.

✔ **Internet method:** To use the Internet to request your grant money, you first need to set up an online account with the federal agency that awarded you the money; you do this by creating a password and user ID. Note that periodically you'll be prompted to change your password.

Of course, you need to keep your current password and user ID in a secure place so you can find them quickly. After all, you don't want to be in the middle of processing your payment when the system times out because you can't find your password (the Internet *times out* when you take too long to complete a certain action). Make sure your information is handy so you can successfully complete the process.

Unlike the telephone method, the Internet method enables you to print out a receipt of your request. For this reason, I prefer the Internet method.

Sometimes you're given a choice as to which method you want to use. Look in your Notice of Grant Award for specific instructions on how to draw down funds.

Documentation is very important when working with a large agency like the federal government. Keeping copies of all transactions and communications, especially the drawdowns you've requested and received, is essential to proper documentation. Doing so also helps you track and monitor your grant balances. So if you choose the telephone method, create your own records of the transactions you make.

Tracking the electronic transfer

One way to track electronic transfers is to create a spreadsheet of every drawdown requested. In this spreadsheet, you want to record the date of the request, the time of the request, the amount requested, and the time period covered (flip to Chapter 4 for pointers on creating a spreadsheet). Updating your spreadsheets at least on a monthly basis is a good idea. Waiting longer than one month can cause you to get behind and lose track of what's what. These up-to-date spreadsheets help you when you have to fill out your quarterly financial reports. See the "Reporting Requirements" section for more about filling out your financial reports.

In addition to the spreadsheet, you should print out and create a hard-copy file of every transaction you request. This file needs to coincide with your budget balance for the grant.

If you want assurance that you and your award agency have the same balances, you can request a grant summary from your federal program manager. A *grant summary* is a printout of all of your grant transactions according to the awarding agency's records. You can double-check your records against the government's records anytime you need to.

Knowing when to request a drawdown

If your budget is tight, you need to carefully track how much time the U.S. Treasury can take to move the money to your bank account. In today's age of electronics, things can be transmitted instantly, but sometimes the government doesn't move that fast. So you need to pay attention to the timing.

Sometimes the last five days of the month are the busiest for the federal agency because everybody is trying to close out the month and process payments. For this reason, you shouldn't wait until the last week of the month to request a money transfer. If you do wait until the end of the month to request your grant money, expect to wait a little longer to receive it. Like banks, the U.S. Treasury isn't open every day. Most agencies tell you that moving money takes five working days, but sometimes you have to wait a little longer.

How long processing a payment request takes depends on whether your nonprofit is the grantee or the subgrantee. If you're the subgrantee, you have to wait for the grantee to receive payment from the grantor before you receive your money. How fast the grantee receives payment depends on the accounting procedures your awarding agency has in place. For instance, if your awarding agency is a large state agency that has a separate finance department, you may find that the department takes more time to process the reimbursement than does a smaller agency with fewer requests.

Reporting Requirements

Everyone has to report to someone, and that's especially true when you're spending Uncle Sam's money. After reading your grant agreement and/or award letter, you should know how many reports you have to submit and when you need to submit them. You can't avoid the paperwork. The Office of Management and Budget (OMB) hands down these requirements. The OMB sets the standards for administering, managing, and auditing federal dollars.

Most grants require that you submit the following two reports to the awarding agency:

> ✔ **A financial status report, called the Standard Form 269:** Your financial status report gives a brief summary of how much money was awarded, how much money was spent, and how much money you have left in your budget. This report is filed quarterly and when you close out your grant.
>
> ✔ **Progress reports, called the Standard Form PPR (Performance Progress Report):** These reports tell the feds whether you're making progress toward the program's goals and objectives. These reports are submitted semiannually.

You have to file these financial status reports even if you don't spend any money during the given quarter. Just fill in zeros if you haven't spent any money. Your program manager will keep a close eye on your program's progress. If you have questions about anything pertaining to your grant, contact your program manager. In the following sections, I explain in detail how to complete and submit both of these reports.

Most federal programs have an annual grant management meeting where you're given guidelines about how to manage your grant and have an opportunity to meet folks from other nonprofits that received the same grant. These annual meetings can help you manage your programs better and offer networking opportunities for you to find out more about other grants that may be available for your nonprofit.

You must file reports on time. The consequences of not filing your reports on time can be detrimental to your organization. If you stop the flow of paperwork, the federal government stops the flow of money. Therefore, if you don't submit reports, you don't receive your money. Mark your calendar, program your PDA, send yourself reminders, do whatever you need to do to remember what is due and when.

Financial Standard Form 269

The most important report you have to submit to your federal grantor is the *Financial Status Report,* which you complete using Standard Form 269 (SF-269). Financial Status Reports (FSRs) tell your grantor how much you've spent in the current quarter versus prior quarters and how much you have left in your budget. Financial Status Reports are due quarterly and when the grant period expires. For copies of FSRs, go to www.whitehouse.gov/omb/grants/sf269a.pdf.

Financial Status Reports come in both a short form (SF-269A) and a long form (SF-269). Each federal awarding agency requires using the SF-269 or SF269-A to report your financial status. I outline steps to help you fill out the short form of the grant Financial Status Report in the following sections. See Figure 11-1 for a copy of SF-269A.

FINANCIAL STATUS REPORT
(Short Form)
(Follow instructions on the back)

1. Federal Agency and Organizational Element to Which Report is Submitted	2. Federal Grant or Other Identifying Number Assigned By Federal Agency	OMB Approval No. 0348-0038	Page of pages

3. Recipient Organization (Name and complete address, including ZIP code)

4. Employer Identification Number	5. Recipient Account Number or Identifying Number	6. Final Report ☐ Yes ☐ No	7. Basis ☐ Cash ☐ Accrual

8. Funding/Grant Period (See instructions) From: (Month, Day, Year)	To: (Month, Day, Year)	9. Period Covered by this Report From: (Month, Day, Year)	To: (Month, Day, Year)

10. Transactions:	I Previously Reported	II This Period	III Cumulative
a. Total outlays			0.00
b. Recipient share of outlays			0.00
c. Federal share of outlays			0.00
d. Total unliquidated obligations			
e. Recipient share of unliquidated obligations			
f. Federal share of unliquidated obligations			
g. Total Federal share(Sum of lines c and f)			0.00
h. Total Federal funds authorized for this funding period			
i. Unobligated balance of Federal funds(Line h minus line g)			0.00

11. Indirect Expense	a. Type of Rate (Place "X" in appropriate box) ☐ Provisional ☐ Predetermined ☐ Final ☐ Fixed			
	b. Rate	c. Base	d. Total Amount	e. Federal Share

12. Remarks: Attach any explanations deemed necessary or information required by Federal sponsoring agency in compliance with governing legislation.

13. Certification: **I certify to the best of my knowledge and belief that this report is correct and complete and that all outlays and unliquidated obligations are for the purposes set forth in the award documents.**

Typed or Printed Name and Title	Telephone (Area code, number and extension)
Signature of Authorized Certifying Official	Date Report Submitted February 3, 2009

NSN 7540-01-218-4387   269-202   Standard Form 269A (Rev. 7-97)
Prescribed by OMB Circulars A-102 and A-110

Figure 11-1: Financial Status Report — Standard Form 269A.

Filling out SF-269A

According to the OMB, the SF-269A takes about 90 minutes to complete. Each item on the form has a number or letter, which makes explaining it rather easy. The top portion of the form (numbers 1 through 9) covers information that identifies the federal agency, nonprofit organization, funding period, payment accounting method, and period (month or quarter, for example) covered by the financial report.

The following steps explain the items on the SF-269A and what to do for each one:

1. **Federal Agency and Organizational Element to Which Report Is Submitted:** Insert the name of the federal agency that awarded the grant.

2. **Federal Grant or Other Identifying Number Assigned by Federal Agency:** Write the grant number assigned by the federal agency, which you can find in your grant award package.

3. **Recipient Organization (Name and complete address, including zip code):** Write the name of your nonprofit and its complete address.

4. **Employer Identification Number:** Write your nonprofit's federal employer identification number (FEIN or EIN).

5. **Recipient Account Number or Identifying Number:** Write your non-profit's self-identifying number (only if it has one).

The *recipient account number* is a self-designated number you use in your nonprofit. If you're managing several projects and need to separate them, you should assign each project an account number to help you. You can leave this box blank if it doesn't apply to you.

6. **Final Report:** Check yes only if this is the final report.

Financial Status Reports are submitted quarterly and at the close of the grant. At the end of a project, two reports are due: a report for financial quarterly activities and a final report. Usually these two reports have the same financial information. The only difference is that you check Yes on the final report.

7. **Basis:** Check either the Cash or Accrual box, depending on which method of accounting you use.

If you account for transactions when cash changes hands or use your checkbook as your primary accounting system, check the cash box. If you record transactions when they take place, regardless of whether any cash has exchanged hands, check the accrual box. (See Chapter 2 for more about cash and accrual methods of accounting.)

8. **Funding/Grant Period:** Write the beginning date of the grant in the From box and the ending date of the grant in the To box.

Make necessary adjustments for any grant extensions you've received.

If you need an extension, request it at least three months before the grant closing date. Most federal programs run a little behind schedule at the beginning, so extensions are common. Most federal agencies are willing to grant up to a one-year extension.

9. **Period Covered by This Report:** Write the dates of the period you're covering with this report in the To and From boxes. Financial Status Reports are usually reported quarterly unless otherwise noted. See

the chart of reporting periods and due dates in the "Submitting SF-269" section.

If this is your final report, your time period is the entire grant period, from the beginning date to the closeout date, including all extensions.

10. **Transactions:** Fill out the following three columns:

   I. **Previously Reported:** The cumulative amounts from the previous report. If this is the first report, this amount is zero.

   II. **This Period:** The current amount expended for the reporting quarter.

   III. **Cumulative:** The previously reported amount plus the amount for the current reporting period.

   For the following categories of transactions, you enter the amount of the transaction in one of the first two columns, depending on when the money was spent, and you enter the total for that category in the third column.

   a. **Total outlays:** Enter the total amounts spent on the grant during the reporting quarter. Consider that your nonprofit spends $5,500 in January, $6,500 in February, and $6,000 in March. Enter the total of $18,000 in the total outlays box for this period.

   b. **Recipient share of outlays:** If you have a cost-sharing or matching grant — in which you pay an agreed portion — you enter the amount you paid, according to agreement in the grant budget. If it's not a cost-sharing or matching grant, enter zero.

   Sometimes the federal government doesn't award the total cost to operate a program. Instead, you may be asked to pay a percentage of the cost. Grants in which you pay a portion of the costs are called *cost-sharing* or *matching grants* (see Chapter 10 for more on this concept).

   c. **Federal share of outlays:** If this is not a matching grant, enter the amounts from a. If this is a matching grant, enter the amount charged to the grant and expected to be reimbursed by the federal agency.

   d. **Total unliquidated obligations:** Enter the expenses that your sub-grantees have incurred but that you haven't yet paid. If you don't have any, leave this box blank.

   e. **Recipient share of unliquidated obligations:** Enter your portion of the total amount obligated if this is a matching grant. If this isn't a matching grant, leave this box blank.

   f. **Federal share of unliquidated obligations:** Enter the amount paid by the awarding agency for expenses that the subgrantees have incurred but that the agency hasn't yet paid. If you don't have any or if it's a cost-sharing grant, leave this box blank.

Although these expenses occurred within the Financial Status Report period, you may not have requested or paid the amounts yet. Reporting all expenses and allocating them to the quarter in which they occur is important.

g. Total federal share: Enter the sum of boxes c and f, for the current period.

h. Total federal funds authorized for this funding period: Enter your total grant amount awarded.

i. Unobligated balance of federal funds: Subtract line g from line h and enter that amount. This is your grant balance for this period.

Most nonprofits fill in only a, b, c, g, h, and i.

11. **Indirect Expense:** Check the appropriate type of rate. This rate, commonly called an *indirect cost rate,* is a cost rate that helps cover some overhead administrative costs. Check with your program manager to get an allowance to pay indirect expenses. (See Chapter 10 for more about indirect cost rates.)

Also, number 11 asks questions about your rate, base, total amount, and federal share of indirect cost rate. For 11(b), enter your current indirect cost rate. For 11(c), enter the amount you used to calculate your rate. For 11(d), enter the total amount of indirect costs. For 11(e), enter the federal share of the amount in 11(d).

12. **Remarks:** This box is usually not applicable. However, if your awarding agency has asked for any additional explanations, provide them here.

13. **Certification:** Be sure to acquire the correct signature on the SF-269A. Auditors will write you up if your Financial Status Reports aren't signed, so make sure your director signs them. The signature certifies that the report is correct and that grant money has been spent according to guidelines.

When you account for grant expenditures on a monthly basis, you can copy the information for the SF-269 from your accounting system onto the form.

Submitting SF-269

Back in the day, we submitted the SF-269 by mail. After September 11, 2001, sending mail to the government became a difficult task. Often mail is returned with a black mark over it. Since then, many awarding agencies require that all grantees submit their financial reports electronically or by fax machine.

Unless otherwise noted, financial status reports are due according to the following table:

Reporting Quarter	Due Date
January 1–March 31	May 15
April 1–June 30	August 14
July 1–September 30	November 14
October 1–December 31	February 14

If you have the option to fax your financial status report, don't wait until the due date to fax it. Not surprisingly, the fax machines usually go crazy on the due dates.

Sometimes fax machines jam and lock up, and federal employees have to turn them off. So, if your report is transmitting and the machine is off, your report probably won't make it to the agency on time.

I once sent financial reports all three ways, by mail, fax, and the Internet, because I wanted to cover all the bases. No one wants to receive the dreaded message when she tries to draw down money — the message that states the government didn't receive your Financial Status Reports, and, therefore, the government can't process your request for grant money. I suggest that you do your reports online to expedite the process.

Progress reports

Your awarding agency wants to know how you're doing with your grant project, so periodically you have to submit a progress report. The progress report, which comes in many forms, states the status of achievements in accomplishing project goals. The progress report indicates the status of the following:

- Equipment purchases
- Number of people served
- Amount of money spent
- Plans for spending the grant money
- Overall status of the grant project

Some reports include corrective actions or plans to resolve problems. After all, seldom does a program run according to schedule. The progress report provides you a place where you can explain program problems and ask for technical assistance from the grantor.

You can download the OMB's progress reports, called the Performance Progress Reports (SF-PPRs), at `www.whitehouse.gov/omb/grants/grants_forms.html`.

Some federal agencies have their own reports, so check with your federal program manager about where to find copies of progress reports. You submit most progress reports online, and you can download them from your awarding agency's Web site.

Completing your progress report

Filling out progress reports is fairly straightforward. Refer to Figure 11-2 for an example of a Performance Progress Report (SF-PPR). The top third of the form asks for basic information about you, your project, and the period covered. The middle section of the report is considered the narrative section. Here you provide specific details about your project's progress within the last period. The bottom section is where you put your contact information and sign certifying that the report is correct and complete.

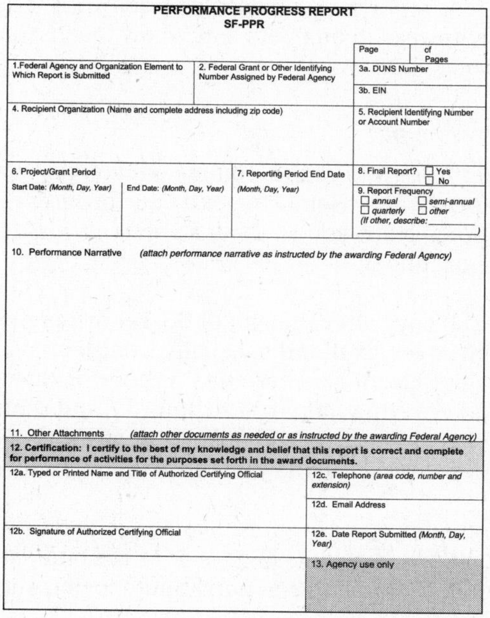

PERFORMANCE PROGRESS REPORT
SF-PPR

Page | of Pages

1.Federal Agency and Organization Element to Which Report is Submitted

2. Federal Grant or Other Identifying Number Assigned by Federal Agency

3a. DUNS Number

3b. EIN

4. Recipient Organization (Name and complete address including zip code)

5. Recipient Identifying Number or Account Number

6. Project/Grant Period
Start Date: (Month, Day, Year) | End Date: (Month, Day, Year)

7. Reporting Period End Date (Month, Day, Year)

8. Final Report? ☐ Yes ☐ No

9. Report Frequency ☐ annual ☐ semi-annual ☐ quarterly ☐ other (If other, describe: ___)

10. Performance Narrative (attach performance narrative as instructed by the awarding Federal Agency)

11. Other Attachments (attach other documents as needed or as instructed by the awarding Federal Agency)

12. Certification: I certify to the best of my knowledge and belief that this report is correct and complete for performance of activities for the purposes set forth in the award documents.

12a. Typed or Printed Name and Title of Authorized Certifying Official

12c. Telephone (area code, number and extension)

12d. Email Address

12b. Signature of Authorized Certifying Official

12e. Date Report Submitted (Month, Day, Year)

13. Agency use only

Figure 11-2: A Performance Progress Report (SF-PPR).

Talk to your program manager about how much information you need to include in this report. Basically, your awarding agency wants to know numbers: how many people you served through your program, how many people participated, how many people directly benefited from your program, and so on. These numbers provide outcome measurements, which help the awarding agency decide your project's overall efficacy so far.

I like to use brief condensed sentences that get to the point on these progress reports. Your awarding agency won't be impressed with a novel about your program. One thing I've learned from dealing with federal employees is that they want only prevalent information. I suggest that you state the facts in numbers and percentages that indicate a reasonable amount of progress.

Refer back to your award letter and grant agreement for specific instructions about how often your program manager wants to know your status. Usually, progress reports cover a six-month period. Keep in mind, though, that some agencies may require progress reports on a different schedule, or they may ask for additional information (not covered on the progress report) about your project.

Pay attention to any special conditions listed in your award document. Special conditions deviate from the norm. For example, your awarding agency may want you to submit progress reports on a monthly or quarterly basis instead of semiannually. Read your award documents and follow the instructions the awarding agency gave you.

Submitting your progress report

Most grantees submit their progress reports online. As you do with SF-269, you have to set up a password and user ID to send your progress report online. Your awarding agency gives you all the instructions you need to submit your progress report online.

Progress reports are due 30 days after the end of the reporting period. Progress reports typically cover six months, usually from January through June and from July through December. Therefore, a report is due no later than July 30 for the period covering January 1 to June 30, and January 30 for the period covering July 1 to December 31. Look at your award letter to see exactly when your awarding agency wants you to submit all reports.

In addition to the semiannual progress reports, you have to do a final report at the closeout of the grant, which is due 90 days after the end date of the grant. See the next section for more information about closing out your grant.

Some agencies allow you to send progress reports by mail or fax machine. Keep in mind, though, that your program is just one of many programs overseen by the federal government. Sometimes paperwork gets lost in the shuffle. Keep copies of everything you send or receive concerning your grant program, especially your financial and progress reports.

Closing Out a Grant

Closeout of a grant occurs when the awarding agency determines that all applicable administrative actions and all required programmatic work under the grant have been completed, with the possible exception of the final audit (see Chapter 12 for more on this). The closeout process completes the grant agreement between the awarding agency and you, the grant recipient.

Usually, you're required to submit a final SF-269 and SF-PPR to close out the grant. You must submit these reports within 90 days after the expiration or termination date of the grant award. And yes, even if you've already submitted a quarterly report, you still need to submit a final report with the same information.

After the grant period has ended, the awarding agency may allow you to keep property purchased with the grant. Deposition of property varies among different agencies. You want to talk to your federal program manager about how to handle any property and equipment purchased with grant money. Your program manager can help you follow your agency's property disposition procedures.

After a grant is closed out, your awarding agency sends you a grant adjustment notice indicating that your grant has expired. This notice also indicates whether all funding was spent or whether some of the money was returned to the U.S. Treasury.

You should keep all records pertaining to grant activities for three years after the expiration of the project. Keep the following records:

- Application
- Award documents
- Canceled checks
- Correspondence
- Deposit slips
- Financial Status Reports (SF-269s)
- Grant adjustment notices (GANs)

- Invoices
- Paid bills
- Performance Progress Reports (SF-PPRs)
- Receipts
- Sales slips
- Supporting documentations

Chapter 12

Getting Ready for the Grant Audit

As the executive director or manager of a nonprofit, you probably already know that audits are a part of business. An audit doesn't mean that you're doing anything wrong. It's simply an evaluation of what's taken place. An auditor looks at events to determine the degree to which the information presented corresponds with established guidelines. After completing the audit, the auditor prepares a report with the details of his findings. Audits are done to verify whether you're doing what you're supposed to do.

Although audits come in many forms, including financial (see Chapter 20 for more on dealing with a financial audit), the audit I'm talking about in this chapter takes a look at your grant documents and budgets to verify that your nonprofit is properly using grant money.

The grant audits I outline in this chapter not only ensure that financial statements are presented in accordance with generally accepted accounting principles (GAAP), but they also analyze procurement practices, property management, cash management, and internal controls of grant programs.

All state, local, or tribal governments, nonprofit organizations, educational institutions, and hospitals that receive grant money must comply with auditing rules handed down by the federal government. In this chapter, I talk about what you need to do to prepare for a grant audit, what the program manager monitors, what the program officers audit, what happens if the Inspector General is called, and the classifications of grant audit findings.

Understanding the Purpose of the Grant Audit

When your nonprofit receives federal money, a grant audit determines whether your organization performed and complied with the federally funded grant. Basically Uncle Sam wants to make sure you're following the rules and to ensure you're being a good steward of federal funds.

The purpose of the grant audit is to assess and evaluate your progress. Each federal agency has *program managers* who are your primary points of contact. Your program manager monitors and oversees your progress by communicating with you. She'll occasionally pay you a personal visit to assess your progress. Before she arrives, your program manager will notify you of plans for an onsite visit and tell you which documents will be evaluated.

Some programs have very detailed monitoring guidelines. Whether you have a detailed monitoring visit is left up to the federal agency. If your program manager believes you're having problems managing the grant, some corrective actions will be suggested.

In addition to program managers, federal agencies have *program officers* who perform grant audits by visiting your site and doing a thorough evaluation of your grant files. Program officers are auditors who work for the federal agency that awarded you the grant.

The federal agency that gave you the grant will decide when you are audited or paid a visit. Just rest assured, you'll be notified in advance of the visit and have plenty of time to get everything in order.

Auditing Yellow Book style

Government auditors use government auditing standards (GAS) to perform governmental audits. The color of the GAS book cover is yellow, so it's often called the Yellow Book. Grant recipients are subjected to the rules of the Yellow Book when they receive $500,000 or more of government money. The government is concerned not just with a nonprofit's financial statements, but also with how it complies with laws and regulations. Accounting done by the Yellow Book is consistent with GAAS (generally accepted auditing standards), but broader in scope. For example, the Yellow Book has a lower threshold for misstatements because of government public accountability.

The major difference between the Yellow Book audit and GAAS is the reporting requirements. For example, the auditor must state in the audit report that the audit was done according to GAAS and GAS. One other difference is GAAS permit identifying material weaknesses, but the Yellow Book requires it.

To complete the audit, the program officer verifies that your nonprofit adheres to the following three circulars. These *circulars* outline the rules a nonprofit has to follow if it receives federal money. Chapter 10 highlights some of the specifics about the different rules. The following is a quick overview of these three circulars that the program officer uses during the audit:

- ✔ **OMB Circular A-133:** Different types of nonprofits have different rules to follow. However, all do have some of the same marching orders. The Office of Management and Budget (OMB) issues audit rules to federal agencies in the form of OMB Circular A-133 that all nonprofits that have federal expenditures of $500,000 or more have to follow.

- ✔ **OMB Circular A-122:** OMB A-122 outlines what's considered reasonable, allowable, allocable, and necessary for grant expenditures. Some costs are uniformly treated across the board for all organizations receiving grant money. For example, purchasing alcoholic beverages is not allowable with grant money.

- ✔ **2 CFR 215:** Every nonprofit organization should have written policies and procedures for accounting, procurements, inventory, personnel, and travel. You can find the administrative requirements for nonprofit organizations in this circular. *CFR* stands for the Code of Federal Regulations, which is the codification of general and permanent rules and regulations (sometimes called administrative law) handed down by the executive branch.

Check out the "Knowing What the Auditor Looks For" section later in this chapter for specific areas the program officer looks at during the audit.

Who Should Undergo an Audit?

All nonprofits should undergo some type of audit. What type of audit you need depends on whether you receive more or less than $500,000 of grant money in a year.

If your nonprofit receives less than $500,000 in grants in a year, you need to make your records available for review or audit by the federal awarding agency and General Accounting Office (GAO).

If you receive $500,000 or more in a year from grants, your nonprofit should have a program-specific audit conducted in that same year. A *program-specific audit* is conducted according to the guidelines in the general accepted government auditing standards (GAGAS).

For grant-related purposes, any nonprofit organization receiving at least $500,000 in a given year should have an independent audit of its financial statements, performed by a CPA (see Chapter 20 for more about these types of audits).

When You're Notified: Comprehending the Nitty Gritty of the Audit

You'll find out you're due for an audit by letter. It will include details about the type of audit (see the next section for more on the types of grant audits) and who will perform it. The letter will also give you details about what you need to do to prepare your nonprofit. Sometimes you may have to present information about your grant's progress; this can be something as simple as a PowerPoint presentation. You'll have anywhere from six weeks to a few months to prepare for an audit.

When the time for the audit arrives, your auditor will meet with your executive director and the executive staff that manages the grant before and after she evaluates your grant files. During the first meeting, the auditor introduces herself, talks about what will take place, and gives a general overview of how long the audit may take. During the closing meeting, the auditor lets you know that the audit is complete and the findings will be mailed after the report is complete. No results or findings are discussed during this closing meeting.

How long the audit takes depends on how much grant money you've received and if you have a good grant management system that allows you to quickly locate the paperwork and files the auditor wants to see. Some audits may take only a couple of hours, while others may take up to a week to complete.

Identifying the Types of Grant Audits

Just like nonprofits vary in their purpose and scope, so do audits. Audits can range from the "What? Me worry?" audit that involves a short phone call, to an audit in which a representative from the Government Accounting Office (GAO) shows up with a fine-tooth comb to review your records. If you've broken out in a sweat thinking about that latter type of audit, you're right to do so. It's the most serious type, so you want to do everything you can to avoid it.

The Government Performance and Results Act (GPRA) states that federal agencies must show how the money they spend actually furthers their mission, goals, and objectives. The government measures the success of each grant program through quantitative outcomes measures. GPRA evaluates whether the grant program accomplished its objectives as stated in the project narrative you submitted when you applied for the grant.

You need to know the proper way to administer and manage your grant. Make sure you read over the cost principles and administrative requirements (contained in the OMB circulars; see Chapter 10 for more info) of your grant so you're prepared for an audit. Not knowing what to do or doing the wrong thing sends up a red flag to the folks in D.C.

The following sections give you the lowdown on the four types of grant audits.

The relatively painless desk audit

A *desk audit* is the simplest kind of grant audit. Your program manager calls you with a series of questions about your grant. You answer the questions honestly, and it's over. This audit can take anywhere from 5 to 30 minutes, depending on the nature of the questions. Of course, you're given a heads-up on what to expect from your program manager beforehand.

Be prepared to answer questions about your federal programs. You may get questions such as

- How much grant money have you spent and what is your present balance?
- Have you expended $500,000 of grant funds within the current year?
- Have you made necessary corrective action steps from the last monitoring visit?
- What, if any, problems are you experiencing while implementing the grant project?

Based on your answers during the desk audit, your program manager may schedule a monitoring site visit (see the next section). Your program manager wants to help you be successful in implementing your grant. To ensure your success, she'll periodically visit you to check on things.

The desk audit is done more frequently of subgrantees by the nonprofit that received the grant from the federal agency. *Subgrantees* are the agencies that partnered with you to get the grant. (See Chapter 11 to understand the relationship between grantor, grantee, and subgrantees.)

Knock, knock: Knowing what to expect during a monitoring site visit

More than likely, your program manager skips the desk audit (see the preceding section) and schedules a *monitoring site visit*. During this type of audit, an evaluation is made of all grant-supported activities to determine the progress you've made toward achieving project objectives; to verify your compliance with the terms, conditions, and purpose of grant; and to identify technical assistance needs.

Your monitoring site visit will be scheduled at a good time for you and your federal program manager. He doesn't just show up at your door. This gives you ample time to make sure everything is in order. After the program manager leaves, you'll receive a corrective action plan (CAP) about how to fix any problems the monitor finds. (Refer to the "Following the corrective action plan" section later in this chapter for more info about the CAP.)

A program monitoring visit can be as casual and brief as one hour or it can last a couple days. The length of the visit is based on whether you're experiencing problems managing your program's progress and/or spending the grant money or if you're managing a large sum of grant money. If you're managing several million dollars with several partners, then your program manager will evaluate your project and meet you and your partners in person. The program monitoring visit is to check on you and to offer technical assistance.

Your program manager will oversee the day-to-day operations of your grant-supported activities, but he's not going to get too detailed about how your entire management system operates. When a more complex audit is desired by the federal agency, you'll get a visit from an accounting team of professionals called program officers (see the next section).

Preparing for the program officer's perusal of your procedures

Your federal agency may send one person, called a program officer, or a team of people to audit your grant files. (*Program officers* are accountants who work for the federal agency.) Sometimes one person may show up, or a team of four people will come in and audit your files in one day. The complexity of the audit and how long it takes depend on how much money is handled.

As executive director of your nonprofit, you can't do everything. The same is true of your program manager. She can't be responsible for every aspect of your grant. Therefore, each federal agency has program officers on staff to audit the records of grant recipients. These program officers are professional auditors with a background in accounting and finance and a thorough understanding of the rules governing grant recipients.

The story of a compliance audit neophyte

When I started my job as a grants accountant, my supervisor gave me seven three-ring binders to read. The notebooks were 3 inches thick with more than 300 pages each. The names written on the outside of the notebooks were "Complying with Federal Grant Guidelines," "Meeting Uniform Administrative Requirements," "Understanding Cost Principles," "Personnel Policies and Procedures," "Financial Policies and Procedures," "Managing Subgrantees," and something called "Auditing." I thought I would just die. For two weeks I did all I could to stay awake. I thought to myself, "I'm in the wrong field."

Two weeks later my supervisor told me, "You have a monitoring visit by our federal program manager in two weeks." That's why he wanted me to read about financial, performance, and compliance audits. He told me I had to prepare the files and get ready to explain what, why, and how we spent more than $10 million in grant money.

In the back of my mind, I was thinking, "I'm not responsible for anything. I've only been here for one month." When the federal program manager showed up, we had an initiation meeting to discuss what he would do for the next three or four days. I quickly discovered an important lesson: A grantee is not just responsible for covering its butt, but it's responsible for monitoring its subgrantees.

The accounting staff had a very clear paper trail of everything pertaining to the grants, files were updated monthly, and everything appeared to be in order. Our accounting system, procurement system, travel system, and personnel system all checked out okay.

But we failed to do one important thing: track the inventory of our subgrantees. I never thought the program manager would ask to visit one of our subgrantees. Then he decided to have a look at the equipment. Well, unknown to me, the equipment, which had been purchased a year before with the grant for $27,000, was still in the box. The subgrantee representative said the equipment hadn't been set up because the software was incompatible with the current computer system, and the agency was keeping it until it could upgrade its computer system.

As grantee, I was responsible for making sure the subgrantees didn't misuse or abuse grant money. This oversight was clearly unintentional by my agency and its partners, but it didn't look good. We weren't making any progress or accomplishing anything, other than spending the money.

When this team is scheduled to pay you a visit is left up to your program manager and the federal agency that awarded the grant. During this auditing site visit, your program officer checks out the following:

- Program compliance
- Subgrantee monitoring

- Financial system (internal control system)
- Procurement system (policy and procedures)
- Travel system (policy and procedures)
- Personnel system (time and attendance reports)
- Property management or inventory system
- Project performance (Government Performance and Results Act)
- Financial status, progress, and closeout reports

Make sure you tag all equipment purchased with a unit cost of $5,000 or more with grant money and give it an inventory control ID number that clearly indicates that the equipment was purchased with grant money. Not only do you have to look out for yourself, but you're responsible for any other agencies that partnered with you to get the grant. If you received federal money that you're sharing with other agencies, follow up with your partners and make sure that any equipment they've purchased isn't sitting in a box. For more about keeping tabs on equipment, see the government rules for nonprofits found at www.whitehouse.gov/omb/fedreg/2004/040511_grants.pdf.

Inspector general audit: When the situation is really serious

The *inspector general audit* is the FBI of audits. Your nonprofit gets an inspector general audit only when you're in major trouble. "Major trouble" can include suspicions of fraud, waste, abuse, and misconduct. If the desk audit reveals some problems and the site visit indicates that you have significant material differences, then the Office of Inspector General investigates the case. This type of audit is very serious.

The Office of Inspector General falls under the U.S. Department of State. It's responsible for promoting effective management and accountability in the federal government. The office conducts independent evaluations and audits that identify problems and provide solutions.

The purpose of an inspector general audit is to evaluate whether your nonprofit has spent the government's money for its intended purposes, has accurately accounted for it, and has adequate controls in place that comply with laws and regulations.

If you face an inspector general audit, you have been accused of some wrongdoing. This accusation may have been the result of you not responding to corrective actions advised by your program manager or program officers, or a concerned citizen may have reported you. If an investigation reveals the accusations to be true, you'll probably have to pay the money back, and you may be hit with heavy penalties and ordered to serve jail time.

Universities pay back millions

For years universities operated on the honor system because the federal government trusted institutions of higher education to do the right thing. But then the government decided to examine how these institutions were spending their federal dollars. From about 2003 to 2005, the following universities paid millions to settle abuse of and misconduct in regard to government grant money: Mayo Clinic paid $6.5 million, Northwestern paid $5.5 million, the University of Alabama paid $3.4 million, Johns Hopkins paid $2.6 million, and Harvard paid $2.4 million.

I've worked with universities that slip a few things through the cracks. One area in which they tend to deviate from the rules is when hiring consultants at expensive, unreasonable rates for work that is paid for out of grant money, but the work is never done. I've witnessed some behavior that I refused to put my signature on for approval.

Now that the Office of Inspector General is investigating universities, we can expect to see more cases of mismanaged government funds.

Knowing What the Auditor Looks For

If you've ever put your house on the market, you know how people come in and look in closets, open up cabinets, pull out drawers, and see what's what (which you may not be very comfortable with). Well, your auditor will look through everything to make sure your nonprofit is following the rules. The auditor performs three general tasks:

- ✔ **Look for improper payments:** All grants have rules about how to allocate expenses, what you can buy, and what you shouldn't buy. These are called *cost principles*. Your auditor will look for improper payments and determine whether costs were allowable according to cost principles.

- ✔ **Look at internal controls:** To ensure your organization has taken steps to protect its assets, the grant auditor determines whether you've established internal controls, or checks and balances. You have to follow the rules about administering the grant program. The auditor checks your use of internal controls to make sure you're following the rules.

- ✔ **Assess the risk factor:** Based on your purchasing, accounting, and inventory systems, your auditor will assess the risk for problems. It doesn't take a rocket scientist to detect trouble, especially if your accounting system is inadequate and you're not keeping up with things.

For your organization to have a successful audit, you need to make sure the program manager can access everything. The following sections explain the importance of getting your books in order, preparing other important documentation, and presenting the grant expenses that you've kept track of so your audit can go off without a hitch.

In real estate, agents determine the odds of selling your home by three things: location, location, location. In the world of grants, successfully passing an audit also depends on three important things: documentation, documentation, documentation.

Preparing the books for audit review

In order for your program manager to monitor your grant's progress, you need to make sure your records are accessible. Get all of your records in order so when the program manager comes knocking, he has everything he needs at his fingertips. He'll tell you what will be examined. Of course, one thing can lead to another, so I suggest that you only give him what he asks for.

Be sure to make and keep copies of everything pertaining to the grant, including financial and progress reports (see Chapter 11), to make the program manager's job easier. Keeping good records is important because you want the audit to move like clockwork. If your program manager has a difficult time making sense of your documentation, you may prolong the audit process.

For every grant you receive, you should keep the following in a hard-copy file:

- ✔ Copy of the grant application
- ✔ Copy of all letters and correspondence (including e-mails)
- ✔ Copy of the grant award document
- ✔ Copy of the grant budget
- ✔ Copy of all grant adjustment notices (including subgrantees)
- ✔ Copy of all receipts, invoices, bills, canceled checks, and so on
- ✔ Copy of the grant employees' payroll information
- ✔ Copy of time and attendance reports

Your program manager will look at these records to make sure you're in compliance with the intended purposes for the grant award.

If you have well-organized and adequate records of all grant activities, you're sure to breeze through the grant audit process. The only thing an audit does is verify that you've followed the grant guidelines. It's virtually impossible to verify what you've done without documentation.

Before you destroy any grant files, contact your program manager. All records of grant activities should be kept on file for three years after the close-out of the grant period, unless an investigation is under way. If you're under investigation, you'll need to keep the records until after the investigation is over.

Proving your agency's existence with organizational records and documents

You know your nonprofit exists; I trust that your nonprofit exists. But Uncle Sam wants unquestionable proof that your nonprofit is what you say it is. Your program officer will want to see records that verify how and when your organization was structured. In addition, the officer will ask for documents about your financial structure, personnel policies, and procedures. Make sure you have the following papers readily available:

✔ **IRS letter of determination:** Your IRS letter of determination is the letter you received when you established your nonprofit. It indicates that your organization is exempt from federal corporate income taxes. It contains important information regarding the basis for your exemption and the requirements associated with maintaining it.

✔ **Articles of incorporation and organizational bylaws:** The articles of incorporation and bylaws are documents you set up when you started your organization. If you've made any amendments to your bylaws, make sure to attach those to your original bylaws.

✔ **Names and addresses of board members:** An up-to-date list of your current board members may be needed for an evaluation of members' political affiliations. (Remember, there's not supposed to be any undue influence made by anyone to get grant money.) It's best to have information about the other boards your members sit on and where your members are employed available just in case you're asked for it. Contact information, including e-mail addresses and telephone numbers, for board members may be required. The best solution is to have resumes of all board members on file.

✔ **Organization operating budget:** Your program officer probably will want to see your operating budget for the current or upcoming program year. This organizational budget differs from the grant project budget. It allows the auditor to put the grant money in a larger context and see the big picture. He can use this budget to determine how much you're relying on grant funding to run your programs. (See Chapter 8 for more on operating budgets.)

✔ **Indirect cost rate:** The auditor will need a copy of your organization's indirect cost rate (if you have one) to verify that the correct percentages have been allocated to the grant. (Your indirect cost rate assigns a percentage of your general overhead and administrative expenses to the grant. See Chapter 18 for more info about this.)

✔ **Financial statements:** Your program officer will want to review your financial statements and Form 990s to determine whether you're financially stable. If you're over your head in debt, your organization may not be the best investment of grant dollars. On the other hand, if you're stable financially, it proves that the government made a good choice in selecting you to receive grant money. Check out the chapters in Part IV for how to create these statements.

Having all of these documents and information at your fingertips when the auditor arrives saves time, and it shows that you're organized and a good record-keeper.

Tracking all grant expenses

The federal government has given your organization money, and it expects you to use it properly. To prove that you spent the money in accordance with the government's expectations, you need to track all expenses back to the invoice and to the request for bid if more than $25,000. For every federal dollar you spend, you should keep the receipt and anything else pertaining to the purchase. When your program manager shows up at your office, he's not just going to take your word that you paid certain amounts for certain items out of your grant budget. You have to have documentation to support every transaction.

A *request for bid* advertises that you need professional services or plan to purchase something from an outside vendor. Be careful with requests for bids because your program manager will want to verify that it was handled correctly.

Your program manager should be able to take a charge allocated to grant funds and track it back to the request for bid. Copies of checks written and rebate checks should correspond to purchases. Your manager will want to see how you account for grant expenditures and how you keep them separate by account numbers from your regular normal nonprofit expenses. (See Chapter 11 for more on keeping grant expenses separate from other expenses.)

You need to pay particular attention to employee salaries paid from grant money. Your accounting system should have accounting codes that separate and allocate grant employees' pay to a designated grant account. You may want to set up a spreadsheet that shows that you keep up with employees paid from the grant. (See Chapter 4 for information about using spreadsheets.)

Time and attendance reports should be recorded and kept on file for every employee paid from the grant. These reports should be signed by the employee's immediate supervisor. One of the most common audit findings is the lack of time and attendance reports. (See Chapter 18 for more about these reports.)

Auditing Cash Management

During the audit, the program manager checks your nonprofit's cash management. In fact, having excess cash on hand is a common audit finding. A good system of cash management helps determine how much cash is needed to take care of immediate needs.

As a director or manager of a small- to medium-sized nonprofit, you need to have a system of cash management because having excess cash in your bank account is a sign of poor cash management. This section helps you reduce the amount of cash on hand and discusses the importance of protecting the money in-house.

Minimizing cash on hand

The key to drawing down federal grant dollars from the U.S. Treasury is to not have more money in your checking account than you need (see Chapter 11 for more on drawing down grant money). Your auditor will review all drawdowns to determine whether you're properly managing federal dollars by keeping the money on hand for a minimum amount of time.

Most people don't have excess cash in their personal checking accounts. The same should go for your nonprofit and its grant money. Your grant money should not lie in your bank account long enough to draw substantial amounts of interest. The main reason: The federal government is giving you this grant money to use on your programs and services, not to sit in your checking account. The money requested from the U.S. Treasury should pass through your checking account quickly.

You need to remember two things about having cash on hand:

✔ **Up to $100 per year may be kept for administrative expenses.** *Administrative expenses* are the costs to oversee the administration of a project, such as the time spent processing payments. As with all things grant-related, verify this with your program manager.

✔ **Interest earned on federal fund balances in excess of $250 is required to be returned to the federal agency.** If you earn interest, you should report it to your program manager and make her aware of why it happened. You're not supposed to hold the money in your bank account for extended periods of time during which it can collect interest.

You're not supposed to use the grant money for anything other than to support the program for which the money is intended. So you can't borrow money from the grant funds to pay for things and then put it back. It's not excess cash.

Segregating duties through internal controls

Internal controls provide reasonable assurance that the spending of grant money complies with laws and regulations. In layman's terms, this would be called a system of checks and balances. As the director or manager, you need to make sure your nonprofit has internal controls in place to protect the organization's finances and assets.

Your auditor will review your entire management system and look at the internal controls you've established. No audit is complete without checking for protective measures that safeguard you from possible theft or embezzlement. Your accounting, procurement, personnel, property, and travel systems are all interrelated, so your auditor will check the adequacies of these areas.

I suggest you implement the following internal controls in your organization to protect not only the grant money you receive, but all donations and assets you have:

✓ Have your in-house project manager (not to be confused with the program manager from the federal agency that issued your grant) be the person who authorizes payments and charges against the grant budget.

✓ Segregate duties within your organization. The person who writes checks shouldn't be the same person who balances the books. Furthermore, the person counting the money shouldn't make deposits, approve payments, and request money from the federal government. This is why some companies have separate accounts receivables and accounts payables departments. Separating duties safeguards your money.

✓ Require two signatures on all checks over a certain amount. You can also have your bank call you for checks over a set amount. Decisions about these amounts depend on your accounting activities and size of your overall budget. For example, if your organization seldom writes a check for more than $500, you may want to place restrictions on all checks written above this amount. Discuss this with your board if you're not sure about what amount to use.

✓ Have internal auditors on staff. You save time and money when people inside your organization make sure that you're properly accounting for expenditures and check to see that you're in compliance.

Keeping a close watch on your money can protect you from theft or embezzlement. A weak internal control system opens up the possibility that your nonprofit will be stolen from.

Make sure you don't supplant any grant money. To *supplant* grant money means to use grant money for something that's already in your budget. Grant funds should be used to supplement — not supplant. For example, if you receive a donation to hire a new secretary but you use grant money to pay the secretary's salary, you've supplanted grant funds. If you're unsure about how to allocate expenses to your grant, ask your program manager about training opportunities offered by the federal agency.

With no internal controls, you have no control

I got a call about a year ago from a desperate woman who owned a boating company and was in crisis mode. She had trusted her accountant to take care of all of her business's bookkeeping and accounting, no questions asked. Well, the accountant owned a check-cashing business and had no problems writing and cashing checks. The accountant had stolen more than $80,000.

By the time the woman discovered what her accountant had done, it was too late to do anything about it. The accountant was the only person balancing the books, writing the checks, approving payments, and using his check-cashing company to cash them. No one had established any internal controls for the woman's business.

The woman wanted to know if I could write a grant to get her stolen money back because she believed (incorrectly) that grant money could be used for anything.

I had to explain to her how grant money is used to fill a gap in society and that for-profit businesses like hers seldom qualify for grant money. I helped her understand how grant money is used in communities to provide jobs; to assist the elderly, needy families, and at-risk children; or to deter criminal behavior.

In the end I told the caller to apply for a Small Business Administration (SBA) loan. She thanked me, and we hung up.

Receiving the Report of Audit Findings

When the auditor is finished with the audit, she issues an *audit report,* which tells your organization the results of the audit. The audit report is the final stage of the audit process, and it communicates audit findings. *Audit findings* are what the auditor discovers after careful evaluation and comparison of your grant activities to the rules, standards, and circulars. When you get your audit findings depends on how long it takes the auditor to prepare it. As with all things government-related, it can take a while.

Auditors are required to report any questionable costs totaling $10,000 or more for known or likely noncompliance issues. The report includes the method used to calculate the questionable costs and the facts supporting the identified deficiency. Government threshold and tolerance for audit findings are stringent. If the program officer discovers anything that indicates you haven't handled the grant money according to the guidelines, you'll be made to pay back the funds.

The following sections give you the lowdown on how audit findings are classified and how to take corrective action to ensure your nonprofit gets back on your program manager and program officer's good side.

Classifying the audit finding

Anytime something is wrong in a court of law, juries, judges, and prosecutors consider the intent behind the misconduct. This is true with audit findings as well. If your auditor finds something wrong with your federal grant records, she will specify how the mistake came to be. Consider the following:

- **Error:** This is when you unintentionally fail to comply with laws, regulations, or terms and conditions of a grant agreement, or you unintentionally omit amounts or disclosures in financial statements.

- **Irregularity:** An irregularity is an intentional misstatement or omission on a financial statement.

- **Illegal act:** This is an outright violation of law or regulations. Whether an act is illegal may have to await a final decision by a court of law.

- **Improper conduct:** An agency employee, contractor, supplier, or recipient is said to have exhibited improper conduct when he performs his duties in a manner that contributes to the abuse or waste of grant money, but that isn't a criminal violation.

- **Abuse:** Abuse is defined as conducting a government program in a manner that doesn't meet the public's expectations for prudent behavior, but which doesn't violate any law, regulation, agreement, or contract.

- **Fraud:** You've committed fraud if you're found guilty of an illegal act that involves obtaining something of value through willful misrepresentation.

- **Waste:** This is when you overspend for items that can be purchased for less.

- **Noncompliance:** Your agency is found to be in noncompliance when you deviate from the laws and regulations governing the administration of grant funds.

These classifications are listed in your audit report according to the dollar value of the findings.

Late-night infomercials have done severe damage to the perception of federal grants. Many people have been misinformed, and the general public believes that you can get a grant to do anything. There are consequences for every choice you make when managing your grant.

Following the corrective action plan

After your program manager leaves, you'll receive a written report of problems to fix. You'll have to respond with the steps you'll take to correct problems. These steps are called your *corrective action plan (CAP)*.

Some common findings included on a corrective action plan are the need to monitor subgrantees and to establish segregation of duties. As a grant recipient, you need to take the actions specified in the corrective action plan. If you need help, contact your program manager for suggestions or technical support. Your program manager will ask for a report from you that explains how the corrective measures are being implemented.

It's in your best interest to respond promptly to the corrective action plan. The consequences of not responding can be detrimental to your current funding and all future funding. If you fail to follow your corrective action plan, you're not cooperating with the terms of the grant agreement, and this makes it difficult for all parties involved.

Chapter 13

Accounting for Payroll and Payroll Taxes

....

In This Chapter

▶ Creating payroll accounts for employees

▶ Calculating federal, state, and local taxes

▶ Paying quarterly payroll taxes

▶ Submitting IRS payroll requirements

▶ Reporting info about contract employees

....

*Y*ou're the executive director or manager at a small- to medium-sized nonprofit, so you may assume that because of your organization's nonprofit status, you don't have to pay any taxes. After all, your status does mean your organization owes no corporate income taxes. However, you're still responsible for paying federal payroll taxes for your employees.

The good news is that you can account for payroll and payroll taxes for nonprofit employees similarly to how other for-profit organizations do so. As an employer, you're required to withhold and/or pay state and federal payroll taxes on behalf of your employees.

You can easily set up your organization's payroll accounting yourself. Or if you prefer, you can hire some part-time help or buy prepackaged software for nonprofits. Regardless of the method you choose, you're responsible for accounting for payroll, taking out the right amount of taxes, and submitting taxes with the required paperwork on time.

Not to worry, though. This chapter shows you how to account for your payroll taxes and all other deductions for the federal, state, and local governments. After reading this chapter, you'll know how to file the necessary paperwork, where to send forms, and when to file forms so you stay current with your paperwork — not to mention keep your nonprofit status.

As an employer, you need to concern yourself with establishing and paying a fair rate of pay and submitting payroll tax payments on time. Some issues, such as minimum wage, have already been decided for you.

Setting Up Payroll Accounts for Nonprofit Employees

Before you can pay federal and state payroll taxes for your employees, you need to make sure you have the proper records and documentation. To do so, establish payroll accounts for your employees by creating a file for each employee. These files can be either electronic or hard copies, depending on your preference. If you use computer software to set up your payroll, your computer walks you through this process. Only your personnel clerk, book-keeper, accountant, supervisor, and executive director should have access to payroll files. You should keep these files under lock and key because of the private information they contain.

Federal law requires all employers to keep records of total wages and hours worked by employees, but it doesn't specify how to keep these records. A great place to keep track of hours and wages is in your employee personnel files, which you can create on an employee's first day. Set up a file for each employee with the following information:

- Employee's name, Social Security number, home address, job title, gender, and birth date
- Workweek hours and dates
- Total hours worked each workday
- Total daily or weekly regular time earnings
- Regular hourly pay rate
- Total overtime pay for the workweek
- Deductions from wages
- Additions to wages
- Pay date and pay period

Make sure you include Form W-4, Employee's Withholding Allowance Certificate, in the paperwork you give your new employees to fill out on their first day of work. Form W-4 indicates filing status, exemptions, and any extra taxes to be taken out of an employee's salary. The purpose of Form W-4 is to tell you how much federal income tax to withhold from your employee's pay-check. Figure 13-1 shows an example of Form W-4.

Cut here and give Form W-4 to your employer. Keep the top part for your records.

Form **W-4**	**Employee's Withholding Allowance Certificate**	OMB No. 1545-0074
Department of the Treasury Internal Revenue Service	▶ Whether you are entitled to claim a certain number of allowances or exemption from withholding is subject to review by the IRS. Your employer may be required to send a copy of this form to the IRS.	20**08**

1 Type or print your first name and middle initial.	Last name		2 Your social security number
Mary	Smith		000 : 00 : 0000

Home address (number and street or rural route)	3 ☑ Single ☐ Married ☐ Married, but withhold at higher Single rate.
7550 Mojo Lane	Note. If married, but legally separated, or spouse is a nonresident alien, check the "Single" box.
City or town, state, and ZIP code	4 If your last name differs from that shown on your social security card,
Selma, AL 36701	check here. You must call 1-800-772-1213 for a replacement card. ▶ ☐

5	Total number of allowances you are claiming (from line **H** above **or** from the applicable worksheet on page 2)	5	
6	Additional amount, if any, you want withheld from each paycheck	6	$
7	I claim exemption from withholding for 2008, and I certify that I meet **both** of the following conditions for exemption.		
	● Last year I had a right to a refund of **all** federal income tax withheld because I had **no** tax liability **and**		
	● This year I expect a refund of **all** federal income tax withheld because I expect to have **no** tax liability.		
	If you meet both conditions, write "Exempt" here . . . . ▶	7	Exempt

Under penalties of perjury, I declare that I have examined this certificate and to the best of my knowledge and belief, it is true, correct, and complete.

Employee's signature
(Form is not valid
unless you sign it.) ▶   Date ▶

8	Employer's name and address (Employer: Complete lines 8 and 10 only if sending to the IRS.)	9 Office code (optional)	10 Employer identification number (EIN)
	Mentoring America, Inc., 8800 Watchman Curve, Selma, AL 36701	00	0000000

For Privacy Act and Paperwork Reduction Act Notice, see page 2.   Cat. No. 10220Q   Form **W-4** (2008)

Figure 13-1: Form W-4, Employee's Withholding Allowance Certificate.

Keeping employee time sheets can help you justify why you paid what to whom to assure both the government and your employees that you're adhering to federal employer-employee guidelines. The Department of Labor oversees these federal guidelines concerning employer and employee relationships. The Department of Labor enforces laws established by the Federal Standards Labor Act, which ensures that employees receive fair wages and overtime pay. The act also requires employers to allocate and pay payroll deductions in a timely manner.

Deducting the Right Amount of Taxes

Before you start calculating how much to deduct from your employees' paychecks for payroll taxes, you need to know how much to deduct for federal and state income taxes. Don't worry. You don't have to be a math whiz to do so. The IRS and state governments offer you tax tables to tell you how much to deduct for federal and state taxes.

You calculate the amount of federal income tax to withhold from each employee based on a federal income tax table, which takes into account the information your employees put on the Form W-4 they fill out on their first day of work. This information includes how many dependents they want to claim, what their filing status is (single, married, and so on), and if they want extra money taken out of their checks.

Don't forget to get the current tax tables for the year in which you're filing. The laws change constantly, so the tables that you used last year aren't valid this year. To find out where you can get copies of these tax tables and all other tax forms, see Figure 13-2 for federal information. Contact your state department of revenue for state information.

Quick and Easy Access to IRS Tax Help and Tax Products

Internet

You can access the IRS website 24 hours a day, 7 days a week, at *www.irs.gov* to:

- E-file your return. Find out about commercial tax preparation and *e-file* services available free to eligible taxpayers;
- Download forms, instructions, and publications;
- Order IRS products online;
- Research your tax questions online;
- Search publications online by topic or keyword;
- Send us comments or request help by email; and
- Sign up to receive local and national tax news by email.

Phone

Order current year forms, instructions, and publications, and prior year forms and instructions by calling 1-800-TAX-FORM (1-800-829-3676). You should receive your order within 10 days.

Walk-In

You can pick up some of the most requested forms, instructions, and publications at many IRS offices, post offices, and libraries. Some grocery stores, copy centers, city and county government offices, credit unions, and office supply stores have a collection of reproducible tax forms available to photocopy or print from a CD-ROM.

Mail

Send your order for tax products to:
National Distribution Center
P.O. Box 8903
Bloomington, IL   61702-8903

You should receive your products within 10 days after we receive your order.

CD/DVD For Tax Products

You can order Publication 1796, IRS Tax Products CD/DVD, and obtain:

- Current-year forms, instructions, and publications.
- Prior-year forms, instructions, and publications.
- Bonus: Historical Tax Products DVD – Ships with the final release.
- Tax Map: an electronic research tool and finding aid.
- Tax law frequently asked questions.
- Tax Topics from the IRS telephone response system.
- Fill-in, print, and save features for most tax forms.
- Internal Revenue Bulletins.
- Toll-free and email technical support.

The CD is released twice during the year. The first release will ship the beginning of Jaunary and the final release will ship the beginning of March.

Purchase the CD/DVD from National Technical Information Service at *www.irs.gov/cdorders* for $35 (no handling fee) or call **1-877-CDFORMS** (1-877-233-6767) toll-free to purchase the CD/DVD for $35 (plus a $5 handling fee). Price is subject to change.

Figure 13-2:
Quick and easy tax information.

When figuring out how much to pay in federal payroll taxes for each employee, salary is by far the most important factor to consider. However, it's not the only one. This section highlights the areas you need to consider when determining how much to pay in federal payroll taxes.

Salaries and wages

Before you determine how much to pay in federal payroll taxes for your employees, you need to know the IRS's two main classifications of employees. These classifications significantly impact when and how much you pay in taxes. The two types of employees are

- ✔ **Exempt:** These employees are paid a set salary and don't qualify for overtime pay.

- ✔ **Nonexempt:** These employees are paid an hourly rate and do qualify for overtime pay.

According to federal law, nonexempt workers are entitled to a minimum wage of at least $6.55 per hour (effective July 24, 2008). Beginning July 24, 2009, the per hour minimum wage rate is $7.25.

An automatic way to give and receive

Some donors give organizations contributions via *authorized payroll deductions,* which are deductions right from their paychecks. They're like money in your bank account because you receive the money in a systematic way around the same time after each pay period. Donors choose which paychecks you receive donations from. For instance, some donors allow you to take deductions out of their second checks if they're paid twice a month.

Larger nonprofits have been using authorized payroll deductions for years. For example, United Way takes authorized payroll deductions right out of its donor's payroll checks. Doing so works well for both the person giving and the organization receiving because it spreads the donations out over longer periods of time for the donor and gives the recipient, United Way in this example, a solid projection of expected revenues.

Minimum wage laws are preset by the federal government, but most states also have minimum wage laws. An employer can never pay an employee less than the minimum wage set by the federal government.

You figure out how much you need to pay in payroll taxes by multiplying the salary amount by the federal payroll tax rates, which are established by law. You can find payroll tax rules, rates, withholding tables, and reporting instructions in IRS Publication 15, Employer's Tax Guide, also known as Circular E. You can find Publication 15 and any other IRS publication at www.irs.gov/app/picklist/list/publicationsNoticesPdf.html.

Overtime and cash advances

When calculating how much tax to deduct from your employees' paychecks, you need to consider two important areas other than salary: overtime and cash advances. *Overtime* is the amount of time an employee works beyond normal working hours. According to federal law, employers must pay workers overtime pay at a rate of at least one and a half times their regular pay rate when the workers work more than 40 hours in a given workweek.

For example, if an employee works 48 hours in a workweek and is paid $15.00 per hour, the employee is entitled to $22.50 per hour for each hour of overtime ($15.00 × 1.5). The employee's regular pay for 40 hours is $600. For 8 hours of overtime, the pay rate is $22.50 × 8, which equals $180. This employee is entitled to $600 plus $180 for a total of $780.

For questions about overtime pay, call the Wage and Hour Division of the Department of Labor at 866-4-US-WAGE (866-487-9243).

Don't worry about these benefits with the IRS

Lucky for you, you don't have to be overly concerned with certain payroll benefits from a federal standpoint. Federal laws do not regulate the following:

- ✔ Paid sick and vacation leave
- ✔ Holiday pay
- ✔ Pay raises
- ✔ Immediate payment of final wages to terminated employees

However, check with your CPA, because you may need to familiarize yourself with state laws that do affect these benefits.

Furthermore, the IRS isn't concerned with whether employers pay fringe benefits to employees; fringe benefits include day-care services, company cars, bonuses, expense accounts, medical insurance, or retirement benefits. According to federal laws, you don't have to pay fringe benefits to your employees.

In addition to overtime, cash advances are an important factor in determining tax deductions. *Cash advances* are loans that the employer gives to an employee that will be repaid from the employee's future pay. Giving cash advances to your nonprofit employees is a subject for board discussion and approval. Use your own discretion when loaning or giving employees advances on their pay. If you have the money in your personal account, you can decide whether to give an advance from your own account, not the nonprofit's. But, I suggest that you not use your organization's income for employees' personal use.

However, if you do decide to give cash advances, don't confuse advances and wages. Advances aren't taxed; they're loans. The employee's wages are taxed. The employer withholds the amount advanced to an employee from the employee's paycheck as repayment of the advance. Before you decide to give cash advances, be sure to check with your board of directors.

Calculating Specific FICA Payroll Taxes and Deductions

Before you start calculating payroll taxes and posting them in the books, you need to know the details about each employee's withholding allowances or exemptions. After you've pulled this information from each employee's Form W-4, you need to compute each employee's gross pay for the pay period. After doing so, you're ready to calculate payroll taxes and deductions.

The Federal Insurance Contributions Act (FICA) is a federal payroll tax that both employees and employers have to pay. The funds collected from FICA are used to fund Social Security and Medicare retirement benefits and to provide for disabled workers and children of deceased workers.

Employees pay 7.65 percent of their gross income for FICA, and their employer matches by also paying 7.65 percent. Self-employed people pay the total 15.3 percent (the employer's 7.65 percent plus the employee's 7.65 percent) of total gross income for FICA. The total FICA rate for employers in 2009 was 7.65 percent of gross salary up to $102,000.

So, for example, if you have an employee who makes $500 a week, you — as the employer — have to pay $38.25 (7.65 × $500) for FICA taxes. Your employee has to pay the same $38.25 to match yours. If you're self-employed and make $500 a week, you owe the total $76.50 ($38.25 plus $38.25) in FICA taxes.

The IRS calculates FICA taxes at the same rate on regular pay, overtime pay, and bonus pay. When you have to pay payroll taxes to the IRS depends on whether your organization is just starting out or you've been operating for a few years. For example, as a rule of thumb, the IRS requires all new nonprofits to pay payroll taxes on a monthly basis for the first year. After your first year, the IRS tells you how often you need to pay payroll taxes — weekly, biweekly, monthly, quarterly, or annually. The determining factor is how much money you owe in a given week, month, or quarter. For example, if you owe $2,500 or less, the IRS will probably have you pay on a quarterly basis. Most organizations pay payroll taxes quarterly. See the "Paying Quarterly Payroll Taxes with Form 941 and Form 8109" section for more on making payments on a quarterly basis.

By law, religious groups have the option to oppose paying Social Security taxes. If you make more than $100 per year and you work for a religious organization that doesn't participate in paying Social Security and Medicare taxes (FICA), you're considered self-employed, which means you have to pay the IRS 15.3 percent of your gross income for Social Security and Medicare. If you're in this situation and you make $500 a week, you owe the total $76.50 ($38.25 plus $38.25) in FICA taxes. Remember that the 15.3 percent that you pay is the combination of your employer's 7.65 percent and your 7.65 percent as the employee.

If you're a lower-level manager at your nonprofit and the nonprofit doesn't take taxes out of your paycheck, you may think you've hit the jackpot. But eventually you have to render to Caesar that which is Caesar's, or the United States government in this case. The best approach is to save and pay your taxes monthly or quarterly to relieve some of the burden of waiting until the end of the year. The IRS charges heftier penalties and much higher interest rates than credit card companies, so saving and paying are good ideas.

As for paying taxes on federal unemployment benefits, I have some good news. You don't have to worry about paying taxes on them if your organization holds an IRC Section 501(c)(3) exemption status under IRC Section 501. To verify your exemption, take a look at your letter of determination from the IRS to find out how the IRS classified your nonprofit status and under which code it established your nonprofit status.

Churches don't have to pay

Churches and religious organizations are exempt from paying income taxes and filing Form 990. They're protected by the First Amendment of the Constitution. Unlike other chief executive officers, churches are not required to withhold income tax from their ordained, commissioned, or licensed ministers for performing services in the exercise of their ministry.

In addition, a minister who's furnished a parsonage or housing allowance doesn't have to report it as part of his gross income. A minister can choose to voluntarily pay income tax if he wants to, but he doesn't have to.

The only time a church can be investigated by the IRS is when someone files a written complaint. If you need more information about churches and religious organizations, call 800-829-3676 and ask for the IRS Tax Guide for Churches and Religious Organizations, or find a copy at www.irs.gov.

Paying Quarterly Payroll Taxes with Form 941 and Form 8109

Quarterly payroll taxes are taxes that your nonprofit owes to the IRS for your match portion of FICA and the amount you withheld from your employees for their portion of FICA and for federal income taxes. As an employer, you're responsible for matching your portion of the FICA tax (7.65 percent of wages). Making your payments to the federal government on time is very important.

You use Form 941, employer's Quarterly Federal Tax Return, to report your quarterly wages and payroll taxes to the IRS, and then depending on the type of depositor you are, you either use Form 941 or Form 8109 to make your payments. See the "Completing Form 8109 (Making tax deposits)" section for more about this form.

Form 941 includes the following information:

- ✔ Wages you've paid
- ✔ Tips your employees received
- ✔ Federal income taxes you withheld
- ✔ Employer's and employee's shares of Social Security and Medicare taxes
- ✔ Advance earned income tax credit (EIC) payments
- ✔ Adjustments for prior quarterly payroll taxes

I can't stress enough how important paying these quarterly taxes is. If you fall behind, catching up can be extremely difficult. If you do fall behind on payroll taxes, talk with your tax accountant for clarity on what steps to take. You may want to go to your local bank and borrow the money. The penalties and interest on IRS outstanding debts is higher than any credit card on the market.

The following sections walk you through Form 941 and Form 8109 and helps you complete them. I also explain how to file the forms and where to send them and your payment.

Create a file with copies of all the forms, checks, and everything else you send to the IRS. Sometimes the IRS makes mistakes. Plus, you need to keep up with what you've paid.

Completing Form 941

As an employer, you withhold federal taxes from your employees for the federal government. Form 941 (see Figure 13-3) is your explanation to the IRS of how much you've deducted from your employees' paychecks and held for the federal government in federal income taxes, Social Security, and Medicare taxes.

According to the IRS, preparing, copying, assembling, and sending Form 941 takes just two hours of your time every three months. You can find a copy of Form 941 online at www.irs.gov/pub/irs-pdf/f941.pdf.

To save time, you can save a copy of the online form on your computer so that each quarter you need to fill in only the information that has changed since the last quarter.

Complete the following simple steps to correctly fill out Form 941:

1. **Fill in the top portion of the form.**

   Fill in your EIN (employer identification number), the name of your organization, your business address, and the reporting quarter.

2. **Complete Part 1.**

   Part 1 is the meat of the form. Answer the questions about how many employees you have, how much they've earned, and how much federal income tax you've withheld. If working through this part by yourself doesn't work for you, consider contracting out your payroll services to a book-keeper or accountant. You can even bite the bullet and hire a CPA — if you can afford it.

Form **941 for 2008: Employer's QUARTERLY Federal Tax Return** 950108
(Rev. January 2008) Department of the Treasury — Internal Revenue Service OMB No. 1545-0029

(EIN) Employer identification number: 88-8888888

Name (not your trade name): Mentoring USA, Inc.

Trade name (if any):

Address: 1000 Safeway Avenue (Number, Street, Suite or room number)
Mobile (City) AL (State) 36601 (ZIP code)

Report for this Quarter of 2008 (Check one.)
- ☑ 1: January, February, March
- ☐ 2: April, May, June
- ☐ 3: July, August, September
- ☐ 4: October, November, December

Read the separate instructions before you fill out this form. Please type or print within the boxes.

Part 1: Answer these questions for this quarter.

1	**Number of employees who received wages, tips, or other compensation for the pay period including:** *Mar. 12* (Quarter 1), *June 12* (Quarter 2), *Sept. 12* (Quarter 3), *Dec. 12* (Quarter 4)	1	1
2	**Wages, tips, and other compensation**	2	6,376 .
3	**Total income tax withheld from wages, tips, and other compensation**	3	391 .
4	**If no wages, tips, and other compensation are subject to social security or Medicare tax**		☐ Check and go to line 6.

5 **Taxable social security and Medicare wages and tips:**

	Column 1		Column 2
5a **Taxable social security wages**	6,376 .	× .124 =	791 .
5b **Taxable social security tips**	.	× .124 =	.
5c **Taxable Medicare wages & tips**	6,376 .	× .029 =	185 .

5d	**Total social security and Medicare taxes** (*Column 2,* lines 5a + 5b + 5c = line 5d)	5d	976 .
6	**Total taxes before adjustments** (lines 3 + 5d = line 6)	6	1,367 .
7	**TAX ADJUSTMENTS** (read the instructions for line 7 before completing lines 7a through 7g):		
7a	**Current quarter's fractions of cents**		.
7b	**Current quarter's sick pay**		.
7c	**Current quarter's adjustments for tips and group-term life insurance**		.
7d	**Current year's income tax withholding** (attach Form 941c)		.
7e	**Prior quarters' social security and Medicare taxes** (attach Form 941c)		.
7f	**Special additions to federal income tax** (attach Form 941c)		.
7g	**Special additions to social security and Medicare** (attach Form 941c)		.
7h	**TOTAL ADJUSTMENTS** (combine all amounts: lines 7a through 7g)	7h	.
8	**Total taxes after adjustments** (combine lines 6 and 7h)	8	1,367 .
9	**Advance earned income credit (EIC) payments made to employees**	9	.
10	**Total taxes after adjustment for advance EIC** (line 8 – line 9 = line 10)	10	1,367 .
11	**Total deposits for this quarter, including overpayment applied from a prior quarter**	11	.
12	**Balance due** (If line 10 is more than line 11, write the difference here.) For information on how to pay, see the instructions.	12	1,367 .
13	**Overpayment** (If line 11 is more than line 10, write the difference here.) . Check one ☐ Apply to next return. ☐ Send a refund.		

▶ You **MUST** fill out both pages of this form and **SIGN** it. Next ➔

For Privacy Act and Paperwork Reduction Act Notice, see the back of the Payment Voucher. Cat. No. 17001Z Form **941** (Rev. 1-2008)

950208

Name (not your trade name): Mentoring USA, Inc. Employer identification number (EIN): 88-8888888

Part 2: Tell us about your deposit schedule and tax liability for this quarter.

If you are unsure about whether you are a monthly schedule depositor or a semiweekly schedule depositor, see *Pub. 15 (Circular E),* **section 11.**

14 A L **Write the state abbreviation for the state where you made your deposits** OR **write "MU" if you made your deposits in** *multiple* **states.**

15 **Check one:** ☑ **Line 10 is less than $2,500.** Go to Part 3.

☐ **You were a monthly schedule depositor for the entire quarter. Fill out your tax liability for each month.** Then go to Part 3.

Tax liability: Month 1 .
Month 2 .
Month 3 .
Total liability for quarter . **Total must equal line 10.**

☐ **You were a semiweekly schedule depositor for any part of this quarter.** Fill out *Schedule B (Form 941): Report of Tax Liability for Semiweekly Schedule Depositors,* and attach it to this form.

Part 3: Tell us about your business. If a question does NOT apply to your business, leave it blank.

16 **If your business has closed or you stopped paying wages** ☐ Check here, and enter the final date you paid wages / /

17 **If you are a seasonal employer and you do not have to file a return for every quarter of the year** ☐ Check here.

Part 4: May we speak with your third-party designee?

Do you want to allow an employee, a paid tax preparer, or another person to discuss this return with the IRS? See the instructions for details.

☐ Yes. Designee's name and phone number ( ) –

Select a 5-digit Personal Identification Number (PIN) to use when talking to IRS.

☐ No.

Part 5: Sign here. You MUST fill out both pages of this form and SIGN it.

Under penalties of perjury, I declare that I have examined this return, including accompanying schedules and statements, and to the best of my knowledge and belief, it is true, correct, and complete.

✗ **Sign your name here**

Print your name here: James Oliver
Print your title here: Executive Director

Date / / Best daytime phone (334) 555 – 5555

Part 6: For paid preparers only (optional)

Paid Preparer's Signature
Firm's name (or yours if self-employed)
Address EIN
ZIP code
Date / / Phone ( ) – SSN/PTIN

☐ Check if you are self-employed.

Page **2** Form **941** (Rev. 1-2008)

Figure 13-3: Form 941, Employer's Quarterly Federal Tax Return.

3. **Complete Part 2.**

   Part 2 determines your tax liability for the quarter. If you're a small nonprofit, you probably owe less than $2,500; if you do, you can check the first box next to number 15 and go on to Part 3. (You can pay your payroll taxes when you submit Form 941.) If you owe more than $2,500, fill out the rest of this part. If you need help, you may want to hire an accountant.

4. **Complete Part 3.**

   Part 3 asks you whether you're still in business.

5. **Complete Part 4.**

   Part 4 asks you whether you authorize someone else to discuss your taxes with the IRS.

6. **Complete Part 5.**

   Provide your signature, printed name, date, and daytime phone number.

Filing Form 941

After you complete Form 941, you need to file it with the IRS, and if you haven't made tax deposits or still have a balance due, you need to make a tax payment with the 941. Because Form 941 is only a report, you need to submit a payment voucher — Form 941-V — if you're submitting a payment with your quarterly report.

If you're a new nonprofit with no previous tax payment history, the IRS requires you to pay monthly using Form 8109, Federal Tax Deposit (FTD). Monthly deposits are due by the 15th of the following month. For example, you have to deposit taxes from paydays during December by January 15. (See the "Completing Form 8109 (Making tax deposits)" section for more on Form 8109.) After you've established a payment history with the IRS, it can determine or project what your future payments are likely to be. The IRS then tells you in February how and when you need to file and which method you need to use to make your payments. If the IRS determines based on your monthly payments that you should pay more frequently than quarterly, it will tell you when and how to pay.

If your nonprofit owes less than $2,500 in payroll taxes and isn't new, you can pay your payroll taxes quarterly with a timely filed Form 941 and enclosing your check and payment voucher 941-V. If you owe more than $2,500, however, you need to contact the IRS (or the IRS will contact you after it receives your Form 941) to find out how often you need to pay your payroll taxes. Larger nonprofits pay payroll taxes either weekly, semi-weekly, or monthly by making payroll tax deposits. Most small nonprofits pay quarterly payroll taxes, and even smaller ones pay annually. Those nonprofits that pay annually use an annual payroll tax report called Form 944. Annual Form 944 is due by January 31. Refer to Table 13-1 to find out when your quarterly FICA payroll taxes are due.

Table 13-1	Due Dates for Quarterly Filing of Form 941	
For the Quarter	*Quarter Ends*	*Form 941 Due Date*
January, February, March	March 31	April 30
April, May, June	June 30	July 31
July, August, September	September 30	October 31
October, November, December	December 31	January 31

Don't send a payment with Form 941 unless you're on a quarterly payment schedule. If you owe more than $2,500 and wait to pay it when you file your Form 941 at the end of the quarterly reporting period, you'll have made a late payment and may have to pay a penalty. See the section "Completing Form 8109 (Making tax deposits)" for information on how to pay your payroll taxes.

The IRS tax line is open Monday through Friday from 7 a.m. to 10 p.m. EST to order tax deposit forms and to answer your questions. That number is 800-829-4933. You can also visit www.irs.gov to download copies of Form 941, the quarterly report, and Form 944, the annual report.

When paying your payroll taxes with Form 941, write a check or money order payable to the "United States Treasury." Where you send your payment and Form 941 depends on where you live. Large nonprofits make their payments electronically using the Electronic Federal Tax Payment System (EFTPS). Small nonprofits can choose to make tax payments electronically or at a bank using Form 8109. Even smaller nonprofits can make payments by mail using Form 941-V. If you're paying by mail, see Figure 13-4 for where you can send your Form 941.

Completing Form 8109 (Making tax deposits)

The IRS has made paying your payroll taxes a fairly easy task. When you register with the IRS and indicate you'll need to report payroll, you'll be enrolled in the Electronic Federal Tax Payment System (EFTPS). You'll be sent information on how to activate your enrollment. You'll also be able to get a booklet of preprinted Federal Tax Deposit Coupons (Form 8109) by calling 800-829-4933. These coupons allow you to make deposits either electronically or at a bank.

If you live in		Without a payment	With a payment
Connecticut Delaware District of Columbia Illinois Indiana Kentucky Maine Maryland Massachusetts Michigan New Hampshire	New Jersey New York North Carolina Ohio Pennsylvania Rhode Island South Carolina Vermont Virginia West Virginia Wisconsin	Dept of Treasury IRS Cincinnati, OH 45999-0005	IRS P.O. Box 70503 Charlotte, NC 28201-0503
Alabama Alaska Arizona Arkansas California Colorado Florida Georgia Hawaii Idaho Iowa Kansas Louisiana Minnesota Mississippi	Missouri Montana Nebraska Nevada New Mexico North Dakota Oklahoma Oregon South Dakota Tennessee Texas Utah Washington Wyoming	Dept of Treasury IRS Ogden, UT 84201-0005	IRS P.O. Box 105083 Atlanta, GA 30348-5083

Figure 13-4:
Where to
send your
Form 941.

You can use Form 8109 (refer to Figure 13-5) to make your payroll tax payments called Federal Tax Deposits (FTDs) at a financial institution. When you make your tax payment using Form 8109, record the amount of tax, the type of tax (Form 941), and the quarter you're paying for on a coupon, and then present that coupon with your payment to a bank that's authorized to accept FTDs. The bank will give you a receipt. You report your deposits on Form 941.

To pay electronically, go to www.eftps.gov and follow the steps on the screens. Remember to record your electronic payment in your checkbook register.

The IRS imposes a deposit requirement on some organizations. But smaller organizations typically can choose whether they want to mail Form 941 with a 941-V payment voucher attached to their payment, use Form 8109 to make a deposit at a bank, or pay electronically.

Most banks are authorized to collect this coupon along with your payment and make the deposit to the IRS. Ask your local bank if it's authorized to make the transaction for you.

Figure 13-5:
Form 8109,
Federal Tax
Deposit
Coupon.

What's new. The oval for Form 990-C has been deleted. Form 990-C has been replaced by Form 1120-C, U.S. Income Tax Return for Cooperative Associations. Filers of Form 1120-C must use the 1120 oval when completing Form 8109-B.

The type of tax ovals for the 1120, 1042, and 944 have been moved on the coupon. Read the type of tax to the right of the oval before you darken the oval.

Note. Except for the name, address, and telephone number, entries must be made in pencil. Use soft lead (for example, a #2 pencil) so that the entries can be read more accurately by optical scanning equipment. The name, address, and telephone number may be completed other than by hand. You cannot use photocopies of the coupons to make your deposits. Do not staple, tape, or fold the coupons.

The IRS encourages you to make federal tax deposits using the Electronic Federal Tax Payment System (EFTPS). For more information on EFTPS, go to *www.eftps.gov* or call 1-800-555-4477.

Purpose of form. Use Form 8109-B to make a tax deposit only in the following two situations.

1. You have not yet received your resupply of preprinted deposit coupons (Form 8109).

2. You are a new entity and have already been assigned an employer identification number (EIN), but you have not received your initial supply of preprinted deposit coupons (Form 8109). If you have not received your EIN, see *Exceptions* below.

Note. If you do not receive your resupply of deposit coupons and a deposit is due or you do not receive your initial supply within 5–6 weeks of receipt of your EIN, call 1-800-829-4933.

How to complete the form. Enter your name as shown on your return or other IRS correspondence, address, and EIN in the spaces provided. Do not make a name or address change on this form (see Form 8822, Change of Address). If you are required to file a Form 1120, 1120-C, 990-PF (with net investment income), 990-T, or 2438, enter the month in which your tax year ends in the MONTH TAX YEAR ENDS boxes. For example, if your tax year ends in January, enter 01; if it ends in December, enter 12. Make your entries for EIN and MONTH TAX YEAR ENDS (if applicable) as shown in Amount of deposit below.

Exceptions. If you have applied for an EIN, have not received it, and a deposit must be made, do not use Form 8109-B. Instead, send your payment to the IRS address where you file your return. Make your check or money order payable to the United States Treasury and show on it your name (as shown on Form SS-4, Application for Employer Identification Number), address, kind of tax, period covered, and date you applied for an EIN. Do not use Form 8109-B to deposit delinquent taxes assessed by the IRS. Pay those taxes directly to the IRS. See Pub. 15 (Circular E), Employer's Tax Guide, for information.

Amount of deposit. Enter the amount of the deposit in the space provided. Enter the amount legibly, forming the characters as shown below:

Hand print money amounts without using dollar signs, commas, a decimal point, or leading zeros. If the deposit is for whole dollars only, enter "00" in the CENTS boxes. For example, a deposit of $7,635.22 would be entered like this:

Caution. *Darken only one space for TYPE OF TAX and only one space for TAX PERIOD. Darken the space to the left of the applicable form and tax period. Darkening the wrong space or multiple spaces may delay proper crediting to your account. See below for an explanation of Types of Tax and Marking the Proper Tax Period.*

Types of Tax

Form 941	Employer's QUARTERLY Federal Tax Return (includes Forms 941-M, 941-PR, and 941-SS)
Form 943	Employer's Annual Tax Return for Agricultural Employees
Form 944	Employer's ANNUAL Federal Tax Return (includes Forms 944-PR, 944(SP), and 944-SS)
Form 945	Annual Return of Withheld Federal Income Tax
Form 720	Quarterly Federal Excise Tax Return
Form CT-1	Employer's Annual Railroad Retirement Tax Return
Form 940	Employer's Annual Federal Unemployment (FUTA) Tax Return (includes Form 940-PR)
Form 1120	U.S. Corporation Income Tax Return (includes Form 1120 series of returns, such as new Form 1120-C, and Form 2438)
Form 990-T	Exempt Organization Business Income Tax Return
Form 990-PF	Return of Private Foundation or Section 4947(a)(1) Nonexempt Charitable Trust Treated as a Private Foundation
Form 1042	Annual Withholding Tax Return for U.S. Source Income of Foreign Persons

Marking the Proper Tax Period

Payroll taxes and withholding. For Forms 941, 940, 943, 944, 945, CT-1, and 1042, if your liability was incurred during:

● January 1 through March 31, darken the 1st quarter space;
● April 1 through June 30, darken the 2nd quarter space;
● July 1 through September 30, darken the 3rd quarter space; and
● October 1 through December 31, darken the 4th quarter space.

Note. If the liability was incurred during one quarter and deposited in another quarter, darken the space for the quarter in which the tax liability was incurred. For example, if the liability was incurred in March and deposited in April, darken the 1st quarter space.

Excise taxes. For Form 720, follow the instructions above for Forms 941, 940, etc. For Form 990-PF, with net investment income, follow the instructions on page 2 for Form 1120, 990-T, and 2438.

Department of the Treasury
Internal Revenue Service

Form **8109-B** (Rev. 12-2006)
Cat. No. 61042S

After you notify the IRS that you're going to make payments using Form 8109, the IRS will send you preprinted copies of Form 8109 within six weeks. The information on Form 8109 is straightforward. Simply fill out the form. Make sure you use a No. 2 pencil for everything but your name, address, and telephone number, for which you can use ink. The first box asks for the month that the tax year ends. If your accounting period starts in January and ends in December, enter 12 in the first squares on the form. Fill out the rest of the form according to the amount of tax, the type of tax, and the quarter for which you're paying.

Completing End-of-Year Forms

At the end of the year, you have your paperwork cut out for you. You need to fill out Forms W-2 and W-3. This section gives you an overview of these two forms and what you have to do with each one.

Filling out the W-2

Form W-2 (see Figure 13-6) is the Wage and Tax Statement for a given year. Employees usually receive three copies. The employee files one copy with the federal return (Copy B) and one copy with the state return (Copy 2). The employee keeps the third copy (Copy C) in her personal records. The W-2 Wage and Tax Statement summarizes all tax deductions for a given year.

22222	a Employee's social security number		
	OMB No. 1545-0008		
b Employer identification number (EIN)		1 Wages, tips, other compensation	2 Federal income tax withheld
c Employer's name, address, and ZIP code		3 Social security wages	4 Social security tax withheld
		5 Medicare wages and tips	6 Medicare tax withheld
		7 Social security tips	8 Allocated tips
d Control number		9 Advance EIC payment	10 Dependent care benefits
e Employee's first name and initial Last name Suff.		11 Nonqualified plans	12a
	13 Statutory employee / Retirement plan / Third-party sick pay	12b
	14 Other	12c
		12d
f Employee's address and ZIP code			
15 State Employer's state ID number	16 State wages, tips, etc.	17 State income tax	18 Local wages, tips, etc.	19 Local income tax	20 Locality name

Form **W-2** Wage and Tax Statement   2008   Department of the Treasury—Internal Revenue Service
Copy 1—For State, City, or Local Tax Department

Figure 13-6:
Form W-2,
Wage
and Tax
Statement.

You find the following information on a W-2 Wage and Tax Statement:

- ✓ Employer's federal identification number
- ✓ Employer's name, address, and zip code
- ✓ Employee's Social Security number
- ✓ Employee's name, address, and zip code
- ✓ Taxable wages, tips, and other compensation
- ✓ Federal income tax withheld
- ✓ Social Security wages
- ✓ Social Security tips
- ✓ Social Security tax withheld
- ✓ Medicare wages and tips
- ✓ Medicare tax withheld
- ✓ Name of state of employment
- ✓ Employer's state identification number
- ✓ State wages, tips, and other compensation
- ✓ State income tax withheld

Form W-2 Wage and Tax Statement consists of the following copies:

- ✓ **Copy A:** Sent by employer to Social Security Administration.
- ✓ **Copy 1:** Sent by employer to state, city, or local tax department if required.
- ✓ **Copy B:** Filed by employee with employee's federal tax return.
- ✓ **Copy C:** Kept by employee in employee's records.
- ✓ **Copy 2:** Filed by employee with employee's state, city, or local income taxes.
- ✓ **Copy D:** Kept by employer in employer's records.

As an employer, you need to fill out a W-2 for each employee. After you've completed all of your W-2s, you need to fill out a Form W-3, too. See the next section for more about Form W-3.

Filling out the W-3

Form W-3 (see Figure 13-7) is the Transmittal of Wage and Tax Statements, which the employer has to submit to the Social Security Administration. The

Wage and Tax Statements are your W-2s; the W-3 transmits them. Your W-3 totals and reports the amounts for all the W-2s it transmits, so both the W-3 and W-2s are filed with Social Security.

Figure 13-7: Form W-3, Transmittal of Wage and Tax Statements.

DO NOT STAPLE							
33333	a Control number		For Official Use Only ▶ OMB No. 1545-0008				
b Kind of Payer ▶	941 ☐ Military ☐ 943 ☐ 944 ☐ CT-1 ☐ Hshld. emp. ☐ Medicare govt. emp. ☐ Third-party sick pay ☐			1 Wages, tips, other compensation		2 Federal income tax withheld	
				3 Social security wages		4 Social security tax withheld	
c Total number of Forms W-2		d Establishment number		5 Medicare wages and tips		6 Medicare tax withheld	
e Employer identification number (EIN)				7 Social security tips		8 Allocated tips	
f Employer's name				9 Advance EIC payments		10 Dependent care benefits	
				11 Nonqualified plans		12 Deferred compensation	
				13 For third-party sick pay use only			
				14 Income tax withheld by payer of third-party sick pay			
g Employer's address and ZIP code							
h Other EIN used this year							
15 State	Employer's state ID number			16 State wages, tips, etc.		17 State income tax	
				18 Local wages, tips, etc.		19 Local income tax	
Contact person				Telephone number ( )		For Official Use Only	
Email address				Fax number ( )			

Under penalties of perjury, I declare that I have examined this return and accompanying documents, and, to the best of my knowledge and belief, they are true, correct, and complete.

Form W-3 is for information purposes only, it just transmits Forms W-2. You don't need to attach any payment to the W-3, but you do have to enclose the W-2s the W-3 transmits.

The Social Security Administration is very picky about the physical state of this form when it arrives. Apparently, Social Security only accepts an original copy of this form. The online version is an information-only copy; Copy A of this version isn't clear enough to be scanned properly. So if you download and try to submit the online version, you may be charged a $50 penalty if the IRS can't scan your form.

If you want to send your W-3 and W-2s by mail, you can order an official IRS form W-3 by calling 800-TAX-FORM (800-829-3676). Most payroll software generates these forms, and you can obtain originals from the IRS walk-in offices. You can also file your W-2s and W-3 electronically on the Social Security Administration's Web site at www.socialsecurity.gov/employer.

Where to send the W-2s and W-3s

After you complete these two forms, be sure to send all Copy A's of Form W-2 along with Form W-3 by regular mail to the Social Security Administration by the due date:

> **Social Security Administration**
> Data Operations Center
> Wilkes-Barre, PA 18769-0001

If you file electronically, you don't have to mail forms to Social Security, but you still need to file these forms by their due dates.

The due dates change from year to year by a day or two. For any tax year, you have to file Copy A of Form W-2 and Form W-3 with the Social Security Administration by March for the previous year. For more on due dates, go to www.irs.gov.

Remember, even though you file Forms W-2 and W-3 electronically with Social Security, you'll still have to distribute the W-2s to your employees and you may have to mail forms to your state tax department.

Keeping up with your paperwork is important because the IRS matches the amounts reported on your quarterly payroll taxes (Forms 941) with the W-2 amounts totaled on Form W-3. If, however, you do make a mistake when figuring your taxes, you can amend your forms and make corrections by using Form 941c, the Supporting Statement to Correct Information. To download Form 941c, go to www.irs.gov/pub/irs-pdf/f941c.pdf. Make sure you submit Form 941c with the next payroll tax Form 941 you file. The corrections are detailed on Form 941c and are treated as adjustments to the amount due with the current Form 941 you're filing.

Accounting for Contract Employees: Form 1099-MISC

The only employees you don't have to worry about paying payroll taxes for are contract employees because they aren't your employees; they're self-employed. You pay contract employees in full, and at the end of the year, you report what you've paid them to the IRS on Form 1099-MISC, Miscellaneous Income (see Figure 13-8). Then they — not you — have to pay the piper.

☐ VOID   ☐ CORRECTED

PAYER'S name, street address, city, state, ZIP code, and telephone no.		1 Rents $	OMB No. 1545-0115 2009 Form **1099-MISC**	**Miscellaneous Income**
		2 Royalties $		
		3 Other income $	4 Federal income tax withheld $	**Copy 1**
PAYER'S federal identification number	RECIPIENT'S identification number	5 Fishing boat proceeds $	6 Medical and health care payments $	**For State Tax Department**
RECIPIENT'S name		7 Nonemployee compensation $	8 Substitute payments in lieu of dividends or interest $	
Street address (including apt. no.)		9 Payer made direct sales of $5,000 or more of consumer products to a buyer (recipient) for resale ▶ ☐	10 Crop insurance proceeds $	
City, state, and ZIP code		11	12	
Account number (see instructions)		13 Excess golden parachute payments $	14 Gross proceeds paid to an attorney $	
15a Section 409A deferrals $	15b Section 409A income $	16 State tax withheld $	17 State/Payer's state no.	18 State income $

Form **1099-MISC**   Department of the Treasury - Internal Revenue Service

Figure 13-8:
Form 1099,
Miscella-
neous
Income.

Contract employees offer creative specialties and are not ordinary employees. For example, some organizations hire accountants, bookkeepers, grant writers, and computer experts on contract. Many organizations go through temporary agencies to test employees out before they formally hire them. In these cases, the contract is with the temporary agencies, not the employees. Other organizations place employees on probationary periods of three, six, or twelve months before they hire them as permanent employees.

One of the greatest advantages of hiring contract employees is that they represent no tax liability for you. Also, if you're not pleased with their work, you can easily let them go. However, most contract employees require signed contracts outlining the terms of dismissal, so you may be better off waiting until their contract expires before letting them go. The good news is that after the contract expires, the employer-employee relationship ends.

At the end of the year, all you have to do for contract employees is give them a Form 1099-MISC. Compared to everything you have to do for regular employees, filling out the lone Form 1099-MISC is a piece of cake. Take a look at Form 1099-MISC in Figure 13-8.

You can complete Form 1099-MISC in just three simple steps before giving it to your contract employees:

1. **At the top of the form underneath Payer's, write your name, address, telephone number, and federal identification number.**

2. **Underneath Recipient's, write the contract employee's identification number, name, and address.**

3. **In box number 7, which is labeled Nonemployee compensation, write the amount of compensation the contracted employee received in that year.**

Form 1099-MISC consists of the following copies:

- ✔ **Copy A:** Sent by nonprofit to the IRS
- ✔ **Copy 1:** Sent by nonprofit to the state tax department if required
- ✔ **Copy B:** Sent by nonprofit to contract employee (recipient)

For the tax year ending in December, Form 1099-MISC Copy B is due by February of the following year. Copy A of Form 1099-MISC is due by March of the following tax year.

The Copy A's of Form 1099-MISC sent to the IRS are transmitted by Form 1096 just as Form W-3 transmits Copy A's of Form W-2. Refer to the instructions to Form 1096 to find out where to mail your Copy A's of Form 1099-MISC with Form 1096. You can obtain instructions for Forms 1099-MISC and Form 1096 at www.irs.gov/app/picklist/list/formsInstructions.html and type "1099-MISC" or "1096" in the Find window. You can order an official IRS form by calling 800-TAX-FORM (800-829-3676). Most payroll software generates these forms, and you can obtain originals from the IRS walk-in offices. You can file Forms 1096 and 1099-MISC with the IRS electronically if you have specialized software.

Staffing only contract employees sounds like a great way to save money, doesn't it? Well, unfortunately, Uncle Sam doesn't let you hire only contract employees, so you have to find other ways to save money. The Department of Wage and Labor has its own auditors who pay close attention to payroll taxes, how they're paid, when they're paid, and how small establishments handle their payroll accounting. If the IRS determines that your contract employees (self-employed) are actually statutory employees (your employees), you'll be on the hook for back payroll taxes and penalties. Publications 15 and 15-A provide you with info to determine who is a statutory employee. Go to www.irs.gov/app/picklist/list/publicationsNoticesPdf.html and type "Publ 15" in the Find window.

Chapter 14

Doing the Accounting for Tax Form 990

*Y*our nonprofit organization is tax exempt, so you're probably wondering why I include a chapter on filing a tax report. You may be surprised to find out that even though you don't have to pay federal income taxes, your organization does have to file a return. IRS Form 990, Return of Organization Exempt from Income Tax, is an annual information return that most tax-exempt organizations must file. Although this is a topic most people, including myself, may prefer to ignore, failure to accurately complete this form leads to repercussions none of us want. The information a tax-exempt organization provides on this form serves as the primary source of information for the public about that particular organization. Therefore, the information you provide on this form becomes the basis for how the public and the government perceive your organization.

Which version of this form your organization needs to complete depends on your organization's gross receipts. Before getting too worried about this form, check out this chapter to find out the steps you need to follow to prepare your information form for the IRS. I wish you could spend all your time running the programs that benefit our communities, but there's a time for everything. And right now, it's tax time!

Be prepared for that first phone call or e-mail from a concerned citizen requesting your Form 990. Your Form 990 is considered public record and must be made available to the public upon request. You have to give your Form 990 to whoever requests it with only a minimal charge equal to the cost of copying the form. To save paper and time, you can post your Form 990 on your Web site. When someone requests a copy, you can simply tell that person how to locate the forms on your Web site.

Choosing the Right Form: Which One Do You Need?

Your gross receipts and total assets from grants, donations, contracts, and so on determine which version of Form 990 your organization must file with the IRS. Your organization may be exempt from income tax, but you have to file one of the following three forms:

✔ **Form 990-N:** Form 990-N, e-Postcard, is for small nonprofits.

✔ **Form 990-EZ:** Form 990-EZ, Short Form Return of Organization Exempt from Income Tax, is for medium-sized nonprofits.

✔ **Form 990:** Form 990, Return of Organization Exempt from Income Tax, is for large nonprofits.

The thresholds that determine which version of Form 990 your organization needs to fill out change often, so make sure you check the IRS's Web site, www.irs.gov/charities/article/0,,id=184445,00.html, for the most up-to-date information. See Table 14-1 for the tax thresholds for tax years 2008 to 2010.

Table 14-1	Tax Thresholds for Form 990		
Form to File	2008 Tax Year (Filed in 2009 or 2010)	2009 Tax Year (Filed in 2010 or 2011)	2010 Tax Year (Filed in 2011 or later)
990-N	Gross receipts normally less than or equal to $25,000	Gross receipts normally less than or equal to $25,000	Gross receipts normally less than or equal to $50,000
990-EZ or 990	Gross receipts greater than $25,000 and less than $1 million and total assets less than $2.5 million	Gross receipts greater than $25,000 and less than $500,000 and total assets less than $1.25 million	Gross receipts greater than $50,000 and less than $200,000 and total assets less than $500,000
990	Gross receipts greater than or equal to $1 million or total assets greater than or equal to $2.5 million	Gross receipts greater than or equal to $500,000 or total assets greater than or equal to $1.25 million	Gross receipts greater than or equal to $200,000 or total assets greater than or equal to $500,000

Knowing What Happens If You Don't File Form 990

If you don't file your personal income taxes, you know Uncle Sam gets upset. The same is true for your organization. Although your nonprofit isn't required to pay federal taxes, you still need to file Form 990. If you don't file, you put yourself and your organization on Uncle Sam's bad side. Make sure you file Form 990 to avoid any repercussions and dire consequences for your nonprofit.

What happens when you don't file Form 990 or you send in an incomplete form? You pay the following penalties:

✔ The IRS charges smaller organizations a penalty of $20 a day, not to exceed the lesser of $10,000 or 5 percent of the gross receipts of the organization for the year, when you file a return late, unless you can show that the late filing was the result of a reasonable cause. Organizations with annual gross receipts exceeding $1 million are subject to a penalty of $100 for each day they fail to file (with a maximum penalty of $50,000 for any one return). The penalty begins on the due date. Additionally, the organization can lose its exempt status.

✔ If your organization doesn't file a complete return or doesn't furnish correct information, the IRS sends the organization a letter that includes a fixed time period during which you can resubmit the form. After that period expires, the IRS charges the person who fails to comply a penalty of $10 a day, with a maximum penalty of $5,000 for any one return.

You only have to give up information about your nonprofit; you don't have to include a check with this return.

Others will play finance detective

With the availability of your Form 990 on the Internet, donors can easily investigate whether your organization has been a good steward of donor investments. They look up your IRS Form 990 to see how much money you brought in, what you did with the money, and how much you paid your executive director. Many donors are skeptical about giving to charitable organizations because some aren't doing the right thing. Donors want to know that they're giving to a reputable organization; they don't want to worry about misuse of their money.

Donors may decide whether to donate to your organization based on the financial picture they glean from reviewing this form. Your Form 990 reveals the same information found on financial statements; the form just makes it easier for the government and public to analyze your numbers.

You can find Form 990s online at www.charity navigator.org, www.guidestar.org, and www.foundationcenter.org.

Understanding the Minimal Requirements: Form 990-N (e-Postcard)

The IRS created Form 990-N specifically for small, tax-exempt nonprofit orga-nizations that gross less than $25,000 a year. See Table 14-1 in the "Choosing the Right Form: Which Form Do You Need?" section of this chapter for more information on the gross receipts you need to use this form. Form 990-N is an electronic notice and very easy to complete, which is why it's also called the e-Postcard. You need to file this form every year by the 15th day of the fifth month after the end of a tax-exempt organization's fiscal year. For a calendar year, the deadline is May 15.

For many years, the IRS didn't require small nonprofits that made less than $25,000 a year to submit any paperwork, but things have changed. Don't fret, though. Filling out Form 990-N is quick and simple. Here's what you must provide:

- ✔ Organization's employer identification number (EIN)

- ✔ Organization's name

- ✔ Any other names your organization uses

- ✔ Organization's mailing address (usually the board secretary's address)

- ✔ Organization's Web site address (if applicable)

- ✔ Name and address of a principal officer of your organization (usually the executive director)

- ✔ Organization's annual tax period

- ✔ A confirmation that your organization's annual gross receipts are nor-mally $25,000 or less

If applicable, indicate whether your organization is going out of business. The IRS needs to know if your nonprofit is no longer operating because it regu-lates nonprofits.

The IRS requires that Form 990-N be filed electronically. No paper form is avail-able. To file Form 990-N, you must have access to the Internet, but you don't have to download any software. If your nonprofit doesn't have a computer, you can fill out Form 990-N using the computer of a friend, a relative, or your public library. You can find Form 990-N at http://epostcard.form990.org.

If you don't file your e-Postcard on time, the IRS sends you a reminder notice, but the IRS won't assess a penalty for filing the e-Postcard late. However, an organization that fails to file required e-Postcards (or Forms 990 or 990-EZ, for that matter) for three consecutive years automatically loses its tax-exempt status. The revocation for the organization's tax-exempt status doesn't take place until the filing due date of the third year.

Filling Out Form 990-EZ

Form 990-EZ (see Figure 14-1) is an annual information return that many organizations exempt from income taxes have to file with the IRS. To find out if
your organization can file Form 990-EZ rather than Form 990, see Table 14-1
in the "Choosing the Right Form: Which Form Do You Need?" section of this
chapter. Basically, Form 990-EZ is a less detailed version of Form 990.

Figure 14-1:
Form
990-EZ,
Return of
Organization
Exempt from
Income Tax.

All filing organizations must complete the top portion of the form and Parts I through V. The top portion of the form is self-explanatory with simple questions that identify you by name and EIN. Just fill in the blanks.

Parts I through V require information about the organization's exempt and other activities, finances, compliance with certain federal tax filings and requirements, and compensation paid to certain people. These five parts, along with the information you need to include in each part, are as follow:

- ✔ **Part I — Revenue, Expenses, and Changes in Net Assets or Fund Balances:** This part is basically your nonprofit organization's statement of activities. Part I is logically divided into revenues, expenses, and net assets.

- ✔ **Part II — Balance Sheets:** This part provides your organization with a simplified version of its statement of financial position (see Chapter 16 for more information on this statement). You can use the numbers from your statement of financial position to fill in some of the info in this part.

- ✔ **Part III — Statement of Program Service Accomplishments:** Here you get to showcase your major accomplishments during the year. In this part, you report organizational and financial accomplishments that relate to your nonprofit's core program areas. Your responses to the questions in this part highlight your accomplishments. Just answer the questions, and before you know it, you're moving on to Part IV.

- ✔ **Part IV — List of Officers, Directors, Trustees, and Key Employees:** In this part, your organization has to report the income for its most highly compensated employees. If your organization provides no compensation, you should list the top three officers, such as president or executive director, treasurer, and secretary.

- ✔ **Part V — Other Information:** In this part, you have to answer a series of questions according to each question's specific instructions. Understanding all these questions is important because they disclose information about unrelated business income, the person who takes care of your books, and any new activities not reported in the prior year.

Only Section 501(c)(3) organizations have to complete Part VI. The questions in Part VI ask about your political activities, changes to your bylaws, unrelated business income, and so on. Because these questions are fairly basic, you can answer them rather easily. For example, one question asks you for the five highest paid employees. All the questions in Part VI are straightforward.

Furthermore, you may need to complete additional schedules depending on the type of your organization and its activities. A *schedule* is a supplemental form with questions pertaining to a specific subject or topic that the IRS requires you to fill out, depending on your responses on other tax forms. Form 990-EZ requests information regarding specific activities on two schedules:

- ✔ **Schedule A** requests information regarding compensation of independent contractors and highest compensated employees, the basis for an organization's public charity status, a private school's nondiscrimination policies and practices, lobbying, specified activities posing compliance concerns, and transactions or relationships with noncharitable exempt organizations.

✔ **Schedule B** requests certain charitable contributions and contributor information.

You can find Form 990-EZ at www.irs.gov/pub/irs-tege/f990rez.pdf. (See the "Submitting Form 990" section for details on what to do with the form after you complete it.)

Filling Out Form 990

Form 990 is the primary reporting mechanism for all organizations that are exempt from federal income tax (see Figure 14-2). Every exempt organization that doesn't meet the requirements for the shorter Form 990-N or Form 990-EZ has to file Form 990 and must complete the top portion of the form and Parts I through XI. See Table 14-1 in the "Choosing the Right Form: Which Form Do You Need?" section of this chapter for the requirements of the three versions of Form 990.

The next sections help you understand how to complete Form 990 and how to submit it.

Walking through Form 990

Form 990 isn't an overly complex form to complete. You can find a lot of the information you need on your nonprofit's financial statements. First, you have to fill out the top portion of the form by following the directions and reporting general information about your organization, such as its name, address, EIN, and so on. The specific parts of Form 990 are as follows. Note that you can use Part IV, Checklist of Required Schedules, to determine which schedules, if any, you must complete in addition to the form itself (see the "Filling Out Form 990-EZ" section for more on schedules).

✔ **Part I — Summary:** This part basically asks you to summarize your organization. It requests details regarding your organization's activities and governance, revenue, expenses, and net assets.

✔ **Part II — Signature Block:** This part requires your signature to verify that the information on this form is correct to the best of your knowledge.

✔ **Part III — Statement of Program Service Accomplishments:** Simply put, this part is where the organization describes its accomplishments in the services it provides. It requests the amount of grant money and allocations your organization received for the services provided, along with all expenses related to the programs.

Form **990**

Return of Organization Exempt From Income Tax

Under section 501(c), 527, or 4947(a)(1) of the Internal Revenue Code (except black lung benefit trust or private foundation)

OMB No. 1545-0047

2008

Open to Public Inspection

Department of the Treasury
Internal Revenue Service (77)

▶ The organization may have to use a copy of this return to satisfy state reporting requirements.

A For the 2008 calendar year, or tax year beginning _____ , 2008, and ending _____ , 20 ___

B Check if applicable:
- ☐ Address change
- ☐ Name change
- ☐ Initial return
- ☐ Termination
- ☐ Amended return
- ☐ Application pending

Please use IRS label or print or type. See Specific Instructions.

C Name of organization

Doing Business As

Number and street (or P.O. box if mail is not delivered to street address) | Room/suite

City or town, state or country, and ZIP + 4

F Name and address of Principal Officer:

D Employer identification number

E Telephone number
( )

G Enter gross receipts $

H(a) Is this a group return for affiliates?   ☐ Yes   ☐ No

H(b) Are all affiliates included?   ☐ Yes   ☐ No
If "No," attach a list. (See instructions)

H(c) Group Exemption Number ▶

I Tax-exempt status: ☐ 501(c) ( ) ◀ (insert no.) ☐ 4947(a)(1) or ☐ 527

J Website: ▶

K Type of organization: ☐ Corporation ☐ trust ☐ association ☐ Other ▶ | **L** Year of Formation: | **M** State of legal domicile:

Part I   Summary

Activities & Governance	1	Briefly describe the organization's mission or most significant activities:	
	2	Check this box ☐ if the organization discontinued its operations or disposed of more than 25% of its assets.	
	3	Enter the number of voting members of the governing body (Part VI, line 1a)	3
	4	Enter the number of independent voting members of the governing body (Part VI, line 1b)	4
	5	Enter the total number of employees (Part V, line 2a)	5
	6	Enter the total number of volunteers (estimate if necessary)	6
	7a	Enter total gross unrelated business revenue from Part VIII, line 12, column (C)	7a
	b	Enter net unrelated business taxable income from Form 990-T, line 34	7b

			Prior Year	Current Year
Revenue	8	Contributions and grants (Part VIII, line 1h)		
	9	Program service revenue (Part VIII, line 2g)		
	10	Investment income (Part VIII, lines 3, 4, and 7d)		
	11	Other revenue (Part VIII, lines 5, 6d, 8c, 9c, and 10c of column (A), and 11e)		
	12	Total revenue—add lines 8 through 11 (must equal Part VIII, column (A), line 12)		
Expenses	13	Grants and similar amounts paid (Part IX, lines 1–3, column (A))		
	14	Benefits paid to or for members (Part IX, line 4, column (A))		
	15	Salaries, other compensation, employee benefits (Part IX, lines 5–10, column (A))		
	16a	Professional fundraising expenses (Part IX, line 11e, column (A))		
	b	(Enter amount from Part IX, line 25, column (D))		
	17	Other expenses (Part IX, lines 11d, 11f–24f)		
	18	Total expenses—add lines 13–17 (must equal Part IX, line 25, column (A))		
	19	Revenue less expenses—line 12 minus line 18		

			Beginning of Year	End of Year
Net Assets or Fund Balances	20	Total assets (Part X, line 16)		
	21	Total liabilities (Part X, line 26)		
	22	Net assets or fund balances, line 20 minus line 21		

Part II   Signature Block

Under penalties of perjury, I declare that I have examined this return, including accompanying schedules and statements, and to the best of my knowledge and belief, it is true, correct, and complete. Declaration of preparer (other than officer) is based on all information of which preparer has any knowledge.

Please Sign Here

▶ Signature of officer | Date

▶ Type or print name and title

Paid Preparer's Use Only

Preparer's signature ▶ | Date | Check if self-employed ▶ ☐ | Preparer's PTIN (See Gen. Inst.)

Firm's name (or yours if self-employed), address, and ZIP + 4 ▶ | EIN ▶
Phone no. ▶ ( )

May the IRS discuss this return with the preparer shown above? (See instructions) . . . . ☐ Yes ☐ No

For Privacy Act and Paperwork Reduction Act Notice, see the separate instructions.   Cat. No. 11282Y   Form **990** (2008)

Figure 14-2:
The first page of Form 990.

✔ **Part IV — Checklist of Required Schedules:** This part determines whether you need to complete any schedules in addition to Form 990 itself.

✔ **Part V — Statements Regarding Other IRS Filings and Tax Compliance:** This part alerts your organization to other potential federal tax compliance and filing obligations it has.

✔ **Part VI — Governance, Management, and Disclosure:** This part contains three sections: governing body and management, policies, and disclosure. These sections pose questions concerning the organization's conflict of interest policies and monitoring system. This part also asks about the review of Form 990 by voting members of the organization's governing board.

✔ **Part VII — Compensation of Officers, Directors, Trustees, Key Employees, Highest Compensated Employees, and Independent Contractors:** This part requires the organization to report the calendar-year amounts paid to compensate employees and independent contractors, taken from W-2 and 1099 forms (see Chapter 13 for more about these forms).

✔ **Part VIII — Statement of Revenue:** Just as its title states, this part is where you state all your organization's sources of revenue, including contributions such as grants and gifts, program service revenue, and fundraising revenue.

✔ **Part IX — Statement of Functional Expenses:** This part requires you to list your organization's expenses by category. The expense categories include program service, management, and fundraising.

✔ **Part X — Balance Sheet:** This part requires you to fill in the information found on your statement of financial position. Refer to your own statement to help you fill out this part (see Chapter 16 for more information on statements of financial position).

✔ **Part XI — Financial Statements and Reporting:** This part asks questions regarding the organization's accounting methods, and financial statement reporting and preparation.

Submitting Form 990

Whew! The worst is over. You've completed Form 990. Now all you have to do is turn it in on time to avoid late fees. Form 990 is due by the 15th day of the fifth month after your organization's fiscal year ends. If you fail to turn it in on time, you have to pay fees of $20 a day up to the amount of $10,000 or 5 percent of your organization's gross receipts, depending on which amount is lower.

Be sure to review the form for any omitted information so you don't have to pay the fee for incomplete returns (a fee of $10 a day up to $5,000).

Your organization can file Form 990 and related forms, schedules, and attachments electronically or by private delivery service. However, if an organization files 250 returns of any type during the calendar year and has total assets of $10 million or more at the end of the tax year, that organization must file Form 990 electronically. If your organization meets this requirement but does not file electronically, the IRS does *not* recognize that your organization filed its return, even if you submitted a paper return.

Completing Form 990-T (Reporting Unrelated Business Income)

Your nonprofit may be subject to corporate income taxes if you engage in for-profit business enterprises in which you gain unrelated business income. *Unrelated business income* is any income generated by a business that is *regularly* carried on and *unrelated* to the exempt function of your nonprofit.

The IRS rule states that all nonprofits that have $1,000 or more in gross receipts from an unrelated business transaction must file Form 990-T, Exempt Organization Business Income Tax Return (see Figure 14-3). You have to file Form 990-T to provide the IRS information about your nonprofit's

- ✔ **Unrelated business income:** If your nonprofit conducts a trade or business that produces income by selling merchandise or providing a service that isn't related to the cause or purpose of your organization, the income generated is considered unrelated business income if the trade or business activity takes place on a regular basis.

- ✔ **Unrelated business income tax liability:** This tax liability is the amount over $1,000 that your nonprofit earns for unrelated business transactions. This includes all gross income less deductions directly connected with producing the income.

- ✔ **Proxy tax liability:** This deals with notice requirements of nondeductible lobbying and political campaigning activities engaged in by certain membership associations that hold a tax-exempt status such as, 501(c)4, 501(c)(5), and 501(c)(6).

You can find Form 990-T online at www.irs.gov. After you log on to the Web site, type **Form 990-T** in the Search box. As with all tax forms, you can call the IRS for technical assistance, but if you're not comfortable with the answers you get from the IRS, consult a tax accountant or CPA.

Be careful with activities outside the scope of tax-exempt purpose. These unrelated business transactions can come back to bite you in the butt. Engaging in excessive unrelated business transactions (50 percent or more of your total transactions) can change the status of your organization from a nonprofit to a for-profit, which means you lose your exempt status. As long as you stay within the scope of the tax-exempt purpose of your nonprofit, though, you don't have anything to worry about.

Form **990-T** Department of the Treasury Internal Revenue Service

Exempt Organization Business Income Tax Return
(and proxy tax under section 6033(e))
For calendar year 2007 or other tax year beginning ...., 2007, and ending , 20 . ▶ **See separate instructions.**

OMB No. 1545-0687
2007
Open to Public Inspection for 501(c)(3) Organizations Only

A ☐ Check box if address changed
B Exempt under section ☐ 501( )( ) ☐ 408(e) ☐ 220(e) ☐ 408A ☐ 530(a) ☐ 529(a)
C Book value of all assets at end of year

Print or Type: Name of organization (☐ Check box if name changed and see instructions.)
Number, street, and room or suite no. If a P.O. box, see page 9 of instructions.
City or town, state, and ZIP code

D Employer identification number (Employees' trust, see instructions for Block D on page 9.)
E Unrelated business activity codes (See instructions for Block E on page 9.)

F Group exemption number (See instructions for Block F on page 9.) ▶
G Check organization type ▶ ☐ 501(c) corporation ☐ 501(c) trust ☐ 401(a) trust ☐ Other trust
H Describe the organization's primary unrelated business activity. ▶
I During the tax year, was the corporation a subsidiary in an affiliated group or a parent-subsidiary controlled group? . ▶ ☐ Yes ☐ No
If "Yes," enter the name and identifying number of the parent corporation. ▶
J The books are in care of ▶ Telephone number ▶ ( )

Part I Unrelated Trade or Business Income

		(A) Income	(B) Expenses	(C) Net
1a Gross receipts or sales ___ b Less returns and allowances ___ c Balance ▶	1c			
2 Cost of goods sold (Schedule A, line 7)	2			
3 Gross profit. Subtract line 2 from line 1c	3			
4a Capital gain net income (attach Schedule D)	4a			
b Net gain (loss) (Form 4797, Part II, line 17) (attach Form 4797)	4b			
c Capital loss deduction for trusts	4c			
5 Income (loss) from partnerships and S corporations (attach statement)	5			
6 Rent income (Schedule C)	6			
7 Unrelated debt-financed income (Schedule E)	7			
8 Interest, annuities, royalties, and rents from controlled organizations (Schedule F)	8			
9 Investment income of a section 501(c)(7), (9), or (17) organization (Schedule G)	9			
10 Exploited exempt activity income (Schedule I)	10			
11 Advertising income (Schedule J)	11			
12 Other income (See page 11 of the instructions; attach schedule.)	12			
13 **Total.** Combine lines 3 through 12	13			

Part II Deductions Not Taken Elsewhere (See page 12 of the instructions for limitations on deductions.) (Except for contributions, deductions must be directly connected with the unrelated business income.)

14 Compensation of officers, directors, and trustees (Schedule K)	14	
15 Salaries and wages	15	
16 Repairs and maintenance	16	
17 Bad debts	17	
18 Interest (attach schedule)	18	
19 Taxes and licenses	19	
20 Charitable contributions (See page 14 of the instructions for limitation rules.)	20	
21 Depreciation (attach Form 4562) 21		
22 Less depreciation claimed on Schedule A and elsewhere on return 22a	22b	
23 Depletion	23	
24 Contributions to deferred compensation plans	24	
25 Employee benefit programs	25	
26 Excess exempt expenses (Schedule I)	26	
27 Excess readership costs (Schedule J)	27	
28 Other deductions (attach schedule)	28	
29 **Total deductions.** Add lines 14 through 28	29	
30 Unrelated business taxable income before net operating loss deduction. Subtract line 29 from line 13	30	
31 Net operating loss deduction (limited to the amount on line 30)	31	
32 Unrelated business taxable income before specific deduction. Subtract line 31 from line 30	32	
33 Specific deduction (Generally $1,000, but see line 33 instructions for exceptions.)	33	
34 **Unrelated business taxable income.** Subtract line 33 from line 32. If line 33 is greater than line 32, enter the smaller of zero or line 32	34	

For Privacy Act and Paperwork Reduction Act Notice, see instructions. Cat. No. 11291J Form **990-T** (2007)

Form 990-T (2007) Page **2**

Part III Tax Computation

35 **Organizations Taxable as Corporations.** See instructions for tax computation on page 15. Controlled group members (sections 1561 and 1563) check here ▶ ☐ **See instructions** and:		
a Enter your share of the $50,000, $25,000, and $9,925,000 taxable income brackets (in that order): (1) $ (2) $ (3) $		
b Enter organization's share of: **(1)** Additional 5% tax (not more than $11,750) $ **(2)** Additional 3% tax (not more than $100,000) $		
c Income tax on the amount on line 34 ▶	35c	
36 **Trusts Taxable at Trust Rates.** See instructions for tax computation on page 16. Income tax on the amount on line 34 from: ☐ Tax rate schedule or ☐ Schedule D (Form 1041) ▶	36	
37 **Proxy tax.** See page 16 of the instructions ▶	37	
38 Alternative minimum tax	38	
39 **Total.** Add lines 37 and 38 to line 35c or 36, whichever applies	39	

Part IV Tax and Payments

40a Foreign tax credit (corporations attach Form 1118; trusts attach Form 1116) 40a		
b Other credits (see page 17 of the instructions) 40b		
c General business credit. Check here and indicate which forms are attached: ☐ Form 3800 ☐ Form(s) (specify) ▶ 40c		
d Credit for prior year minimum tax (attach Form 8801 or 8827) 40d		
e **Total credits.** Add lines 40a through 40d	40e	
41 Subtract line 40e from line 39	41	
42 Other taxes. Check if from: ☐ Form 4255 ☐ Form 8611 ☐ Form 8697 ☐ Form 8866 ☐ Other (attach schedule)	42	
43 **Total tax.** Add lines 41 and 42	43	
44a Payments: A 2006 overpayment credited to 2007 44a		
b 2007 estimated tax payments 44b		
c Tax deposited with Form 8868 44c		
d Foreign organizations: Tax paid or withheld at source (see instructions) 44d		
e Backup withholding (see instructions) 44e		
f Other credits and payments: ☐ Form 2439 ___ ☐ Form 4136 ___ ☐ Other ___ Total ▶ 44f		
45 **Total payments.** Add lines 44a through 44f	45	
46 Estimated tax penalty (see page 4 of the instructions). Check if Form 2220 is attached ▶ ☐	46	
47 **Tax due.** If line 45 is less than the total of lines 43 and 46, enter amount owed ▶	47	
48 **Overpayment.** If line 45 is larger than the total of lines 43 and 46, enter amount overpaid ▶	48	
49 Enter the amount of line 48 you want: **Credited to 2008 estimated tax ▶** **Refunded ▶**	49	

Part V Statements Regarding Certain Activities and Other Information (see instructions on page 18)

	Yes	No
1 At any time during the 2007 calendar year, did the organization have an interest in or a signature or other authority over a financial account (bank, securities, or other) in a foreign country? If YES, the organization may have to file Form TD F 90-22.1. If YES, enter the name of the foreign country here ▶		
2 During the tax year, did the organization receive a distribution from, or was it the grantor of, or transferor to, a foreign trust? If YES, see page 5 of the instructions for other forms the organization may have to file.		
3 Enter the amount of tax-exempt interest received or accrued during the tax year ▶ $		

Schedule A—Cost of Goods Sold. Enter method of inventory valuation ▶

1 Inventory at beginning of year	1		6 Inventory at end of year	6	
2 Purchases	2		7 **Cost of goods sold.** Subtract line 6 from line 5. Enter here and in Part I, line 2	7	
3 Cost of labor	3		8 Do the rules of section 263A (with respect to property produced or acquired for resale) apply to the organization?	Yes	No
4a Additional section 263A costs (attach schedule)	4a				
b Other costs (attach schedule)	4b				
5 **Total.** Add lines 1 through 4b	5				

Sign Here Under penalties of perjury, I declare that I have examined this return, including accompanying schedules and statements, and to the best of my knowledge and belief, it is true, correct, and complete. Declaration of preparer (other than taxpayer) is based on all information of which preparer has any knowledge.
▶ Signature of officer Date ▶ Title
May the IRS discuss this return with the preparer shown below (see instructions)? ☐ Yes ☐ No

Paid Preparer's Use Only Preparer's signature ▶ Date Check if self-employed ☐ Preparer's SSN or PTIN
Firm's name (or yours if self-employed), address, and ZIP code ▶ EIN Phone no. ( )

Form **990-T** (2007)

Figure 14-3: Form 990-T, Exempt Organization Business Income Tax Return.

Handling IRS Form 990 Extensions and Mistakes

Sometimes you may need a little extra time to file Form 990. Or, perhaps you noticed an error after submitting it. So what happens when you can't finish completing the form on time or you do complete the form on time, but you later discover you made a mistake? Don't worry — all is not lost. The following sections provide you with solutions to both of these issues.

Requesting an extension

If you find you're running out of time and you can't meet the IRS's deadline for filing Form 990, you can request an extension. Use Form 8868, Application for Extension of Time to File an Exempt Organization Return, to request an automatic three-month extension (see Figure 14-4). You can also use this form to apply for an additional three-month extension if the original three months aren't enough. This second extension is not automatic; to obtain a second extension, your organization must show reasonable cause for the additional time requested. This is a fairly easy form to fill out.

Most nonprofits file extensions because CPA fees are less expensive during less busy times. For example, if you require a CPA during peak season (January 1 through April 15), the hourly rate you have to pay is much higher than it is during the rest of the year. This fact goes back to supply and demand — if the demand for a service is high, the cost to supply it goes up, too.

Correcting Form 990 mistakes

As humans, we all make mistakes. If you need to make a correction to your Form 990, you just need to file a new return (make sure to include any required schedules with it). Use the version of Form 990 applicable to the year of the form being changed. The changed return must provide all the information requested by the form and instructions — not just the new or corrected information.

To correct a mistake:

- Check the amended return box in the heading of the return.
- State in Schedule O which parts and schedules of Form 990 you amended and describe the amendments.

Form **8868**
(Rev. April 2008)
Department of the Treasury
Internal Revenue Service

Application for Extension of Time To File an Exempt Organization Return

▶ File a separate application for each return.

OMB No. 1545-1709

- If you are filing for an **Automatic 3-Month Extension,** complete only **Part I** and check this box . . . . ▶ ☐
- If you are filing for an **Additional (Not Automatic) 3-Month Extension,** complete only **Part II** (on page 2 of this form).
Do not complete Part II unless you have already been granted an automatic 3-month extension on a previously filed Form 8868.

Part I **Automatic 3-Month Extension of Time.** Only submit original (no copies needed).

A corporation required to file Form 990-T and requesting an automatic 6-month extension—check this box and complete Part I only . . . . ▶ ☐

All other corporations (including 1120-C filers), partnerships, REMICs, and trusts must use Form 7004 to request an extension of time to file income tax returns.

Electronic Filing (e-file). Generally, you can electronically file Form 8868 if you want a 3-month automatic extension of time to file one of the returns noted below (6 months for a corporation required to file Form 990-T). However, you cannot file Form 8868 electronically if (1) you want the additional (not automatic) 3-month extension or (2) you file Forms 990-BL, 6069, or 8870, group returns, or a composite or consolidated Form 990-T. Instead, you must submit the fully completed and signed page 2 (Part II) of Form 8868. For more details on the electronic filing of this form, visit *www.irs.gov/efile* and click on *e-file for Charities & Nonprofits.*

Type or print	Name of Exempt Organization	Employer identification number
File by the due date for filing your return. See instructions.	Number, street, and room or suite no. If a P.O. box, see instructions.	
	City, town or post office, state, and ZIP code. For a foreign address, see instructions.	

Check type of return to be filed (file a separate application for each return):
☐ Form 990   ☐ Form 990-T (corporation)   ☐ Form 4720
☐ Form 990-BL   ☐ Form 990-T (sec. 401(a) or 408(a) trust)   ☐ Form 5227
☐ Form 990-EZ   ☐ Form 990-T (trust other than above)   ☐ Form 6069
☐ Form 990-PF   ☐ Form 1041-A   ☐ Form 8870

- The books are in the care of ▶ ....
  Telephone No. ▶ (........) ....   FAX No. ▶ (........) ....
- If the organization does not have an office or place of business in the United States, check this box . . . . . ▶ ☐
- If this is for a Group Return, enter the organization's four digit Group Exemption Number (GEN) .... If this is for the whole group, check this box . . . . . ▶ ☐ . If it is for part of the group, check this box . . . . . . ▶ ☐ and attach a list with the names and EINs of all members the extension will cover.

1   I request an automatic 3-month (6 months for a corporation required to file Form 990-T) extension of time until ...., 20....., to file the exempt organization return for the organization named above. The extension is for the organization's return for:
  ▶ ☐ calendar year 20........or
  ▶ ☐ tax year beginning ...., 20......, and ending ...., 20........

2   If this tax year is for less than 12 months, check reason: ☐ Initial return ☐ Final return ☐ Change in accounting period

3a	If this application is for Form 990-BL, 990-PF, 990-T, 4720, or 6069, enter the tentative tax, less any nonrefundable credits. See instructions.	3a	$
b	If this application is for Form 990-PF or 990-T, enter any refundable credits and estimated tax payments made. Include any prior year overpayment allowed as a credit.	3b	$
c	**Balance Due.** Subtract line 3b from line 3a. Include your payment with this form, or, if required, deposit with FTD coupon or, if required, by using EFTPS (Electronic Federal Tax Payment System). See instructions.	3c	$

Caution. If you are going to make an electronic fund withdrawal with this Form 8868, see Form 8453-EO and Form 8879-EO for payment instructions.

For Privacy Act and Paperwork Reduction Act Notice, see instructions.   Cat. No. 27916D   Form **8868** (Rev. 4-2008)

Form 8868 (Rev. 4-2008)   Page **2**

- If you are filing for an **Additional (Not Automatic) 3-Month Extension,** complete only **Part II** and check this box . ▶ ☐
Note. Only complete Part II if you have already been granted an automatic 3-month extension on a previously filed Form 8868.
- If you are filing for an **Automatic 3-Month Extension,** complete only **Part I** (on page 1).

Part II **Additional (Not Automatic) 3-Month Extension of Time.** You **must** file original and one copy.

Type or print	Name of Exempt Organization	Employer identification number
File by the extended due date for filing the return. See instructions.	Number, street, and room or suite no. If a P.O. box, see instructions.	For IRS use only
	City, town or post office, state, and ZIP code. For a foreign address, see instructions.	

Check type of return to be filed (File a separate application for each return):
☐ Form 990   ☐ Form 990-PF   ☐ Form 1041-A   ☐ Form 6069
☐ Form 990-BL   ☐ Form 990-T (sec. 401(a) or 408(a) trust)   ☐ Form 4720   ☐ Form 8870
☐ Form 990-EZ   ☐ Form 990-T (trust other than above)   ☐ Form 5227

STOP! Do not complete Part II if you were not already granted an automatic 3-month extension on a previously filed Form 8868.

- The books are in the care of ▶ ....
  Telephone No. ▶ (........) ....   FAX No. ▶ (........) ....
- If the organization does not have an office or place of business in the United States, check this box . . . . . . ▶ ☐
- If this is for a Group Return, enter the organization's four digit Group Exemption Number (GEN) .... If this is for the whole group, check this box . . . . . ▶ ☐ . If it is for part of the group, check this box . . . . . . ▶ ☐ and attach a list with the names and EINs of all members the extension is for.

4   I request an additional 3-month extension of time until ...., 20........
5   For calendar year ...., or other tax year beginning......................., 20....., and ending ...., 20........
6   If this tax year is for less than 12 months, check reason: ☐ Initial return ☐ Final return ☐ Change in accounting period
7   State in detail why you need the extension ....
  ....
  ....

8a	If this application is for Form 990-BL, 990-PF, 990-T, 4720, or 6069, enter the tentative tax, less any nonrefundable credits. See instructions.	8a	$
b	If this application is for Form 990-PF, 990-T, 4720, or 6069, enter any refundable credits and estimated tax payments made. Include any prior year overpayment allowed as a credit and any amount paid previously with Form 8868.	8b	$
c	**Balance Due.** Subtract line 8b from line 8a. Include your payment with this form, or, if required, deposit with FTD coupon or, if required, by using EFTPS (Electronic Federal Tax Payment System). See instructions.	8c	$

Signature and Verification

Under penalties of perjury, I declare that I have examined this form, including accompanying schedules and statements, and to the best of my knowledge and belief, it is true, correct, and complete, and that I am authorized to prepare this form.

Signature ▶ ....   Title ▶ ....   Date ▶ ....

Form **8868** (Rev. 4-2008)

Figure 14-4:
Form 8868,
Application
for
Extension of
Time to File
an Exempt
Organization
Return.

Your organization can file an amended return at any time. You have to make your amended return available for public inspection for three years from the date of filing or three years from the date the original return was due, whichever is later.

If you submit supplemental information or file an amended Form 990 or 990-EZ with the IRS, you should also send a copy of the information or amended return to any state with which you filed a copy of your original Form 990 or 990-EZ to meet that state's filing requirements.

State laws vary concerning their treatment of nonprofits. If a state requires your organization to file an amended Form 990 or 990-EZ to correct conflicts with the Form 990 or 990-EZ instructions, your organization must also file an amended return with the IRS.

Keeping in Line with IRS Regulations

Understanding and complying with the rules and guidelines pertaining to nonprofits is important to keeping your nonprofit, tax-exempt status. The board is responsible for ensuring the organization complies with accounting practices, as well as local, state, and federal laws. Nonprofit administrators look to the Internal Revenue Service (IRS) for guidelines regarding unrelated business income and the disclosure of relevant information about revenues.

The IRS granted your tax-exempt status, which relieves you from paying income taxes like those for-profit organizations pay. In exchange for your exemption, you're supposed to enjoy your tax-free status and not compete with for-profits. The IRS has a very detailed schedule (Schedule B to Form 990) for reporting and disclosing information about your donors. I address unrelated business income and donation disclosure in the following sections.

Reporting nonprofit unrelated business income

Before you decide to enter into a money-making venture, evaluate how the venture relates to your mission and how it may affect your nonprofit status. Income earned for activities outside the scope of an organization's tax-exempt purpose is called *unrelated business income (UBI)*. You should ask yourself three questions to determine whether income is unrelated business income:

✔ Is the income earned from a trade or business?

✔ Is the income earned from your regular daily operations?

✔ Is the income unrelated to the tax-exempt purpose of your charitable organization?

If you answer yes to any of these questions, two things could happen: Your nonprofit may owe income taxes, and it could lose its nonprofit tax-exempt status.

If you have more than $1,000 in gross receipts from the sale of goods and services unrelated to your nonprofit status, then you must file Form 990-T, Exempt Organization Business Income Tax Return, and you may have to pay income taxes on those receipts.

If your nonprofit receives 20 percent of its total income from a money-making venture, the IRS may declare your organization a for-profit entity, and you could lose your tax-exempt status.

To access more information from the IRS on tax-exempt organizations, visit its Web site at www.irs.gov/pub/irs-pdf/p598.pdf.

In addition to the federal requirements, you must stay abreast of your state and local laws about earning unrelated business income. Because state laws vary, I suggest that you visit the following Web site to find information about your state: www.irs.gov/charities/article/0,,id=129028,00.html.

Reporting nonprofit contributions

The Financial Accounting Standards Boards (FASB) establishes the standards (GAAP) for recognizing donations and contributions made or received.

The guidelines state that you should keep the following information about all contributions received:

✔ Pledges or promises to give should be recorded in the accounting records if they are deemed *unconditional* (not contingent on some uncertain future event).

✔ Donated services or in-kind contributions of volunteer time or specialized skills, such as those provided by accountants, medical personnel, computer technicians, and others, must be included in the financial statements.

  ✔ Name of person or organization giving the donation.

  ✔ Amount of the donation.

  ✔ Date of the donation.

Your auditor will use the information about your donors to verify contributions received.

You can review the FASB standards in the Financial Accounting Standard Board Statement Number 116, Accounting for Contributions Received and Contributions Made, by visiting the following Web site: www.fasb.org/pdf/fas116.pdf. Or see Chapter 9 for more information about FASB 116.

Part IV
Wrapping Up the Books

The 5th Wave   By Rich Tennant

"Isn't that our bookkeeper?"

In this part . . .

Having a viable set of financial records that reflect your true financial position is your goal. At the end of the year, you want to create a summary of all accounting activities for the current accounting period and prepare the accounts for the next one. Your statement of activities indicates whether you're operating in the black or red. Your statement of financial position shows your solvency versus liquidity. Your cash flow statement routes cash according to activity. Your statement of functional expense evaluates your expenses based on their functions. Finally, your notes to the financial statements summarize any significant changes to accounting methods and all contingent liabilities.

This part explains each of these financial statements in more detail and helps you create each one for your organization.

This part also covers the final step after your accounting period expires — taking your records and financial statements to an independent accounting firm to get an audit. This audit justifies whether your books have been presented according to generally accepted accounting principles (GAAP).

Chapter 15

Analyzing the Statement of Activities

In This Chapter

▶ Knowing what's reported on the statement of activities

▶ Comparing current revenues and expenses to prior periods and other nonprofits

*R*arely do financial disasters happen overnight. When I hear a news report about a nonprofit closing its doors due to lack of funding, I realize that the situation probably could have been avoided with proper financial oversight. Usually the *statement of activities* contains signs that, if properly evaluated, reveal the likelihood of trouble and ways to avoid disaster. Good financial managers use their statement of activities, also referred to as inc*ome statements,* as planning tools and indicators of future events. (For an introduction to the basics of the statement of activities, flip to Chapter 3.)

Information found on a statement of activities provides

✔ A summary of transactions, events, and circumstances that change an organization's net assets

✔ Information about the relationship between transactions and events

✔ How revenues are used to provide program services

By evaluating your statement of activities on a frequent basis, you know where your resources come from, how and when they flow, and how to set your course. Knowing how you're doing compared to what you've planned can help you make necessary changes. In this chapter I explain how to come up with the numbers on your statement of activities and how to use those numbers to strategically plan and carefully forecast and track your donations and expenses.

Understanding the True Meaning of the Statement of Activities

Your *statement of activities* is a summary of all the income that you've earned and every expense that you've incurred for a particular time period. It also shows whether your net assets or equity have increased or decreased over that time period.

Just like large corporations evaluate their expenses and make conscious efforts to downsize, you may need to consider doing the same thing when operating your nonprofit. Choosing what to cut and what to keep requires careful evaluation of your revenue sources, restrictions on those resources, and your expenses. In addition, you can compare planned expenses, just like you compare revenues, to keep your spending on track.

In a nutshell, your statement of activities (see Figure 15-1) indicates whether your nonprofit has extra money to operate with or whether your nonprofit is operating in a deficit position. (A *deficit* is a negative amount that means that you've used all of your revenues and them some, and you're in financial trouble.) Basically the statement of activities indicates whether you've had a good year (ending in the black) or a bad year (ending in the red).

You can use your statement of activities to evaluate ways to downsize or cut expenses and increase revenue streams. When created on a monthly or quarterly basis, your statement of activities can be used to

✔ Focus on peak periods when contributions are up

✔ Plan for the downtimes when contributions come in slowly

Knowing your peak periods and slow periods can help you plan to sustain your nonprofit during the slow periods.

Tracking your revenues and expenses on a monthly, quarterly, and annual basis helps you make better decisions about what expenses to keep and what to give up. When revenues decrease, most organizations look for ways to reduce expenses. As a general rule, most nonprofits try to keep administrative costs down to have more funds available for programs.

You'll need your *chart of accounts* to set up your statement of activities. This chart lists your ledger account names and numbers arranged in the order in which they appear in your financial statements. You use the account numbers instead of the account names when you put together financial statements. (For more about your chart of accounts, see Chapter 5).

Before you can fully use this important statement, you first need a firm grasp of what the statement of activities shows. The following sections reveal what information is found on this statement.

OASIS, Inc.

Statement of Activities

For Year Ended December 31, 20XX

	Unrestricted	Temporarily Restricted	Total
Revenue			
Contributions	$150,743	12,500	$163,243
Event income:			
Annual Conference	47,818		47,818
Mentoring Symposium	64,790		64,790
Special events	23,333		23,333
Christmas Gala	45,833		45,833
Total Event Income	181,774		181,774
Other Programs:	6806		6,806
Interest Income	550		550
Miscellaneous Income	36		36
Total Revenue	339,909	12,500	352,409
Expenses			
Program			
Mentoring Program	155,275		155,275
Tutoring Program	93,535		93,535
Total Program	248,810		248,810
Management and general	57,055		57,055
Fundraising	14,536		14,536
Total Expenses	320,401		320,401
Change in Net Assets	19,508	12,500	32,008
Net assets, beginning	102,992		102,992
Net Assets, End	$ 122,500	$ 12,500	$135,000

Figure 15-1:
A sample statement of activities.

Revenues

Basically, you have two types of donations to account for on the statement of activities:

- ✔ **Unrestricted support:** This money can be used for anything. For example, a donor gives $10,000 to your nonprofit and doesn't specify how you can spend the money.

- ✔ **Restricted support:** These donations have strings attached or imposed sanctions. When your nonprofit receives restricted gifts, you have a legal obligation to comply with the donor's restrictions. There are two types of restricted support:

  - **Temporarily restricted support:** The donor places a short-term restriction on the funds' use.

  - **Permanently restricted support:** The donor places permanent restrictions on the money's usage.

If your board of directors designates a portion of unrestricted support for a specific purpose, it may be called an *appropriation* or *board-designated support.* Board-designated funds aren't restricted in the same way as donor-restricted support. A board can change its mind and remove this self-imposed limit on some resource, but it can't change the limitation placed on resources contributed from an outside donor. Remember boards are inside the organization and they designate; donors are outside the organization and they restrict.

When all the conditions have been met and you've fulfilled the agreement or met the donor's requirements, restricted support is reported as *net assets released from restrictions.* You simply move the amount of the previously restricted funds from one category to another. For example, while the funds were restricted, they were reported as *restricted net assets;* when the restrictions are released, the funds are reported as *unrestricted net assets.* Your overall bottom line doesn't change. You've merely moved funds from one category to another by simultaneously increasing unrestricted net assets and decreasing restricted net assets.

To classify revenues on your statement of activities, you should list the totals from all accounts from your general ledger beginning with the number 4. These will include individual contributions, grant support, special events, ticket revenue, unrelated business income, in-kind contributions, and all other sources of income earned by your nonprofit. After you've listed all your income sources, add them up. In Figure 15-1, you can see from the trial balance how revenue accounts are identified.

When restrictions on gifts are met, the restricted support is simultaneously reported as an increase to unrestricted net assets and a decrease to restricted net assets in the revenue, gains, and support (income) section of the statement of activities.

Expenses

Your nonprofit incurs overhead (operating) and program expenses. Depending on your establishment, you may have program, general management, and fundraising expenses. You won't forget to include your expenses if you refer back to your chart of accounts and your general ledger.

You report all expenses on the statement of activities as decreases in unrestricted net assets. You do this by adding up all of your expenses and subtracting them from unrestricted revenues. For example, look at Figure 15-1 and notice how all the expenses are subtracted from unrestricted support only. The difference between revenues and expenses equals a change in net assets.

Gains and losses

Gains and losses come from activities that are incidental to an organization's central activities or from events and circumstances beyond the organization's control. Gains are reported in the revenue section and losses are reported in the expense section of the statement of activities. Gains increase net assets and losses decrease net assets. There are two types of gains or losses:

- ✔ **Realized gains and losses essentially come from transactions or events that have occurred.** The economic impact has happened and can be felt. A transaction example is the gain or loss from the sale or disposition of an organization's investments or some other asset it owns. You have a gain when you receive more than the asset's cost and a loss when you receive less than its cost. An event example is a loss from a fire where the fire caused a decrease in value of an asset.

- ✔ **Unrealized gains and losses come from the change in fair market value of investments that an organization holds.** The nonprofit hasn't sold the investments so there is no realized gain or loss. However, there has been a gain or loss in the value of the asset, it just hasn't been realized or felt because the asset hasn't been sold, the gain or loss is unrealized. Because GAAP requires investments to be reported at fair market value on the statement of financial position, you have to have a mechanism to reflect the economic change in the statement of activities, which effects net assets and therefore keeps the statement of financial position in balance. Whew, that's why there are unrealized gains and losses!

You record all gains and losses (realized and unrealized) recognized on the statement of activities as increases or decreases in unrestricted net assets unless their use is restricted by stipulation of the donor or by law. (For more on the treatment of gains and losses, see Financial Accounting Standard

Board Statement Number 117, www.fasb.org/pdf/fsp_fas117-1.pdf, and Financial Accounting Standard Board Statement Number 124, www.fasb.org/pdf/aop_FAS124.pdf.)

What this statement doesn't show

There are a few limitations to the statement of activities. You may have a few things of value that you may not be able to accurately measure or report on the statement. These include

✔ **Uncollectible accounts and pledges receivable:** They are assets and potential liabilities, and are reported on the statement of financial position. Changes in the estimate of the amount of uncollectible receivables changes revenue in the statement of activities, but the total value of the estimate is reported on the statement of financial position.

✔ **Accumulated depreciation:** Although you report the depreciation expense for any year on the statement of activities, you report the depreciation expense that has accumulated over the years on the statement of financial position as accumulated depreciation. Accumulated depreciation holds the write-off amount to keep the current value of a fixed asset accurately stated on the books. It reduces the carrying value of the fixed asset. (See Chapter 2 for more about depreciation.)

✔ **People's loyalty and devotion to your organization:** Even if someone tried to measure these attributes, it would be difficult to put a number on them.

Evaluating the Data

You can use your statement of activities to analyze more than just the total revenues earned and expenses incurred for a given period. For example, you can compare the following:

✔ Current month revenues and expenses to prior months

✔ Current quarterly revenues and expenses to prior quarters

✔ Current annual revenue and expenses to prior years

Depending on your scope of services, you can also use your statement of activities to

✔ Compare your data to similar organizations

✔ Track how economic conditions affect your contributions

✔ Evaluate changes in giving trends

- Position yourself to better focus on organization and program efficiency
- Identify programs or areas that need your immediate attention

You can also use information found on the statement of activities to figure out what percentage of your revenues come from

- Individual donors (private)
- Foundations
- Corporate sponsors
- Fundraising
- Grants
- Fees for program goods and services provided

Knowing where your resources come from can help you to assess your capability of generating future revenues.

I cover all of these topics in the following sections.

Analyzing revenues and expenses

The numbers alone on your nonprofit's statement of activities don't have much meaning. You want to analyze and determine the relationship of its parts and how the results affect your nonprofit.

To analyze the numbers on a statement of activities, you need to convert the numbers to percentages, which gives you a better idea of what percentage of revenues come from which sources and which categories of expenses are too high. When the dollar amounts are converted into percentages, it shows how significant the components of your income statement are. Then when you compare revenues and expenses, you can better understand the relationship between the two. Reducing numbers to a simpler form helps you discover the true relationship of the parts of the statement of activities to the whole.

Take a look at the following example, which shows how much money a hypothetical nonprofit collected:

Revenues Collected for 2009

Individual donors	$45,000
Corporate sponsors	$25,000
Foundation grants	$85,000
Government grants	$300,000
Fee for services	$45,000
Total revenues collected	*$500,000*

By converting these figures into percentages, you can evaluate the revenues much easier.

To calculate the percentage for each revenue collected, divide the amount by the total revenues collected. For example, take the $45,000 collected from individual donors and divide it by $500,000, which is the total amount of revenues collected ($45,000 ÷ $500,000 = 0.09 or 9%). This means that $45,000 is 9 percent of $500,000, so you know that 9 percent of the revenues came from individuals.

Be sure to double check your math by adding up the percentages. Your total should equal 100 percent.

The result of converting the revenues from each source into a percentage is shown in the following table:

Percentage of Revenues from Sources

Individual donors	9%
Corporate sponsors	5%
Foundation grants	17%
Government grants	60%
Fees for services	9%
Total revenues collected	*100%*

Based on these percentages, this organization is relying heavily on grants, to the tune of 77 percent of its revenues (17 percent from foundation grants plus 60 percent from government grants).

Although I wouldn't attempt to operate a nonprofit organization without grants because they're important to a nonprofit's funding, having this much money coming from grants can be a good or bad thing. If an aggressive grant writing campaign is ongoing, then it may be okay. But if the nonprofit isn't aggressively seeking new grants, then it's putting itself in a precarious position because grants aren't permanent sources of income. The nonprofit could be in danger of running low on revenues when the grants end. (For more information about applying for grants, see Chapter 10.)

Evaluating your expenses just like the revenues gives you a better indication of how much money is going to administrative, program, and overhead expenses. For more information about administrative expenses, see Chapter 18.

Determining change in net assets

A complete statement of activities indicates whether you've increased or decreased your net assets over a given period. Subtracting total expenses from revenues equals either a positive number or a negative number.

✓ A **positive number** means you've taken in more revenues than you have expenses. This is excess income, a surplus and you're "in the black."

✓ A **negative number** means your expenses are higher than your revenues. A negative number equals a loss, a deficit which means you're "in the red."

For example, if your total revenues are $100,000 and your total expenses are $95,000, then your change in net assets is a surplus of $5,000. But if your total revenues are $100,000 and your total expenses are $105,000, then your change in net assets is a $5,000 loss. ***Remember:*** Revenues − Expenses = Change in net assets

In the private sector, stockholders benefit from the difference between revenues and expenses by collecting dividends paid from the company's profits. In the nonprofit sector, *stakeholders* are the beneficiaries (your donors, as well as the people you help), and the money that's left after you've paid your expenses is reinvested in the nonprofit. When all revenues are collected and all expenses are paid, you need to have a *surplus* to stay afloat. Just because you're a nonprofit doesn't mean you don't need a positive difference between revenues and expenses.

Using the statement to make comparisons

As the world changes, so do your nonprofit's finances. Revenues go up and down; expenses go up (and sometimes down). You can use the data on the statement of activities to compare

✓ Current and historical amounts for your nonprofit

✓ Your nonprofit's finances to other nonprofits in the industry

Seeing how the numbers compare over time

You can compare numbers on your statement of activities on a monthly, quarterly, or annual basis. Looking back at previous time frames helps you gauge how well you're doing in the current period.

Comparing your current-year data to prior years shows trends and can help your nonprofit focus on important contributors (start with your donors list to see how much was given by whom) and high expenses. Of course, some expenses are probably up because of the changes in the economy, and there may be little that you can do to change that, but you may be able to offset other expenses. Take a look at Table 15-1, which compares current year revenues and expenses to prior years.

Table 15-1	Comparing Prior Year Data to Current Year				
	2009	*2008*	*2007*	*2006*	*2005*
Revenues	$500,000	$475,000	$450,000	$425,000	$400,000
Expenses	$450,000	$450,000	$425,000	$400,000	$390,000
Change in Net Assets	$50,000	$25,000	$25,000	$25,000	$10,000

Table 15-1 shows a comparative list covering five years of revenues and expenses and the change in net assets. If you take what's happening in 2009 and compare it to any other year, it gives you a bit more than just looking at the numbers. For example, consider revenues starting with 2005 and look at what was reported in 2009. If you divided the revenues from any year into 2009, it gives you a percentage of change. The same is true for the expenses. By dividing the numbers, you can see that the trend of revenues increased faster than expenses. It appears that expenses plateau from 2008 to 2009; I would investigate why to see if this is the start of a trend or a single occurrence.

Comparing your nonprofit to other nonprofits

Not a day goes by that the weatherman doesn't compare today's temperature with last year's temperature, or even last week's for that matter. A comparison of your nonprofit's finances to other nonprofits gives you something to measure and test your progress by.

Just like people can find your nonprofit's Form 990, Return of Organization Exempt From Income Tax, on the Internet, you can take a gander at other nonprofits' Form 990s too. You can look up your favorite charities and other nonprofits with operating budgets and programs similar to yours. Go to the following Web site: www.guidestar.org.

When comparing your nonprofit to others in the industry, you want to compare apples to apples and oranges to oranges; therefore, try to find a nonprofit of similar size and with similar programs in your city. That way you're both subject to the same economic conditions and environment. Of course, you first have to be around for a few years before these types of assessments and analysis can be compared.

Another factor to consider when comparing your statement of activities to another agency's statement is the accounting method used by the other organization. For example, if the other nonprofit uses the cash method and you're using the accrual basis, then this is not a good comparison. The primary difference in the two methods is timing recognition of revenues and expenses. For more detail information about these two methods, see Chapter 2.

Chapter 16

Reporting Financial Condition on a Statement of Financial Position

....

In This Chapter

▶ Knowing what the statement of financial position reveals

▶ Classifying assets and liabilities

▶ Using the numbers to analyze your position

....

Many experts feel that out of all the financial statements, the statement of financial position is the most important. The *statement of financial position* (also referred to as the *balance sheet*) provides a quantitative report of your organization's financial health. It demonstrates responsibility and accountability. It also monitors the progress of your organization and its financial condition.

This chapter walks you through this important financial statement and shows you how to use the numbers on your statement of financial position to analyze your nonprofit's financial health.

Grasping What the Statement Says about Your Nonprofit

The statement of financial position reveals what your nonprofit owns (the *assets*) and what it owes (the *liabilities*) as of a particular date. The difference between your nonprofit's total assets and total liabilities equals your nonprofit's *net assets* or net worth.

If you're a math person, you can think about what the statement of financial position shows in terms of the following equation:

Assets – Liabilities = Net assets

A statement of financial position reveals the overall value of your organization at a point in time. It shows your organization's *solvency* (its ability to pay its bills) and *liquidity* (how quickly assets can be converted into cash) at a particular point in time.

Internal users (such as board members, accountants, and managers) use the statement of financial position to get information about

- ✔ **Your nonprofit's ability to meet its obligations.** This is revealed by the amount of your current assets, which are used to meet your current liabilities. If your current liabilities are greater than the current assets, then people will wonder whether you're having cash flow problems, making it difficult to pay your debts.

- ✔ **Your organization's net assets (the difference between what is owned and what is owed).** You can find this information at the bottom of the statement of financial position. Net assets represent the net cumulative results of your nonprofit's changes in net assets over the years. You report the change in net assets for any year on the statement of activities; you report the ending net assets on the statement of activities on the statement of financial position. Net assets are the accumulation of surpluses and deficits over your nonprofit's history and help explain how you acquired some of your assets. You acquire assets by either borrowing money to buy them (liabilities) or by spending your own surplus funds (this amount is represented by net assets).

- ✔ **Your agency's progress and ability to continue to provide services.** Simply compare changes in balances from prior periods to the current period.

- ✔ **The need for external financing.** You're in this situation when your current assets won't cover current debts, or if your long-term assets can't be converted into cash in time to pay current liabilities.

- ✔ **The results of economic activity.** This is revealed by the overall financial results as displayed on the statement of financial position as of a certain date.

You can tell a lot about an organization by viewing how its finances are managed. External users (such as bankers, creditors, and private and public donors) use the statement of financial position to evaluate whether your nonprofit's financial position is stable enough to secure a loan or whether your nonprofit is worthy of their investments. These folks may also take an interest in the same information your internal users look at. Additionally, many grant proposals require you to include a copy of all financial statements, including the statement of financial position, with the proposal.

Although a statement of financial position is usually only prepared quarterly or annually, it represents a single point in time. It's subject to change overnight. So if you're having a board meeting and your financial condition has improved or declined significantly due to a large donation or an unexpected large expense, you'll definitely want to reveal the good or bad news by giving your board members copies of the updated statement of financial position.

Creating and Reading a Statement of Financial Position: The How-To

Doing your own statement of financial position is as easy as 1-2-3. The statement tells a story about your position and condition; it's an X-ray of your financial health. It's based on what you own (current and long-term assets), what you owe (current and long-term liabilities), and the difference between the two (net assets).

Creating your very own statement of financial position is simple to do. You can use your chart of accounts to help you identify which accounts should be included. (If you're not sure about your chart of accounts, see Chapter 5.)

Before you can create and read your nonprofit's statement of financial position, you need to know what the different numbers mean. Figure 16-1 shows a sample statement. As you read this section, follow along in this figure to see what the different numbers mean.

Understanding the statement's structure

The top of your statement of financial position should include the name of your nonprofit, the name of the statement (statement of financial position), and the date of the balances reported on the statement.

The statement of financial position is like a scale with two sides. It has a top half and a bottom half. The top half shows assets, and the bottom half shows liabilities and net assets; the two halves have to balance, which is why this statement is sometimes called a *balance sheet*. Take a look at Figure 16-1; the top half equals $175,000, and the bottom half equals $175,000, so everything at OASIS Inc. is balanced.

OASIS, Inc.
Statement of Financial Position
December 31, 20XX

Assets		
Current assets		
Cash:		
Checking Account	$	69,000
Mentoring Checking	$	22,193
Tutoring Checking	$	7,794
Money Market Account	$	13
Total Cash	$	99,000
Certificates of Deposit	$	66,500
Accounts Receivables	$	5,500
Total Current Assets:	$	171,000
Fixed Assets:		
Office Equipment	$	25,000
Less Accumulated Depreciation	$	(21,000)
Net Fixed Assets	$	4,000
Total Assets	**$**	**175,000**

Liabilities and Net Assets		
Liabilities:		
Accounts Payable	$	2,900
Deferred Revenue	$	37,100
Total Current Liabilities	$	40,000
Net Assets:		
Temporary Restricted	$	12,500
Unrestricted:		
Designated for Scholarships	$	45,000
Undesignated	$	77,500
Total Unrestricted	$	122,500
Total Net Assets	$	135,000
Total Liabilities and Net Assets	**$**	**175,000**

Figure 16-1:
A statement
of financial
position
shows your
nonprofit's
financial
position.

Every balance sheet has two main parts:

- ✔ **Assets:** Assets are always shown first on the statement of financial position. Adding all current assets to your fixed assets and other long-term assets gives your total assets. When you've reached your total assets, you've finished half of the statement.

- ✔ **Liabilities and net assets:** In this area on your statement of financial position, you add your current liabilities to your long-term liabilities to get your total liabilities. Notice in Figure 16-1 that this nonprofit doesn't have any long-term liabilities. This is good, because it means that it's not weighted down in heavy debt.

Net assets equals assets minus liabilities. Don't confuse assets with net assets. In Figure 16-1 the total net assets are $135,000.

One way to understand net assets is to compare it to your payroll check. You have gross pay (similar to your nonprofit's assets) less taxes and other deductions (your nonprofit's liabilities), which equals your net pay or the amount you take home (the nonprofit's net assets).

Underneath net assets, you find restricted and unrestricted net assets. Don't get bogged down with the rhetoric of temporarily restricted, permanently restricted, designated assets, and undesignated assets for this discussion. You only need to focus on whether they're restricted or unrestricted. *Restricted* simply means donors have imposed limitations or conditions on gifts that will be met at some future time, while *unrestricted* means there were no limits or restrictions on the resources, and you're free to use them however you'd like.

OASIS Inc.'s statement of financial position in Figure 16-1 shows total net assets of $135,000. The organization's net assets come from $12,500 in restricted net assets and $122,500 in unrestricted net assets.

To finish the bottom half of the statement of financial position you add your total liabilities of $40,000 to your total net assets of $135,000 to get your total liabilities and net assets of $175,000. Notice how this is the same amount of total assets at the top half of the OASIS Inc. statement of financial position. This is how total assets equals total liabilities plus net assets. You've just completed your statement of financial position. You're done!

A good checkpoint to remember is that total assets will always equal liabilities plus net assets.

Your statement of financial position is unique, and it shows what you own and what you owe. No two organizations will have the exact same statement of financial position. So don't worry if you don't have every line item listed on the statement shown in Figure 16-1.

Here I've covered the basics of the statement of financial position and how it has to always stay in balance. The following sections explain the different parts of the statement of financial position and what information to include in the different fields. Here you can see how to create your nonprofit's very own statement of financial position. When you're preparing your own statement, just relax and don't let the numbers throw you off.

Classifying assets

Assets are classified on the statement of financial position in the order of their liquidity. *Liquidity* means how quickly assets can be converted to cash. This section presents asset categories in the order they appear on a statement of financial position.

To come up with the figures for each category, you simply have to add up all the items under each category of assets and take that sum and place it on your statement of financial position.

Current assets

Current assets are those items that can be converted into cash within a year. Current assets are usually listed in the following order:

- ✔ **Cash:** Checking and savings account balances (Because cash is the most liquid type of asset, it's listed first.)

  Petty cash should be included in the cash category.

- ✔ **Marketable securities:** U.S. Treasury bills, certificates of deposit, stocks and bonds

- ✔ **Grants and accounts receivables:** Expected to be collected within the year

  Grants and accounts receivables may also be listed under long-term assets, depending on whether the money will be received in the current period or future periods.

- ✔ **Prepaid expenses:** Prepaid rent, prepaid insurance, and supplies on hand

Long-term assets

Long-term assets are also referred to as *noncurrent assets,* which includes fixed assets. *Long-term assets* are items that you can't convert into cash within a year. Long-term assets consist of the following:

- ✔ **Investments:** In the form of bonds, stocks, and real estate that you don't intend to sell within a year.

- ✔ **Property, plant, and equipment:** Land, buildings, and equipment.

- ✔ **Intangibles assets:** Copyrights, patents, trademarks, trade names, customer lists, and other assets that you own, have cost you money to obtain, and are probably worth more than what they cost you. They're called *intangible* because they usually don't have a physical presence, and there is uncertainty concerning their future benefits.

- ✔ **Other assets:** Anything that's not classified in the other areas.

When talking about long-term assets, you may hear the term *capital expenditures.* These are purchases of fixed assets, renovation costs, equipment, buildings, land, and so on. Often with these purchases you'll owe a payment to a lender for multiple periods. Generally if you buy something that is useful for more than one year, the cost should be capitalized. Capital expenditures are classified as plant, property, and equipment on your statement of financial position.

Net fixed assets

Net fixed assets equals the price of an asset minus the accumulated depreciation. Your *accumulated depreciation* is the total depreciation expense charged to assets over the years. (See Chapter 2 for more information about depreciation.)

Assets are recorded on the statement of financial position at their original cost less depreciation except for investments, which are recorded at fair market value. Your depreciation expense is listed on your statement of activities, but to show the office equipment at its true value on the statement of financial position, you have to subtract the accumulated depreciation amount from the cost. Figure 16-1 shows office equipment purchased at a price of $25,000 less $21,000 (accumulated depreciation) for a value of $4,000.

Total assets

Total assets are your current assets plus long-term and net fixed assets. Your total assets include cash in your bank accounts, CDs (certificates of deposit), accounts receivables, and the value of all equipment and any other long-term assets you have. It's important that you know how much readily available cash you have on hand in order to meet your current obligations on time.

To calculate your total assets, you need to add all current assets to all long-term and net fixed assets. For the balance sheet in Figure 16-1, the total assets are $175,000. The total current assets are $171,000, and the net fixed assets are $4,000.

Classifying liabilities and net assets

Knowing your nonprofit's liabilities is important because you need to have assets available to pay your obligations. Have you ever heard someone say, "We're not broke, but our assets are tied up"? This means the organization doesn't have anything it can quickly and easily convert to cash to cover what it owes. You need to have current assets to meet your current liabilities (liabilities can also be categorized as long term). Not having current assets available to pay the bills can cause serious cash flow problems for your nonprofit.

Furthermore, by identifying your nonprofit's net assets, you can see pretty quickly how stable your organization is. The difference between your total assets and total liabilities gives a quick snapshot of your nonprofit's sustainability. Net assets are the same as net worth for a person, and the two are calculated the same way (total assets minus total liabilities).

In the notes to your financial statements, you should disclose information about the maturity of assets and liabilities and all restrictions on their usage. (See Chapter 19 for more info.)

Current liabilities

Current liabilities represent items that will be paid off within one year. Current liabilities require your nonprofit to have current assets for their payment. Some common current liabilities include the following:

- ✔ **Accounts payable:** These include credit card payments or purchases from vendors on credit.

- ✔ **Salaries payable:** This category is for salary expenses incurred but not yet paid at the end of the period.

- ✔ **Payroll taxes:** These are payable for state and federal taxes owed on salaries.

To identify your current liabilities, just take a look at your chart of accounts. Of course, the specific financial information can be found in your ledger. Just add the totals to get your total current liabilities.

In Figure 16-1, there are two current liabilities, accounts payable and deferred revenue, which total $40,000. (*Deferred revenues* are payments received in advance before a service or product is delivered. Sometimes people will make an annual donation prior to the year to be used. Sometimes these are called *refundable advances.*)

Long-term liabilities

Having too much debt can be risky business. To determine how much of this risky debt your nonprofit has on its books, you can look at the long-term liabilities on the balance sheet. *Long-term liabilities* represent obligations that will be paid in future periods. Some common long-term liabilities are

- **Notes payable** for mortgages and land payments.
- **Equipment payable** for vehicles and heavy-duty copy machines.
- **Bank loan payable** for money borrowed for working capital. *Working capital* is the difference between current assets and current liabilities, and it measures an entity's ability to meet its short-term debts. I explain how to figure this amount in the "Calculating working capital" section later in this chapter.

To come up with long-term liabilities, add up the amounts for all obligations that you owe that aren't due or payable within a year. These consist of long-term debts, such as mortgages, vehicles, heavy machinery, and so on. In Figure 16-1, OASIS Inc. has no long-term debts.

Net assets

Net assets are essentially what you're worth or the difference between your total assets and your total liabilities. Net assets can be classified as restricted or unrestricted, and your donors determine whether net assets are restricted or not; if donors choose to restrict their gifts, they set the terms and length of the restrictions.

In the for-profit world, *retained earnings* is the net difference between liabilities and assets on the balance sheet. In the nonprofit world, we have net assets. First, you should consider the beginning balance in net assets plus or minus current period net assets to get the ending balance of net assets.

Asset accounts (statement of financial position accounts) aren't closed at the end of the accounting year. Statement of financial position accounts are considered real or permanent accounts. The only accounts that are closed are revenue, expense, and income summary accounts.

When preparing financial statements, you always prepare the statement of activities first, because you close the end results of revenues minus expenses to net assets.

There is a direct relationship between what happens on the statement of activities and the statement of financial position. Your end results from the statement of activities accounts (revenues – expenses = increases or decreases in net assets) is transferred to your statement of financial position. This is why the statement of activities is the first financial statement prepared. You can't prepare the statement of financial position until after you have the difference between revenues and expenses.

You need to report your net assets on your statement of financial position. They help keep the statement of financial position (balance sheet) in balance. You calculate and report the beginning net asset balances, the change in those balances, and the ending net asset balances on the statement of activities. These ending net asset balances also appear underneath liabilities on the statement of financial position.

In the OASIS Inc. statement of financial position in Figure 16-1, you see temporary restricted net assets of $12,500 and total unrestricted net assets of $122,500 for total net assets of $135,000.

You can double-check yourself when calculating your net assets by thinking of net assets as the difference between total assets (listed on the top of the balance sheet) and total liabilities. The total assets are $175,000, and the total liabilities are $40,000. Therefore, OASIS Inc.'s total net assets are $135,000 ($175,000 – $40,000 = $135,000). As with all equations, if you have two parts, you can figure out the third number. Also double-check that the net asset balances on the statement of activities agree with the balances on the statement of financial position.

Restricted net assets

Sometimes donors make contributions but place some restrictions on how and/or when the money may be used. These contributions are called *restricted contributions* and create *restricted net assets*. Donors may restrict the money for a wide variety of functions, including to buy a new building, start a new program, or build an endowment. Your donors will tell you if a gift is restricted when they give it to you. It's your responsibility to honor the terms of the gift and to keep accurate records of how you manage the gift.

You need to report on the statement of financial position or in the notes to the financial statements whether donors have imposed restrictions on contributions. Two types of restrictions are:

✔ **Permanently restricted net assets:** The donations in this category generally are used to provide a permanent source of income for your nonprofit. Some donors place conditions on their gifts that prohibit the sale of the contributed asset or that it can be used only for a certain purpose. Some gifts may require you to set up an endowment fund. An *endowment* is a transfer of money or property with a requirement that it be invested and the principal stays intact for a certain period of time.

✔ **Temporary restricted net assets:** These assets may have time or purpose restrictions or both. For example, your donor may tell you that the asset can only be used to support a specific program, invested for a specified term, used at a designated future period, or used to acquire a long-term asset. If a donor gives a gift that has both time and purpose restrictions, it's often referred to as a *term endowment.*

Your donors list is a good starting point to find these nest eggs. In the statement of financial position in Figure 16-1, you can see that OASIS Inc. has $12,500 in temporary restricted net assets.

Borrowing from restricted assets can cause you to lose the entire contribution.

Unrestricted net assets

Unrestricted net assets arise from gifts and other revenue that have no restrictions on their use, or from restricted gifts whose restrictions have been met. Unrestricted income is like gold. It has no pre-imposed terms and generally can be used immediately for anything you want. Some boards place self-imposed or board-designated endowments on themselves. This creates a class of unrestricted net assets called *designated unrestricted net assets.* Make sure the board designations are disclosed in the notes to the financial statements.

In the OASIS Inc. statement of financial position in Figure 16-1, you see total unrestricted net assets of $122,500.

If your nonprofit receives donated gifts with restrictions that limit their usage to long term, you can't classify them with cash or other assets that are unrestricted. It's important that you show available assets and those intended for future use and not mix the two. Normally the assets with use restrictions placed on them are reported in the long-term section of the statement of financial position with the heading assets restricted as to their use. The use descriptions should be disclosed in the notes (see Chapter 19). Readers of your nonprofit statement of financial position need to know what's available to you and what's not.

Total liabilities and net assets

To complete the statement, you need to add together the total liabilities and the total net assets. This number should match the number of the total assets line on the top half of your statement of financial position.

In Figure 16-1, OASIS Inc. has liabilities of $40,000 and net assets of $135,000. When you add the two figures together, you get $175,000, the exact same amount as the total assets. Success!

Evaluating the Numbers

There is more to your statement of financial position than just the numbers or total amount of assets, liabilities, and net assets. Accountants take the numbers from this statement to evaluate how well you're doing. You can do the same: Think of this evaluation of your nonprofit's statement of financial position as a financial checkup.

You can get a sense of whether your organization is in good financial shape just by looking at the lines for total assets and total liabilities and net assets.

If the number on the top half (total assets) of the statement is less than the total liabilities number on the bottom half, you have a problem. How long your problem lasts, or if it worsens, depends on your nonprofit's plans for the future. Some problems are only temporary. For example, you may have experienced unbudgeted increases in expenses. Maybe a water pipe burst and caused you to slip into a different position.

The statement of financial position is always referred to as of a given date because your financial condition is subject to change from day to day and by unplanned circumstances.

The statement of financial position reveals your organization's ability to pay its bills. It also plays a part in determining what interest rate you pay when using credit cards or borrowing money. By analyzing current assets and current liabilities, you can figure out how much cash is on hand to pay liabilities. You can study your nonprofit's financial position and get a crystal-clear picture of how your nonprofit is doing by using the statement of financial position to

✔ Compute working capital

✔ Analyze your debt-paying ability

Internal and external users of your balance sheet are interested in evaluating your financial health. Bankers, vendors, investors, donors, board members, constituents, accountants, and executive directors can easily evaluate your financial position by making a few simple computations. They look at your working capital and debt-to-equity ratio to determine whether to lend you money, issue credit cards, or charge higher interest rates.

This section shows you how to analyze your financial position and how to compute debt-paying ability and working capital.

Calculating working capital

Working capital is the difference between current assets and current liabilities. Working capital indicates how much money you have available after paying your current liabilities and your ability to cover other obligations that may arise in the future. Creditors use working capital to determine interest rates.

To figure out your nonprofit's working capital, you subtract the total current liabilities from the total current assets.

Take a look at Figure 16-1. The total current liabilities for the year are $40,000, and the total current assets are $171,000. Subtracting the total current liabilities from the total current assets gives you a working capital of $131,000 ($171,000 – $40,000 = $131,000).

Working capital is the amount you have left after you've paid your bills. If you have excess working capital, it means you can cover your current liabilities and have cash left over for other needs. Some may call working capital *excess cash.* Excess cash is like spare change.

Calculating a debt-to-equity ratio

Creditors use the numbers on your statement of financial position to determine what percentage of your total assets is used to pay your liabilities. One of the most commonly used ratios is the debt-to-equity ratio. A *debt-to-equity ratio* is total debts (liabilities) divided by total assets. This number shows the percentage of your nonprofit's assets financed by debt. A high number signals that your nonprofit may not be able to pay its bills when they're due. The higher the number, the more highly you are leveraged.

Looking at Figure 16-1, OASIS has a total of $175,000 in assets and a total of $40,000 in liabilities. To calculate the organization's debt-to-equity ratio, you divide the total liabilities by the total assets. The math comes out to 23 percent ($40,000 ÷ $175,000 = 0.23). This is a low debt-to-equity ratio.

Having a low debt-to-equity ratio is a good thing. Anything over 50 percent is considered risky.

Chapter 17

Eyeing the Cash Flow Statement

*T*he cash flow statement is one of the major financial statements required by generally accepted accounting principles (GAAP). This statement basically reveals the inflow of cash to an organization and the outflow of cash from an organization. *Cash inflows* are cash receipts that come from operating, financing, and investing activities. *Cash outflows* are cash payments for operating, financing and investing activities.

The information found on the cash flow statement gives users an idea about your organization's ability to generate positive future cash flows, its ability to pay debts, and a summary of sources (inflows) and uses (outflows) of cash. The cash flow statement is a better indicator of this than the statement of activities because the statement of activities reports transactions on the accrual basis not the cash basis. (See Chapter 15 for more about statements of activities.) In this chapter, I explain the importance of the cash flow statement, how it indicates a nonprofit's ability to pay its debts, and how you can create it and use it to make decisions based on your need for available cash.

Seeing What the Cash Flow Statement Can Tell You about Your Nonprofit

The cash flow statement provides important information about your nonprofit. This statement answers questions about your nonprofit with information not found on other financial statements. It reveals how your organization's growth and expansion were financed. It also identifies cash amounts from operations, selling and acquiring securities, purchasing and selling capital assets, and financing activities with creditors. Your cash flow statement can cover your monthly, quarterly, and annual cash inflows and outflows.

Almost every transaction in an organization affects cash. *Cash* includes balances in your checking and savings accounts, as well as currency and coins. *Cash equivalents* include short-term investments that are quickly and easily turned into a known amount of cash and are so near to maturity that changes in interest rates won't effect their value. Examples of these types of investments are treasury bills, commercial paper, and money market mutual funds.

You can improve your cash flow by keeping cash in an interest-bearing account or buying certificates of deposit.

Using the statement to see the big picture

The cash flow statement summarizes where your cash came from and where it went during the period. Donations of cash, checks, credit card contributions, money collected from fundraising, and grants received from all sources are considered *cash inflows*. *Cash outflows* are all purchases made with cash, payments for salaries and payroll taxes, and outlays paid with cash during the period.

To have a *positive cash flow* means that your inflow exceeds your outflow. One major problem most organizations have is the timing of the cash flow. Unfortunately, cash inflows (revenues) tend to lag behind outflows (expenses), creating a shortage of cash or a *negative cash flow*.

This statement also shows cash flow divided into categories. This is helpful to board members and other users because it breaks down cash inflows and outflows for the differing types of transactions. The statement of cash flow enables users to

- Understand how an organization obtains and uses cash
- Analyze the short-term viability of an organization; it reveals an organization's liquidity or solvency
- Evaluate changes in statement of financial position accounts (assets, liabilities, and net assets; see Chapter 16 for more on these)
- Compare current information to prior statements
- More accurately predict amounts and timing of future cash flows

The cash flow statement does have some limitations. This report doesn't tell the full story of your organization's financial condition; it only explains how your cash balance has changed.

The cash flow statement differs from the statement of financial position and statement of activities because it shows the cash flows of activities during the reporting period. Another difference is that the statement uses the cash basis of accounting, meaning that transactions are recorded when cash is received or paid. Other financial statements reflect the accrual basis of accounting, whereby revenues are matched with expenses in the period earned or incurred, not when cash changes hands. (See Chapter 2 for more information about these two accounting methods.)

Making decisions based on the statement

You should use the cash flow statement along with the statement of financial position and statement of activities when making long-term financial decisions for your nonprofit. Many believe the statement of financial position is the most important financial statement, but you can own millions in assets and have no cash to pay your current liabilities. The statement of activities may include restricted gifts that are outstanding, such as pledges to give. All financial statements indicate performance, and the cash flow statement is sometimes overlooked because many people don't know how to use it.

Proper use of a cash flow statement can help you determine the following:

- ✔ If you need to borrow money
- ✔ When you can make major purchases
- ✔ When you need to consider downsizing

You know what happens when an organization can't pay its debts. It defaults on creditors, borrows money, files for bankruptcy protection, or uses a combination of all three. You can use cash flow ratios to get an early warning about potential cash flow problems in your organizations. I explain two important ratios in the "Analyzing cash flow indicators" later in this chapter.

Understanding How to Create and Use a Cash Flow Statement

The cash flow statement is closely related to what happens in your organization's checkbook. To fully understand the cash flow statement, you must know the extent to which your organization relies on the cash it generates and the extent to which it relies on investments. You should view the cash flow statement alongside your nonprofit's other financial statements (see the other chapters in Part IV for the statements to have) to get the total picture of your nonprofit's financial standing.

The following sections identify the different parts of this statement and explain how to read it so you can fully understand your organization's cash flow status. If you're interested in creating your own cash flow statement, I provide you with some hands-on direction to get you started.

Getting the statement started

Before you can begin creating your organization's cash flow statement, you need to have a battle plan. How do you plan on preparing the statement? You have two basic methods to choose from. Both methods classify and report cash receipts and payments from three activities: operating, investing, and financing activities. Both methods report cash flows from investing and financing activities in exactly the same manner, but they differ from how they report cash flows from operating activities:

✔ The *direct method* reports operating cash receipts and disbursements, such as cash received from donors or from providing services, and cash paid to employees or vendors. *Cash receipts* are what you have coming in; *disbursements* are what you have going out. The net total of these operating receipts and disbursements is *net cash flow from operating activities.* This method focuses on operating cash receipts and payments. Many believe knowing the sources of operating cash receipts and the reasons for making operating cash payments is more useful than just knowing the organization's change in net assets. They also believe knowing operating cash receipts and disbursements from prior periods can help predict future operating cash flows. But the cash flow statement is hard to prepare using this method if your books are kept on a running accrual basis. If you keep your books on the cash basis all year long and post accrual adjustments at the end of the year, using this method shouldn't be too difficult. But books with transactions recorded on the accrual basis have to be adjusted to be reported on the cash basis. Your other choice of methods, the indirect method, adjusts accrual basis records to the cash basis.

✔ The *indirect method* begins with the change in net assets (net income, see Chapter 16 for more on net assets) and makes accrual to cash adjustments for revenues and expenses that didn't arise from the receipt or payment of cash during the reporting period. This method focuses on the differences between changes in net assets (net income) and net cash flow from operating activities. Many users believe that the change in net assets, when adjusted to net cash flow from operating activities, is a more useful predictor of future cash flows than operating cash receipts and payments

GAAP encourages using the direct method, but it allows you to use either method. However, even if you choose to use the direct method, GAAP requires an additional disclosure reconciling the change in net assets to net cash flows from operating activities, which is what the indirect method does.

In practice, almost everybody uses the indirect method. For most organiza tions, the cash flow statement is easier to prepare using the indirect method. And if you use the direct method, you must use the indirect method to reconcile the change in net assets to net cash flow from operating activities. Finally, you don't need the direct method to determine operating cash receipts and payments. You can usually determine specific operating cash flows by using information from the statement of financial position and statement of activities.

Identifying the parts of the statement

To completely grasp the cash flow statement and what it can tell you about your organization, you need to be able to identify its parts. The statement has three sections (see Figure 17-1):

✔ Cash flow from *operating activities* includes operating revenues received and operating expenses paid in cash. If it isn't an investing or financing activity, its an operating activity.

✔ Cash flow from *investing activities* includes cash paid for acquiring and cash received from selling securities and/or assets.

✔ Cash flow from *financing activities* includes obtaining cash from creditors, repaying creditors, and receiving donations with long-term donor restrictions.

Cash flow from operating activities	
Receipts:	
Contributions	157,148
Events Receipts	214,820
Other Receipts	7,475
Total Receipts	379,443
Cash Disbursements	–313,020
Net cash provided by operating activities	**66,423**
Cash flow from investing activities	
Purchases of Fixed Assets	–2,363
Investment in term endowment	–12,506
Net cash used by investing activities	**–14,869**
Cash Flow From Financing Activities	
Contributions restricted for	
investment in endowment	12,506
Principal Payments on Mortgage	–8,716
Net cash provided by financing activities	**3,790**
Net Increase in cash	**55,344**
Cash and cash equivalents, beginning of year	43,656
Cash and cash equivalents, end of year	**$ 99,000**

Figure 17-1: An example of a cash flow statement.

e math

hows, you use the cash flow amounts from three categories to
rganization's cash flow. You add the totals for each section
r organization's increase or decrease in cash for that
organization has net cash provided by operating activities
net cash used by investing activities of –$14,869, and net cash
provided by financing activities of $3,790 to give you a net increase in cash
of $55,344. *Remember:* Parentheses and dashes are negative numbers.

You also have a beginning cash balance from the previous period that you
can use to see how your cash flow has changed over a longer period of time
(the beginning cash balance for a period is actually the ending cash balance
for the previous period). The difference between the beginning cash balance
from the previous period and ending cash balance from the current period
is the net increase or decrease in cash between the two periods.

The cash flow statement yields your organization's change in cash, then the
statement adds the change in cash to the organization's cash balance at
the beginning of the year (last year's ending cash balance) to arrive at
this year's ending cash balance. This year's ending cash balance should equal
the cash balance in the current asset section of the organization's statement
of financial position. This is because the balances on the statement of
financial position are end-of-year balances, so end-of-year cash on the statement of financial position should equal end-of-year cash on the statement
of cash flows.

If you report cash and cash equivalents on the statement of financial position, then the statement of cash flows will show the change in cash and cash
equivalents instead of just cash. The statement still yields the change in cash,
but it adds the change to cash and cash equivalents at the beginning of the
year to get cash and cash equivalents at the end of the year.

The following sections break down these three parts and explain how you
can use these numbers to your advantage.

Operating activities

The operating section of the cash flow statement reports how much money
was collected from operating activities. Remember, if it isn't financing or
investing, then its operating. Nonprofits depend on gifts and contributions
from individuals, corporations, foundations, and government entities. Some
may generate revenue by charging a small fee for the services they provided,
but for the most part, they rely heavily on fundraising activities to raise
the necessary funds for operations. Check out the operating activities part of
the cash flow statement in Figure 17-1. Note that all of the activity here is
reported on the cash basis.

Your cash receipts and cash disbursements (payments) are recorded in your checkbook register. (***Note:*** When I say cash, I'm talking about checks too.) Your checkbook register serves as a cash disbursements journal and a summary cash receipts journal. It's a summary cash receipts journal because only the total cash deposited is recorded in your checkbook register. You keep the detail for your cash deposits in other registers called journals. You can have receipts journals for any kind of income, contributions, special events, grants, and so on. When you receive money, you post the receipt to a receipts journal. The total receipts recorded in the journal is posted to the cash account and related income account (*double-entry accounting*) in the general ledger. If you're using accounting software, the program keeps these journals and does the posting for you.

At the end of each month, you should post the totals from your various cash receipts journals and your cash disbursements journal to the cash (and other) accounts in the general ledger. You summarize each journal by adding the columns, and then use that summary to develop entries to post to your general ledger. (For more about journals and ledgers, see Chapter 5.) The totals in Figure 17-1 would be taken from the activity posted to the cash account in the general ledger, and using the detail for this cash activity found in the cash receipts and cash disbursement journals, amounts are transferred to the cash flow statement. To get your net cash provided by operating activities, add your total receipts for operating activities and subtract your total disbursements for operating activities.

Investing activities

The investment section of the statement of cash flows reveals amounts used to sell or buy securities and to purchase and/or sell property, plant, or equipment. Take a look at the cash flow from investing activities in Figure 17-1. (Note: *Endowments* are transfers of money or donations of property with requirements that the investment principal remains intact.)

Reflected in this section is your investment of the gifts restricted for endowment into your endowment fund. Also listed in this section are your purchases of fixed assets. If you had sold some fixed assets, then the proceeds would have been listed here as well. In our example, you received $12,506 in gifts restricted for investments in endowments (reported in the financing activities section) and you invested the $12,506 in term endowments (reported in the investing activities section). You also used $2,363 to purchase fixed assets yielding $14,869 of net cash used by investing activities. Remember, you get this detailed information from the receipts and disbursement journals that make up the total amounts posted to the cash account in the general ledger.

Financing activities

Financing activities are essentially borrowing money, repaying the debt, and receiving gifts with long-term donor imposed restrictions. Typical long-term credit instruments are mortgages and notes payable. When you borrow money, you receive cash from financing activities, and when you make loan payments you use cash for investing activities. Typical gifts with long-term restrictions are contributions for long-term endowment funds.

You find these amounts in your activity posted to your debt accounts in the general ledger. These numbers were first recorded in your cash disbursement journal (also known as your checkbook journal), and then posted to the cash, debt, and interest expense accounts (remember double-entry accounting) in the general ledger. Take the total amounts posted to the debt accounts in the general ledger and transfer them to the statement of cash flows.

Check out the financing activities section in Figure 17-1. The amounts in this section of the cash flow statement reflect principal payments on the organization's mortgage and the total received from donors' gifts restricted for endowments. (Your restriction is to use the proceeds from the investment and not to touch the principal.) In this example the organization repaid $8,716 of principal on its mortgage, and received gifts restricted for endowment of $12,506, resulting in net cash provided by financing activities of $3,790. If you had borrowed some money, you would have reported the amount of cash received here as well.

One last thing, if you take out a loan to buy some long-term asset and you never receive the cash (think mortgage loan), this transaction will not appear on your cash flow statement because you didn't receive or disburse any cash. However, this non-cash financing activity must be disclosed in your financial statement notes (see Chapter 19).

Analyzing Cash Flow Indicators

Cash flow ratios are used to evaluate an organization's ability to pay its current liabilities given its current assets. Knowing this number tells you how likely it is that your organization can continue to support itself.

If you're experiencing problems meeting your current obligations, you need to call an emergency board meeting. Your board can help you remedy this problem. Some cash flow problems are temporary and can be resolved with a short-term loan. If you think your cash flow problems are more significant, you may want to hire a CPA to help you foresee future cash flow problems.

Although you can calculate several ratios from the cash flow statement, for this discussion, I focus on two of the most important indicators: operating cash flow ratio and free cash flow. The following sections take a closer look at them.

Financial ratios are only meaningful if a reference point is used. You should compare them to historical values and similar organizations. Ratios should be viewed as indicators, and some are limited by different accounting methods.

Calculating the operating cash flow ratio

The *operating cash flow (OCF) ratio* evaluates whether an organization is generating enough cash to meet its short-term obligations.

To calculate the OCF ratio, grab your statement of financial position (see Chapter 16) to get the total current liabilities at the end of the period. Then you divide the net cash flow from operating activities (taken from your cash flow statement) by the current liabilities. Here's the equation:

> Operating cash flow ratio = Net cash flow from operating activities ÷ Current liabilities

For example, Figure 17-1 shows net cash flow from operating activities of $66,423; the total current liabilities is $40,000 (taken from Figure 16-1 in Chapter 16). Dividing $66,423 by $40,000 equals 1.6606. This number is the operating cash flow ratio for OASIS Inc.

When you calculate a ratio, you measure performance. This result indicates whether an organization can sustain itself. As a general rule, a ratio below 1.0 indicates potential problems with paying short-term debt. It signals a need to hold a fundraiser, sell some stock, slow down on spending, tap into your reserves, or borrow money. Any ratio above 1.00 is considered safe for most organizations.

Determining free cash flow

Free cash flow (FCF) tells you how much money you have after paying your bills, including paying for investments in capital assets. I consider this spare change.

To calculate free cash flow, you need to grab your cash flow statement (see Figure 17-1). You subtract cash used for purchases of fixed assets (its in the investing activities section) from net cash flow from operating activities (in the operating activities section of the cash flow statement). Here's the equation:

> Free cash flow = Net cash flow from operating activities – cash used for purchases of fixed assets.

For example, net cash flow from operating activities is $66,423 and cash used for purchases of fixed assets is $2,363. So you subtract $2,363 from $66,423, which equals $64,060.

Many organization's include debt payments made for loans that were taken out to buy fixed assets. If you do this with this example, you also subtract the cash used by principal payments on mortgage (it's in the financing activities section of the statement of cash flows). This is the amount of cash you have after paying all of your operating expenses and your payments for fixed assets. This cash is available for paying other debt and any other investments or expenditures the organization wishes to make. So, for this example, you subtract $2,363 and $8,716 from $66,423, which equals $55,344. This number is excellent. Based on the information provided, OASIS Inc. is stable and has sufficient funds to meet its financial obligations as of the end of the year.

The lower your amount of free cash flow, the less money you have to pay for other debts and other nonoperating activities. If it's zero or negative, you might have cash flow problems! Free cash flow indicates amounts of cash available for expansion of programs, facilities, or endowments. Obviously more is better.

Chapter 18

Organizing the Statement of Functional Expense

Your *statement of functional expense* reveals by line item and category how much you've spent for the different categories of expenses reported on the statement of activities — program costs, management and general expenses, and fundraising expenses. Basically, this statement is an itemized list providing detailed information about the expenses reported on the statement of activities. Overall, it measures your organization's efficiency in fulfilling its mission; it shows how well you've used your funds for their intended purposes.

Right now, the folks who make up the American Institute of Certified Public Accountants (AICPA) are having lengthy discussions about the need for providing a statement of functional expenses. Presently it's only required for certain organizations (voluntary health and welfare groups), but all nonprofits are encouraged to create one. Knowing how much it costs to run your organization and to put on fundraising events is valuable information to have.

In this chapter, I look at how expenses are divided by function into three categories and how to use the numbers to measure efficiency.

Classifying Functional Expense

Your challenges as a nonprofit executive director or manager are to address the needs of your constituents, pay your organization staff, and keep administrative costs down, all while running effective programs. To do so, you can rely on the statement of functional expense. To fully use this statement, you need to know how to classify your organization's expenses.

You classify expenses according to function to measure how well you're doing. In other words, you're figuring out how much of the donors' money is used to run programs versus being spent on other things. Your statement of functional expense breaks down all organization costs by function into three main categories:

- Program expenses
- Management and general expenses
- Fundraising expenses

Sometimes a fourth category, membership development, is reported. This category is used by some larger membership organizations, but most organizations report membership development with their fundraising costs.

Doing the statement of functional expense is a simple task. Take a look at the statement of activities in Chapter 15. See how the expenses are broken down by program, management and general, and fundraising expenses? If you prepare your statement of activities in this manner, you've already done your statement of functional expense (see Figure 18-1).

Keeping track of time

Allocating time and matching it with the correct programs aren't mere suggestions when it comes to federal grant programs. It's required that all employees who are paid from grant funds document their time and attendance. If your nonprofit receives any grant money, you're required to use this statement to record in detail your time expense.

One way to track and allocate employee expense among the categories is by keeping track of how much time is spent doing what. If you make a habit of writing down how you spend your time every day, it removes the guesswork.

If you're like most nonprofits, your agency has three types of workers:

- Employees who are ineligible for overtime pay (paid on salary)
- Employees eligible for overtime pay (paid hourly)
- Unpaid volunteers

The best way to properly allocate expenses is to have staff and volunteers fill out *time and attendance reports (T&A reports)* that indicate which program to charge. Time and attendance reports are also called *time sheets*. They indicate how an employee spent her time. Time sheets also reflect which program or fund will pay the employee's salary.

OASIS, Inc.
Statement of Functional Expense
For Year Ended December 31, 20XX

	Program		Management & General	Fundraising	Total
	Mentoring	Tutoring			
Advertising	400		1,100		1,500
Awards	11,000				11,000
Bank Service Charges			200		200
Board Meeting			3,000		3,000
Speaking Contest	5,500				5,500
Mentor's Sports Day	13,000				13,000
Conference Registration	700	700	600	300	2,300
Credit Card Fee			1,500		1,500
Depreciation	350	350	650	150	1,500
Dues and Subscriptions	700	700	1,250	300	2,950
Equipment	50	50	30	20	150
Interest				5	5
Liability Insurance			900		900
Marketing			400		400
Miscellaneous			600		600
Payroll Taxes	4,500	4,500	1,600	800	11,400
Postage and Delivery	700	700	630	250	2,280
Mentorship Training	17,500				17,500
Mentor's Retreat	12,500				12,500
Printing and Publication	5,000	5,000	650	275	10,925
Rent	2,300	2,300	800	300	5,700
Mentoring Project	8,000				8,000
Tutoring Project		9,500			9,500
Salaries	57,000	57,000	23,000	10,000	147,000
Sponsorship	4,100				4,100
Supplies	300		390		690
Professional Services			1,700		1,700
Telecommunications	1,600	1,600	1,400	400	5,000
Travel	8,800	10,100	11,300	700	30,900
Web Site			3,300		3,300
Totals	$ 154,000	$ 92,500	$ 55,000	$ 13,500	$ 315,000

Figure 18-1:
Sample statement of functional expense.

You should ask each employee to keep a log of how she spends each hour of her workday. She should also record time off for holidays, weekends, sick days, and vacation time. The time and attendance report should be filled out to coincide with your nonprofit's pay period, signed, and dated by the employee. Then you or the employee's supervisor should review, sign, and date the report as verification of the employee's time. This report can be used to allocate the employee's personnel expenses to the various functional categories.

Keeping time and attendance reports yields the following benefits:

- ✔ Helps settle disputes about an employee's pay
- ✔ Creates a paper trail for auditors
- ✔ Verifies how federal dollars are spent
- ✔ Provides a way for management to keep up with employee costs
- ✔ Provides a basis for allocating personnel costs to functional categories

Time and attendance reports are mandatory for employees paid out of federal grants. Federal grants program managers require these reports because they give accountability and add credibility to how the money has been used. Plus, signed time and attendance reports provide documentation for audit use.

Keep completed time and attendance reports with your grant files. Program managers may ask to see them during a monitoring visit or audit. The timesheet in Figure 18-2 displays how to document and track your and your employees' time.

SSN: 000-00-0000		NAME: **Mary Smith**					PERIOD ENDING: **1/15/09**				
DIVISION: Executive Division			EMPLOYEE BASE: Montgomery, AL								

Month January	1	2	3	4	5	8	9	10	11	12	COMP TIME	TOTAL
Tutoring		2.00	1.00	2.00	3.00	2.00	3.00					**13.00**
Mentoring		2.00	2.00	1.00	1.00	2.00	3.00					**11.00**
Fundrasing		3.00	2.00	1.00	1.00	2.00	1.00					**10.00**
General		1.00	3.00	4.00	3.00	2.00	1.00	8.00	8.00	8.00		**38.00**
TOTAL DIRECT HOURS		8.00	8.00	8.00	8.00	8.00	8.00	8.00	8.00	8.00	0.00	**72.00**
ANNUAL LEAVE												0.00
SICK LEAVE												0.00
HOLIDAY LEAVE	8.00											8.00
PERSONAL LEAVE												0.00
MILITARY LEAVE												0.00
COMP LEAVE												0.00
OTHER												0.00
DAILY	8.00	8.00	8.00	8.00	8.00	8.00	8.00	8.00	8.00	8.00	0.00	**80.00**

Mary Smith 1/15/09   *James Oliver* 1/15/09
EMPLOYEE   DATE   SUPERVISOR   DATE

Figure 18-2: A simple timesheet helps you track employees' hours.

You can also ask volunteers to fill out a time and attendance report. If a volunteer donates professional services (such as legal or accounting services) that your nonprofit would otherwise have to pay for, you can account for the volunteer's time as an in-kind donation.

Allocating expenses

The expenses listed on your statement of functional expense are ordinary, day-to-day expenses and cover a wide variety of expenses, including, but not limited to, advertising, awards, conference registration, credit card fees, equipment, marketing, and so on. Any of the many expenses your nonprofit incurs may be charged to program costs, management and general costs, and/or fundraising costs. You just need to make that determination.

Your list of expenses may be different than another nonprofit's because each organization is unique, but overall, every bill paid should be allocated to one of the three categories. Of course, some expenses benefit all three categories. Some may only be charged to one or two. When expenses apply to more than one category, your bookkeeper can allocate an equal share of expenses to the appropriate categories. Some expenses, such as marketing, may be split equally, especially if you're advertising all the programs and services offered by your nonprofit.

Some high-tech devices, such as copiers or printers, can allocate expenses based on actual usage. For example, you can have your copier or printer set up to assign codes to each program and person. Then, each time something is photocopied or printed, the copier or printer matches the expense to the program or person. So when you're making copies of a fundraising event flyer, your copier can assign the cost of printing to fundraising expense.

To help you have a clearer grasp of the three main types of functional expenses, the following sections break them down and help you differentiate between them so you know how to classify them on your statement of functional expense.

Program expenses

Your programs are used to implement your mission. *Program expenses* are the costs of goods and services used to fulfill your purpose and to operate your projects. Some common programs are

- Food pantries and soup kitchens
- Mentoring programs

✔ Tutoring programs

✔ Support groups

Of course many programs benefit people, so these are just a few examples. Program expenses are expenses directly related to a program. Common program expenses are

✔ Supplies

✔ Wages of people working solely or directly for a program

✔ Personnel costs related to the program's direct employees

The total program expense on the statement of functional expense should equal the program expense reported on the statement of activities. The totals for administrative and fundraising expenses should also agree with those amounts reported on the statement of activities.

If an expense is incurred by two or more programs, you can divide it equally by the programs that benefited. For example, consider the cost of labor (salaries, payroll taxes, and fringe benefits). This is usually a high expense for nonprofits. By using time and attendance reports, you can divide the expense up by the hours spent working on each program (see the "Keeping track of time" section earlier in the chapter).

Management and general expenses

The second classification of expenses on the statement of functional expense is *management and general expenses (M&G)*. These costs aren't identifiable to any program, fundraising, or membership development activity. That is, they aren't directly related to an activity nor are they reasonably allocable to an activity. These expenses represent costs that are shared by all activities and are necessary for the organization's operation. Some expenses are general overhead costs of operations like rent and utilities. These costs provide an indirect benefit to your organization as a whole, and you incur them whether you run one or three programs.

Management and general activities include

✔ Accounting staff

✔ Business management

✔ Insurance

✔ Legal expenses

✔ Payroll taxes

✔ Rent/Mortgage

✔ Salaries

✔ Travel

✔ Utilities

✔ Administrative activities of the organization as a whole

For example, you use the phone in your office for day-to-day business. You wouldn't go out and buy a new phone just to operate a new program and to keep expenses separate. You use the phone you have to make the calls needed about the new program, and you allocate a portion of the phone bill to all programs that benefit from its use.

You may be allowed to charge a portion of your M&G to your grants. If you have programs funded by government grants, you may have an allowance for administrative expenses of 5 percent or more that can be allocated to the grant. If you have an *indirect cost rate* (a rate given to government grant recipients for running grant programs), you have an acceptable rate already computed for you. (For more on indirect cost rates, see Chapter 10.)

Your T&A reports are the best way to allocate expenses for salaries and fringe benefits to the right category. Finally, your operating budget separates program costs from M&G and fundraising costs. See Chapter 8 for more about operating budgets.

If you can't identify the cost as a program or fundraising cost, then it's automatically a M&G cost. Make sure the total M&G on the statement of functional expense matches the M&G amount on the statement of activities.

Fundraising expenses

The third group of expenses on the statement of functional expense is for fundraising. You're fully aware of how important fundraising is to your organization. You seek philanthropists who will donate money, goods, services, time, and effort to support your cause with no quid pro quo. Keeping track of the expenses related to fundraising is important to help you determine whether your efforts at raising money are working and whether you're spending money in the right areas.

Fundraising activities include

✔ Advertising and direct mail campaigns

✔ Maintaining donor mailing lists

✔ Conducting fundraising events, including dinners and dances, concerts and fashion shows, sporting competitions, and auctions

✔ Preparing and handing out fundraising materials

✔ Conducting other activities involved with soliciting contributions from individuals, organizations, foundations, corporations, and government entities

The cost of all activities that create support for your nonprofit in the form of gifts, grants, contributions, and services are considered fundraising expenses. Some fundraising expenses stand out. For example, the cost of a direct mail campaign is easy to allocate to fundraising expenses because you know how much postage was used, how many envelopes were mailed, and how many copies you printed.

Many of the fundraising activities held by some nonprofits aren't considered fundraising events by the IRS. According to the IRS, fundraising events don't include

- ✔ Sales of gifts or goods or services unless they're of nominal value (*nominal value* is less than real or market value)

- ✔ Sweepstakes, lotteries, or raffles where the names of contributors or other respondents are entered in a drawing for prizes

- ✔ Raffles or lotteries where prizes have only nominal value

- ✔ Solicitation campaigns that generate only contributions

If need be, check with your accountant to verify you're classifying the expenses correctly.

A new method is emerging to conduct fundraising campaigns over the Internet. This new wave is called *ePhilanthropy,* and it allows you to solicit funds from your Web site, even while you're sleeping.

Using the Statement of Functional Expense to Calculate Ratios

Potential donors typically like to give money to organizations where they know their money is being spent wisely. They sometimes calculate how much of your total expenses are used for programs versus how much is used for management and general expenses. Face it: No one wants to give to an organization and have his gift squandered. You can use the statement of functional expense to show your donors exactly how your nonprofit is spending its money and that you're using your donations to help the people you're trying to reach.

To show how you use your funding, you can calculate different ratios that provide insight into your organization's operating performance and financial position. You calculate ratios to measure your nonprofit's organizational efficiency. The total expenses alone don't give a clear picture of your efficiency, but calculating ratios gives the numbers more meaning. (To calculate a ratio, you divide one number by another number. Ratios indicate the relationship of one thing to another.)

Ratios are only as good as the numbers used to calculate them, so make sure the figures on your statement of functional expense are accurate.

By figuring the ratios in the following sections, you can show that your donors' contributions aren't being used to pay high salaries and other extravagant expenses. You can ideally advertise that your nonprofit has low administrative and fundraising costs. As a general rule, you want to keep your administrative and fundraising costs down and spend donations on their intended purpose of running programs.

Program spending ratio

The *program spending ratio* tells you what percentage of your total spending goes toward programs. Having your program expenses broken down by percentages gives the statement of functional expense more meaning. It allows people to get a quick overview of how much of their donations support programs.

To calculate the program spending ratio, you divide total program expenses by total expenses. Refer to Figure 18-1 to see the two categories for program expense, mentoring and tutoring, for this example.

The total allocated to the mentoring program is $154,000. The total program expense for the tutoring program is $92,500. The total program expense is $246,500.

The total expenses for the year are $315,000. The program spending ratio is 78 percent ($246,500 ÷ $315,000 = 0.78). This means that 78 percent of your total expenses are used to run programs.

Overall you're better off with a high program spending ratio because donors want to fund programs, not the administrative and fundraising costs to operate your nonprofit. If the percentages in this example were the other way around, you probably wouldn't get too many donations if only 22 percent of the total expenses supported programs. Of course, sometimes there's room for exceptions. If you're renovating or upgrading your building, you'll have something to show for the disparity.

Fundraising efficiency ratio

The *fundraising efficiency ratio* tells what percentage of dollars were spent to raise another dollar. Nonprofit managers have a challenging job to raise capital while keeping costs down. This ratio is important because donors like their money to go directly to the programs they're supporting.

You divide fundraising costs by total contributions to get your fundraising efficiency ratio. (You need to refer to your statement of activities to get the total contributions for the year; see Chapter 15 for more on the statement of activities.) To calculate the fundraising efficiency ratio, consider the following hypothetical scenario.

If you received $425,000 in contributions and your fundraising costs were $13,500, your fundraising efficiency ratio is 3 percent ($13,500 ÷ $425,000 = 0.03). It only costs 3 cents to raise a dollar.

A 3 percent fundraising efficiency ratio is considered a good ratio because it shows that you're keeping fundraising costs down. A bad ratio depends on what your board and stakeholders expect from you. Larger organizations can have a higher ratio, but small nonprofits should strive to keep this number as low as possible.

Chapter 19

Closing the Nonprofit Books

In This Chapter

▶ Knowing why you need to close the books

▶ Completing year-end entries

▶ Including notes with your financial statements

As you come to the end of your fiscal year, you need to wrap up your books for previous 12 months and start the books for the next year. Your *fiscal year* may be on a calendar year from January to December or some other 12-month period. No matter when your fiscal year ends, you need to close your books and start a new accounting cycle or year. To do so, you have to make some closing entries to certain accounts. Closing your books is an important process because you need to transfer the balance from statement of activities accounts to another account, so that only statement of financial position accounts remain open.

When you close your books, you need to make sure all of your temporary accounts, such as your revenue and expense accounts, have zero balances so revenues and expenses in the next accounting cycle can be properly recorded and closed.

This chapter discusses how to close the temporary accounts (revenue and expense), how to make some of the necessary notes to your financial statements, how to do reversing entries, how to make the necessary adjustments to your accounts, and how to prepare your books for the next accounting period.

If you're using a manual system, closing the books may turn out to be a little more work than if you were using accounting software because computerized systems close the accounts for you. Regardless of which system you use, you need to understand the procedures to end one accounting period and begin another.

Understanding the Need to Close Your Nonprofit's Books

During the course of the year, you've had money coming in (revenues) and money going out (expenses). This is a continuous cycle that will always take place in your organization. At the end of your fiscal year, you have completed an accounting period and need to close the year.

You close the books to determine your nonprofit's income or losses for the year. If you don't close your books, you have no ending to your accounting period. Without closed books you have no new beginning. Your accounting period had a beginning date and an ending date. At the end of the accounting period, you tab up the totals and prepare financial statements and then move onto the next accounting period.

After your books are adjusted, you can prepare your trial balance and then your financial statements. At this point you can also close your books. After your financial statements are done, you turn your information over to a CPA for an independent audit. But you can't prepare accurate financial statements until your books are adjusted, and you can't start a new accounting period until your books are closed.

To understand how to close the books, you have to know the difference between temporary and permanent accounts:

- ✔ **Temporary accounts:** Revenue and expense accounts are considered temporary accounts. They increase as the year progresses. These accounts are ones you close out at the end of the accounting cycle. The closing process resets these accounts to zero so that only increases for the current accounting period are accumulated in the accounts.

  You find these accounts in the general ledger; they're reported on the statement of activities (also called the *income statement;* see Chapter 15 for more about this statement). They include all revenue you received and every bill you paid for that year. These accounts record your organization's income and expenses.

- ✔ **Permanent accounts:** These accounts are also found in the general ledger and reported on the statement of financial position (also called the balance sheet; see Chapter 16 for more about this statement). They carry over from year to year, so you don't need to worry about closing these accounts. But, you do close your temporary accounts to a permanent account.

When you close the books, you transfer the balances of your revenue and expense accounts to an income summary account. (I explain the particular steps of closing out the books in the following section.) Remember, the balances for all your accounts; revenues, expenses, assets, liabilities, and equity are in you general ledger. An *income summary* account records the closing of expense and revenue accounts for a given period (12 months, in the case of closing the books at the end of the fiscal year).

The income summary account is closed to a statement of financial position account called net assets. The *net assets* account as shown on your statement of financial position is the net assets at the end of year from your statement of financial activities. The difference between total revenues and total expenses gives an increase or decrease in net assets. The net assets at the beginning of the year is added to the increase (decrease) in net assets to give the net assets at end of year. The statement of financial position shows the net assets at the end of year as net assets. The purpose of closing entries is to transfer revenues and expenses to the net asset account.

Closing entries accomplishes two things:

- ✔ **It causes all expense and revenue accounts to begin the new accounting period with zero balances.** Each accounting cycle needs to show performances that took place only during that period. Revenue and expense accounts are only used temporarily to store your accounting activities. After the accounting period ends, you transfer the results of everything that transpired during that cycle to the income summary account.

- ✔ **It transfers the net effect of the past period's revenue and expense transactions to an equity account.** During your accounting cycle you made purchases, you received support and revenue, and you paid bills. Now that this accounting period has expired, you only need to reflect the effect of the activities that happened in it. So by closing revenue and expense accounts to the income summary, the income summary reflects the net effects of your revenues and expenses. This net effect is transferred to an equity account by closing the income summary to net assets.

Adjusting, Closing and Reversing Entries

During your year-end closing process, you'll probably need to adjust some of your accounts to correct some balances and make cash to accrual adjustments. After you've made your adjusting entries, you can prepare an adjusted trial balance which you'll use to prepare your financial statements. Then you need to make closing entries to close your income and expense accounts to the income summary, and close the income summary to net assets. Finally, at the beginning of the next accounting period, you may want to reverse some of the cash to accrual adjustments you made at the end of the previous accounting period.

The following sections walks you through the actual closing process including when you may have to reverse and adjust some entries at year end.

Adjusting entries: Year-end

Adjusting entries are necessary to end the reporting period and to record unrecognized revenues and expenses incurred during the accounting period. When a transaction begins in one accounting period and ends in a later one, adjusting entries are required. Also, adjusting entries are done to make corrections due to mistakes made during the year. These type of adjusting entries are also called *correcting entries*.

Adjusting entries are journal entries that are recorded in a journal called the general journal. You post these entries in chronological order. The general journal is where you post various entries for events that affect accounts but aren't part of the normal transaction process or are somehow special or unusual. Examples are closing entries, correcting entries, and other adjusting entries,

Certain accounts require adjustments at the end of your accounting period due to their nature, like prepaid expenses. Certain things like differing bases of accounting and time-period concepts will require account adjustments. *Prepaid expenses* are assets until they're used in the operation of your organization. Things such as subscriptions to journals or magazines, insurance, and so on are considered prepaid expenses.

Using different bases of accounting may require adjustments if you've kept your books on the cash basis throughout the year because your financial statements must be presented on the accrual basis according to generally accepted accounting principles (GAAP). The cash basis reports revenues and expenses when they're received or paid. GAAP require assigning revenues to the periods in which they're earned and expenses to the period in which they are incurred. Adjusting entries can be made to make cash to accrual adjustments.

When accounts like payroll overlap accounting periods, they require special consideration. The entire adjustment process is based on revenues being recognized in the accounting period in which they are earned and expenses recognized in the period they were incurred.

Say the mortgage payable balance in your general ledger is $4,900 and your interest expense is $900. But your notice from the bank says your mortgage balance is $5,000 and the interest you paid for the year was $1,000. You would make the following entry to correct (adjust) the balances in your general ledger (to increase an expense you debit it and to increase a liability you credit it):

Date		Debit	Credit
20XX			
Dec 31	Interest expense	100	
	Mortgage payable		100

To adjust mortgage payable and interest expense to bank's records.

Or suppose you get paid every two weeks but the end of the year falls right in the middle of the two-week period. Wages for the first week were $2,000. Accrual accounting requires you to recognize the payroll expense when it was incurred, not when it is paid. So to post an adjustment:

Date		Debit	Credit
20XX			
Dec 31	Wages expense	2,000	
	Wages payable		2,000

To accrue the last week's wages for 20XX.

Here's an example for a cash to accrual adjustment. Assume there is a zero balance in accounts payable at the end of the year. However, in early January, you receive a $50 telephone bill for the month of December, which you pay in January. The expense was incurred in December, so the accrual basis of accounting requires you to recognize the expense in December not January. To do this you post the following entry:

Date		Debit	Credit
20XX			
Dec 31	Telephone expense	50	
	Accounts payable		50

To post accounts payable at 12/31/XX

When you record the payment in January, you either debit accounts payable in your cash disbursements journal or debit telephone expense if you reversed the cash to accrual adjustment at the beginning of the year. I talk about reversing entries later in this chapter.

To make the adjustments, at the end of each accounting period or year, you prepare a worksheet called a Working Trial Balance. This worksheet allows you to see what will appear on your financial statements. Follow these steps:

1. **Begin your working trial balance with your unadjusted trial balance.**

   This is the listing of your account balances in the general ledger before you have posted your year-end adjustments to these accounts (first two columns).

2. **Post your adjustments to the accounts (third and fourth columns) and list your adjusted trial balance (columns five and six), which is your unadjusted account balances with your adjusting entries taken into account.**

   The account balances in your adjusted trial balance should equal the balances in the general ledger once you have posted your adjustments to the general ledger. Figure 19-1 shows an example.

Saltwell Community School Work Sheet for Month Ended December 31, 20XX											
	A) Unadjusted Trial Balance		B) Adjustments		C) Adjusted Trial Balance		4) Income Statement		5) Balance Sheet	
Account Titles	Dr.	Cr	Dr.	Cr.	Dr.	Cr	Dr.	Cr.	Dr.	Cr.
Cash	325				325				325	
Prepaid Insurance	1200			50	1150				1150	
Office Supplies	60			23	37				37	
School Library	1440				1440				1440	
Office Equipment	3440				3440				3440	
Account Payable		380				380				380
Unearned Day Care Fees		1500	125			1375				1375
Net Assets		3950				3950				3950
Day Care Fees Earned		1950		125		2175		2175		
				100						
Rent Expense	500				500		500			
Salaries expense	700		105		805		805			
Utilities Expense	115				115		115			
Insurance Expense			50		50		50			
Office Supplies Expense			23		23		22.5			
Depreciation Exp Sch Bks			40		40		40			
Accum Depre Sch Books				40		40				40
Depreciation Ofc Eqp			63		63		62.5			
Accum Depre Ofc Eqp				63		63				63
Salaries Payable				105		105				105
Account Receivables			100		100				100	
TOTALS	7780	7780	505	505	8088	8088	1595	2175	6492	5913
Net Income								580		579
							2175	2175	6492	6492

Figure 19-1: Worksheet.

After all adjustments are made to your books, you should do an adjusted trial balance to verify that everything balances. Your *adjusted trial balance* is the difference between the unadjusted trial balance and your trial balance after adjustments. Take a look at Figure 19-1 to see how the adjusted trial balance helps you complete your financial statements.

When your trial balance is balanced, you can complete your financial statements. All you have to do is move the information from your worksheet into the correct categories on your financial statements. Check out the chapters in Part IV to help you put together the different financial statements you need. Now all you have to do to finish closing out your year is post your closing entries.

Closing entries: A 1-2-3 step

To close out your accounting period, you need to make three important closing entries: one for expenses, one for revenues, and a final one for the income summary. You can't do the income summary without the other two. The steps are as follows:

1. **Close expense accounts.**

   Your expense accounts are found in your general ledger, each one has to be reset to zero. To close an expense account, you need to decrease it or zero it out by doing a credit (**Remember:** Expense accounts have a normal balance of a debit.) Expense accounts are closed by credits equal to the total account's debit balance. To close, you write a closing entry in the general journal listing all the expense accounts such as this:

Date		*Debit*	*Credit*
20XX			
Dec 31	Income summary	WW	
	Telephone expense		XX
	Supplies expense		YY
	(Keep listing expenses)		ZZ

   To close expense accounts to the income summary.

   Note in this example the total of all the credits to the expense accounts equals the debit to the income summary. So for this example, XX + YY + ZZ = WW. Closing the expense accounts transfers the total of expenses to the income summary.

2. Close revenue accounts.

Your revenue accounts are also found in the general ledger and you have to reset each one of them to zero. To close a revenue account, you need to decrease it or zero it out by doing a debit. Revenue accounts have a normal balance of a credit, so you close it out by making a debit equal to the account's credit balance. To close a revenue account, follow this example:

Date		Debit	Credit
20XX			
Dec 31	Contributions	WW	
	Program fee income	XX	
	(Keep listing revenues)	YY	
	Income summary		ZZ

To close expense accounts to the income summary.

In this example the total of all the debits to the revenue accounts equals the credit to the income summary. So for this example, WW + XX + YY = ZZ. Closing the revenue accounts transfers the total of revenues to the income summary.

3. Close the income summary account.

Your income summary account is a temporary account in the general ledger set up to close the revenue and expense accounts. The balance in the income summary equals the total expenses (debits) posted to the account in step one netted against the total revenues (credits) posted to the account in step two. If the income summary has a credit balance, then you had a surplus (increase in net assets) for the year. If it has a debit balance, then you had a deficit (decrease in net assets) for the year. So the last step is to transfer the balance from the income summary to net assets by closing the income summary to net assets. The entry looks something like this:

Date		Debit	Credit
20XX			
Dec 31	Income summary	XX	
	Net assets		XX

To close the income summary.

Notice in this example there was a surplus for the year because I had to debit the income summary to close it. If I had to debit the income summary to close it, then there was a credit balance in the income summary, which means revenues exceeded expenses. If in this scenario, the debits had exceeded the credits, a deficit would have resulted, showing that expenses were more than revenues.

The income summary account is closed to your net assets account on your statement of financial position.

Reversing entries to close temporary accounts

Some accounts tend to overlap the accounting period. For instance, if your accounting period ends December 31 and payroll isn't paid for this period until January 15, the money employees receive in January is for work performed in December. This is considered an *overlap,* and adjustments need to be made at year-end to make sure salaries are charged to the right year.

If you keep your books on the cash basis during the year and make cash to accrual adjustments at the end of the year for your financial statements, you need to reverse those cash to accrual adjustments (the *overlapping* revenue or expense adjustment) at the beginning of the next year. If you don't, then you'll count the overlapping revenue or expenses twice: once in the period you made the cash to accrual adjustment (placed the transaction in the right period), and again in the next period when you receive the accrued revenue or pay the accrued expenses. Reversing the accrual entry subtracts the revenue or expense that was accrued and recognized in the previous period and it eliminates the amount accrued to the related asset or liability account on your statement of financial position

A reversing entry is easy, you record it in the general journal. You debit what was credited and you credit what was debited in your year-end cash to accrual adjustment. Remember the example for an adjusting entry for December's $50 telephone bill received and paid for in January? Well we moved the expense from January into December by making the following adjusting entry:

Date		Debit	Credit
20XX			
Dec 31	Telephone expense	50	
	Accounts payable		50

To post accounts payable at 12/31/XX

I moved the expense into from one period into another. If you run your books on the cash basis in January and don't make any reversing entries, you recognize $50 of telephone expense when you pay December's phone bill in January. You'd end up counting it twice, once in December and once in January. You'll also still show $50 in accounts payable even though the bill has been paid. That's because accounts payable is found on the statement of financial position and is a permanent account; it is not reset to zero at year end. So to prevent all this from happening you post a reversing entry:

Date		Debit	Credit
20XX			
Jan 1	Accounts payable	50	
	Telephone expense		50

To reverse previous year's telephone accrual

See how the accounts payable balance has been eliminated? A $50 debit netted against a $50 credit equals zero. But what about telephone expense? Expenses are temporary accounts that are closed to zero at the end of the year so where is the $50 debit to offset the $50 credit of the reversing entry going to come from? It comes from your cash disbursements journal when you pay the $50 phone bill in January.

So you reverse all of the previous year-end's cash to accrual adjustments. Don't reverse all of the adjustments. Some adjustments correct balances and shouldn't be changed. Some expenses, like depreciation, aren't paid with cash, and so those entries wouldn't be reversed. But entries that move income or expenses from one period to another need to be reversed if you run your books on the cash basis and make year-end accrual adjustments.

Completing the Notes to the Financial Statements

The *notes* (also referred to as *footnotes*) to your financial statements provide additional valuable information about your financial picture that can influence the overall judgment about your organization's future. According to generally acceptable accounting practices (GAAP), all financial statements should contain notes of disclosure (see Figure 19-2 for an example).

OASIS, Inc
Notes To Financial Statements
December 31, 2010

NOTE 1 - Organization and Summary of Significant Accounting Policies

Organization
The OASIS, Inc is a nonprofit organization established under Section 501 (C) (3) of the Internal Revenue Code. The OASIS' purpose is to mentor and tutor middle school children by providing a positive adult role model. The Organization conducts its own programs of mentoring and tutoring within the public school system.

Basis of Accounting
The accompanying financial statements are presented using the accrual method of accounting.

Information regarding the financial position and activities are classified into the applicable classes of net assets: unrestricted net assets, and temporarily restricted net assets.
Unrestricted net assets – these are net assets without donor-imposed stipulations.
Temporarily restricted net assets – net assets that may or may not be met by actions of OASIS and/or the passage of time.

In addition, expenses are classified into mentoring and tutoring program service expenses, management and general and fundraising expenses.

Certain funds have been designated by the Board of Directors for specified purposes. These funds have appropriately been included in the unrestricted net asset classification.

*Currently, OASIS does not have any assets that are permanently restricted.

Accounting Estimates
The preparation of financial statements in conformity with generally accepted accounting principles requires management to make estimates and assumption that affect the reported amounts of assets and liabilities and disclosure of contingent assets and liabilities at the date of the financial statements and the reported amount of revenues and expenses during the reporting period. Actual results could differ from those estimates.

Fixed Assets
Fixed assets are recorded at cost or estimated fair market values at the date of donation. Depreciable assets are being depreciated using the straight-line method over the estimated useful lives of three years.

Contributions
Contribution of noncash assets are recorded at their fair value at date of donation. Contributions received are recorded as unrestricted or temporarily restricted, depending on the existence and/or nature of the donor's gift. If restrictions are fulfilled in the same time period, as the contribution, the donation is reported as unrestricted.

Donated Services
The OASIS has many volunteers throughout the year. Time and values of these services are been tracked, but have not been reported, pending status and passage of Statement of Financial Accounting Standards (SFAS) No. 116.

Functional Allocation of Expenses
The costs of providing the various programs and other activities have been summarized on a functional basis in the statement of activities. Accordingly, certain costs have been allocated among the program and supporting services benefited.

Income Taxes
The Organization is exempt from federal income tax under provision of Section 501 (c) (3) of the Internal Revenue Code. No provisions for income taxes have been provided in the statements.

Funds held as agent
The Organization has acted as a fiscal agent for several other organizations in the past. In prior years, these funds were classified on the statement of financial position as a liability.

Cash and cash equivalents
Cash and cash equivalents are defined as cash on hand, checking accounts, interest bearing money market accounts and certificates of deposit with initial maturities not exceeding three months.

NOTE 2 **Contingencies**

The OASIS participates in grant programs assisted by various government agencies. Those programs are subject to financial and compliance audits by the grantors or their representatives, the purpose of which is to ensure compliance with condition precedent and subsequent to the granting of funds. According to management, any liability for reimbursements which may arise as the result of these audits is not believed to be material.

Figure 19-2:
A sample notes of disclosure.

The following sections give you a better idea of what to include in the notes to your nonprofit's financial statements, how to disclose changes in accounting methods, and how to divulge ongoing lawsuits that your stakeholders need to know about.

Folks inside and outside your nonprofit review your financial statements to figure out how well your organization has done and is doing. However, many consider the notes to financial statements more important than the financial statements themselves because the notes explain things that the numbers can't. Think of your notes as the written story behind the numbers.

Explaining changes in accounting methods

Indicating the accounting method is usually contained in the first note written to your financial statements. Your notes outline the various accounting methods that you've used to prepare your financial records.

Changing accounting methods in the middle of your accounting period can have an adverse effect on your bottom line or income. All changes that bear a significant effect on your reported income or make changes to it should be disclosed.

Some common accounting methods disclosed in your notes are

- ✔ **Inventory methods chosen to record value and cost:** Your chosen inventory method sets the price that you used to value your inventory. You may have recorded it at the cost you paid for it, or its current market value. Whichever method you used should be indicated in the notes to the financial statement. Also, you should disclose in the notes when you make changes.

- ✔ **Depreciation method or writing off of assets:** *Depreciation* is the writing off as an expense the cost of an asset over its useful life. Because depreciation reduces net assets, changing your depreciation method affects your income. Depreciation can present a favorable outcome if you have less expense or an unfavorable outcome if you have more expense.

Within these methods, you can select from various methods that are acceptable policies. So if last year's statements were prepared using a different method, they may not be comparable with the current year's statements. Financial managers like to compare apples to apples and oranges to oranges, but changes to accounting methods will cause you to compare apples to oranges. Even though they're both fruits, they're pretty different. You need to disclose any changes in your accounting methods and the financial impact of those changes in your footnotes.

For example, think of the relationship between your statement of activities and your statement of financial position. Your statement of activities records all expenses and revenues. Your statement of financial position records all assets, liabilities, and equity. The difference between revenues and expenses are closed out to the statement of financial position as an increase or decrease in net assets. So if you change the accounting method for any account tied to an expense, the change in method makes a difference in your net assets.

Two principles shed some light on changes in accounting methods.

- ✔ **The Full Disclosure Principle:** This principle states that investors and creditors have every right to information relevant to the user's decision making.

  Don't get me wrong, this doesn't mean that everything should be disclosed; but anything that may have a material effect on your organization's financial health should be disclosed in the notes to your financial statements.

✔ **The Consistency Principle:** This principle states that consistency should be used with the same accounting events period after period. In other words, don't switch between methods for the same accounting event every time a full moon rolls around.

Noting all lawsuits

Because some lawsuits may have an adverse effect on your nonprofit's finances, you need to disclose any lawsuits in the notes of your financial statements. The disclosure should describe the nature of the litigation, possible outcomes, and financial impact if known. Why do you need to include this information? Your stakeholders need to know who may potentially want to sue you and why because they have a vested interest in your livelihood. Plus, GAAP requires this information. For example, a disgruntled employee may want to sue you seeking damages for injury or workers compensation, or someone may want to take you to court for wrongful death or negligence of someone entrusted in your care. For instance, if you operate a nonprofit daycare facility and one of your employees leaves a child in a van, you could face a lawsuit from a disgruntled parent.

Although you can't prevent lawsuits, you can protect your organization by purchasing liability insurance to offset the effects of someone winning a case against your organization. (Check out Chapter 3 for more info about how to protect your nonprofit with insurance.)

Including all contingent liabilities

You also need to report in the notes information about future events that may occur. It's not pleasant to think about, but anything that could have a material effect on your net assets should be disclosed. A future event that may occur but whose occurrence is not certain is called a *contingency*. Like terrorist threats, contingencies pose a threat to your organization's ongoing concern. Examples of things that could be considered contingencies are

✔ An ex-employee's lawsuit for lost wages or wrongful termination

✔ Not filing Form 990 and forgetting to file an extension that results in penalties

Check out Figure 19-2 for how the wording appears for contingent liabilities in the notes.

Noting conditions on assets and liabilities

Sometimes donors impose restriction on the assets they give your nonprofit, and these restrictions need to be included in the notes to your financial statements. Also, if you have pledged assets as collateral for loans, you should include this in the notes. If you have long-term liabilities, you should disclose the effective interest rate, maturity dates, repayment terms, and so on.

Putting Last Year Behind You and Looking Forward

After you've closed the books, you can prepare your financial statements (see Chapters 15-18). When all of that number crunching is finished, make sure to store the journals, general ledger, and any supporting documentation someplace safe. You never know when you're going to need that info, and you definitely don't want to mix the old records with the new ones.

You also need to start a new set of books for the new fiscal year. Start with journaling, maintain good records throughout the year, and end with polished audited financial statements. When you end the year, you'll find yourself going over the same procedures for the next. Think about how good you'll feel when it's over.

Chapter 20

Preparing for an Accounting Audit

In This Chapter
▶ Understanding the reasons for getting an audit
▶ Meeting the players in the nonprofit audit
▶ Grasping the annual audit process
▶ Ending with a clean bill of health
▶ Bracing for an IRS audit

The very thought of being audited makes most people sweat. However, you don't need to get bent out of shape. Audited financial records add credibility to your organization, especially when you get the green light or a good report. An *audit* is a careful evaluation of your accounting systems to ensure that your financial data is accurate and complete. At the end of the audit process, you're given a professional opinion about your organization's financial practices and statements.

This chapter focuses on the financial audit, which inspects your financial data to report whether the information meets standards and requirements. (Check out Chapter 12 for more information about a grant audit.) This chapter outlines what you can do to ensure your financial books are on the up and up in case you ever face an IRS audit. If you follow my recommendations in this chapter, you can relax. Your audit shouldn't turn up any surprises.

Understanding the Audit Purpose and Need

Getting an audit is like going to the doctor for your annual checkup. You don't want one, but you need one. It's good for you. An *audit* determines whether recorded information properly reflects your nonprofit's economic events and activities that occurred during the accounting period. (The *accounting period* is the same as your fiscal year — whatever 12-month period was established in your bylaws.) It's sort of like a final exam at the end of the accounting period. It tests your accountability in accordance with generally accepted accounting principles (GAAP) using generally accepted auditing standards (GAAS).

Having your bookkeeping and accounting records audited by an external auditor shows good financial management and oversight of your nonprofit and implies that your nonprofit is a reputable organization. You gain credibility when you have someone outside your organization inspect your nonprofit financial activities and give her professional opinion about whether you're doing things right.

The following sections point out who looks at your audit's findings and who's involved in the process, including what you need to do to hire an external auditor.

Considering the nonprofit constituency

Your *constituencies* are your supporters or the groups that your organization helps or impacts — the public. As a nonprofit, it's best to establish and maintain a good reputation with your constituents. Getting a clean bill of health stating that you're operating according to accounting principles appeases your constituents and adds credibility to you.

If you get one bad report, even if it's false, your reputation can be tarnished indefinitely. A lot of people are suspicious or skeptical of how nonprofits use their donations. Some of the larger nonprofits have left a bad taste in the public's mouth. For example, contributions to the United Way of America dropped when it was revealed that the executive director flew first class and enjoyed a lavish lifestyle. This type of behavior by the bigwigs makes people wonder what the smaller nonprofits, which are less prominent in their communities, are doing.

Lots of people depend on you, and many more watch your every move. If you miss a step by not keeping your end of the bargain, you can affect the livelihood of your nonprofit and disappoint a lot of people. The financial audit reveals how well you're keeping your end of the bargain to the following folks:

- ✓ **Stakeholders:** If you were a for-profit entity, you would have stockholders. But nonprofits have *stakeholders,* individuals and groups that benefit from your establishment. When you organized your nonprofit, you made a vow to help society and relieve some of the government's burden for providing services. In other words, the work you do should benefit citizens. Stakeholders use the results of an audit to confirm that you're operating according to the status quo.

✔ **Nonprofit watchdogs:** Naysayers help you stay in line and balance. Nonprofit watchdog groups secretly investigate organizations to find out what they're doing wrong. Most nonprofit watchdog groups report wrongdoing to the media. Nonprofit watchdogs use the results of a bad audit to call your reputation into question.

✔ **IRS:** The IRS is interested in your nonprofit's finances. Although you may never get the dreaded audit letter from the IRS, if you do, you'll hand over your external audit report, and your auditor will work closely with the IRS. (Check out the "If You Get Audited by the IRS" section later in this chapter for more specific info.)

✔ **Grant makers:** Organizations that want to give you funding for your services and programs often request audited financial statements so they can determine whether you'll be a responsible steward of their money.

✔ **Donors:** Individuals may also be interested in the results of your independent audit. If your records show that you're following the rules, donors may consider your organization a wise investment.

Knowing who's involved in the process

The auditing process is more than just a couple of people looking at your nonprofit's books. The process requires two sets of people who must work together to ensure your nonprofit's finances are in good order. They are

✔ **An external auditor:** You need to hire an independent external auditor who can review your financial records. This person ensures that your nonprofit's financial records follow generally accepted accounting principles (GAAP) and generally accepted auditing standards (GAAS). In case the IRS should ever come calling, you'll be prepared.

✔ **An internal auditor and audit committee:** You need internal folks who do checks and balances on in-house practices. You may have one or two bookkeepers or a finance manager who runs regular reports and keeps a close eye on all the records. Furthermore, federal legislation requires that you have an internal audit committee, which is responsible for the nonprofit's financial statements.

To have a successful audit, you need both an external auditor and an internal auditor and audit committee. The following sections help you round up these team members.

If you need to double-check your own accounting system for internal purposes (like if your board of directors requests an audit), you can use your staff to do it. This type of audit is called *internal auditing.* When you need an independent audit of your financial statements, the same person who works in your office doing your everyday bookkeeping and accounting shouldn't turn around and audit those records. If that person audits your financial statement, he loses his independence.

Finding an independent external auditor

One side to the auditing equation is having an independent external auditor examine your books. You should hire a CPA who specializes in public accounting to perform a financial audit. Accountants who pass a comprehensive exam and receive their license as a CPA are the only ones qualified to evaluate your financial position and offer a professional opinion.

Accountants compile financial statements, and CPAs audit them. Don't confuse the two.

An external auditor should have no ties to you, your cause, or your staff and/ or board, personally or professionally (other than doing the audit, of course). This is what's meant by *independent.* You need to avoid conflicts of interest between your auditor and your nonprofit. It's your responsibility, not the auditor's, to determine whether your auditor is associated with you, your colleagues, or your cause in any manner.

Finding the right auditor should be done by your audit committee (see the next section about how to select your audit committee). The best way to find a CPA with experience auditing nonprofit organizations is to ask for referrals from other agencies in your city. You can also call your local chamber of commerce to see if someone there can recommend a good CPA.

Forming an internal audit committee

In addition to hiring an external auditor, you need to have internal auditors and an internal audit committee. The internal auditors may be one or two individuals who regularly check your financial records. More important is your *audit committee,* which is responsible for overseeing the organization's annual audit of financial statements and ensuring those statements accurately represent your organization's financial position.

Whether you need or can afford internal auditors, external auditors, and an audit committee depends on the size of your nonprofit. Some states (like California) offer guidance in how nonprofits are evaluated according to the size of their operating budgets.

✔ A nonprofit budget under $300,000 may be considered small and probably doesn't need an audit committee.

✔ One with a budget between $300,000 and $500,000 may be considered medium size. If this describes your organization, you may want to form an audit committee, but it's not a must.

✔ An organization with an operating budget of $500,000 or more is likely to be considered large and should have an audit committee.

Your internal audit committee works with the external auditor. After the auditor finishes his work, he explains his findings to your audit committee. He should also make recommendations to your committee about how to improve bookkeeping and accounting procedures.

You need at least three people to serve on your audit committee. Your board of directors should elect or appoint individuals to be on the audit committee. The audit committee meets as often as necessary to fulfill its role of selecting, hiring, and ensuring that the external auditor's work is done properly. Members of your internal audit committee include your treasurer and qualified board of directors with a background and professional experience in accounting, general management, finance, or law.

Searching for Accountability: Leaving a Paper Trail

In order for your external auditor to review your nonprofit's finances and issue his opinion, he needs to have access to the proper records and paperwork. You can save yourself some money if you separate your expenses and revenues and record them on a piece of paper, a computer spreadsheet, or preferably a computer program like QuickBooks and give them to your accountant. He'll want to see copies of the following documents to prove what's in your nonprofit's financial records and financial statements:

✔ **Payment receipts:** These include copies of checks or bills stamped paid.

✔ **Vendors' statements:** These are invoices submitted by the people you do business with.

✔ **Bills:** Provide these for utilities, rent, insurance, and other things.

✔ **Donation receipts:** These include copies of checks, letters sent with checks, and anything else a donor may have given when making a donation.

✔ **Donors list and receipts:** Your auditor will verify the accuracy of your donors list by contacting a few people on it. He won't have time to contact every person on the list, but he'll choose a random sampling of names to verify the amount given.

If you find yourself searching for these items as you gather them, resolve to do a better job of keeping and organizing your documents next year. Chapter 4 has loads of helpful tips.

Walking through the Audit Process

Have you ever wondered exactly what auditors do? Although the nitty-gritty of what the auditor does when he reviews your nonprofit's finances is beyond the scope of this book, it's helpful to have a basic grasp of what to expect.

The auditor doesn't use rocket science or some complicated math formula to form an opinion. Rather, the auditor has generally accepted auditing standards (GAAS) and generally accepted accounting principles (GAAP) to guide his analysis. (Refer to Chapter 1 for an introduction to these two sets of guidelines.) The following sections take a look at what the auditor does to get an opinion.

Phase I: Planning and design

During Phase I, your auditor obtains information, such as copies of your articles of incorporation, current bylaws, list of current board members, minutes of the board of directors and committee meetings, and your IRS letter of determination, from you about the background of your organization and your legal liabilities in an attempt to understand your internal controls and assess fraud risk.

Your auditor uses this information to develop an overall audit plan. No two organizations are alike, so no one method works for every nonprofit. The auditor will follow certain steps, but he must plan and design an audit based on your organization's size and scope of work.

Phase II: Calculating audit risk

During Phase II, the auditor assesses the type of audit risk involved and determines how long the audit will last and how much it will cost. Risk falls into two camps:

✔ **Acceptable:** An acceptable audit risk measures the auditor's willingness to accept that the financial statements you gave him may be materially misstated (based on the auditor's professional judgment) after the audit is complete. Think of it like this: The auditor is taking a chance by basing a decision on your information after performing tests on it.

✔ **Inherent:** Inherent risk measures the likelihood that your financial statements have material misstatements *before* considering internal controls. Your auditor has to determine the likelihood that your financial statements may not be legit. Just by looking at your financial statements, some auditors can detect that something isn't right, sort of like the way a dog sniffs out fear.

It's better for you if your auditor determines that the risk involved in auditing your nonprofit is acceptable. It means his neck probably won't be on the line. And because the level of risk determines the cost of an audit, an acceptable audit risk probably will be cheaper for you.

Phase III: Analysis

Your auditor has to assess the overall reasonableness of your transactions by analytical tests or detailed tests of balances. This is done by determining sample items (which items will be evaluated), sample size (how many items will be verified), and reaching an audit conclusion about what to measure, mostly in terms of monetary value. GAAS outline how auditors should perform these tests, which include

✔ Procedures to obtain an understanding of internal controls

✔ Tests of usefulness of policies and procedures

✔ Reasonableness of account balances

✔ Testing balance details to see if the audit objectives have been satisfied by the balances on the accounts

Usually, auditors also ask to see financial statements for more than one period to compare. A good auditor can look at the numbers and detect if something is grossly wrong. If there's a big increase or decrease in your spending, it shows in your expenses. After performing the required tests and looking at your financial statements, an auditor can do a reasonable assessment of your true financial position.

Phase IV: Gathering final evidence and issuing the report

Phase IV is the final phase of the audit. Your auditor gathers financial information to summarize the results and issue the audit report, to review or prepare your financial statements, and to prepare the notes of disclosure (see Chapter 19 for more on notes). During the final review the auditor looks for contingent liabilities to include in the notes. *Contingent liabilities* are pending lawsuits, potential losses, and balloon payments that your nonprofit may have to settle or pay.

Your auditor does a final analysis to evaluate the *going concern concept,* which indicates that your nonprofit will continue for another accounting period. He also writes a letter stating that your financial statements have been audited. And then he reads your annual report to check that it represents what's in the financial statements.

After all of this, your auditor issues a report (see the next section). The *auditor's report* shares your auditor's professional opinion of your nonprofit's financial stability based on information given, a series of audit tests, and a careful analysis of your financial position as stated on your financial statements.

After the Audit Is Finished: Receiving the Auditor's Report

The job of an external auditor isn't glamorous. Believe me, I did it for six months, and I've had root canals that were more exciting. However, an auditor ensures your nonprofit's finances are in order, so he's got a pretty important job. When your auditor is finished reviewing all the numbers, he communicates his findings in the form of an auditor's report. A good auditor will always find something wrong with your records and make suggestions about ways to improve your financial and managerial systems.

As the executive director or manager of your nonprofit, you and your board are responsible for the results of your audit and its findings. It's up to you and your board of directors to take action, as necessary, on the audit findings. Responsibility for the overall nonprofit lies with the board of directors.

The audit is based on information submitted by you. It's your responsibility to make sure the information is accurate. (Check out the earlier section, "Searching For Accountability: Leaving a Paper Trail," for what you need to provide the auditor.) The following sections give you the lowdown on the importance of the auditor's professional opinion and the four types you may encounter.

Eyeing the importance of the opinion

Your auditor hasn't been privy to every transaction that has taken place over the course of the accounting period; therefore, all he can do is issue an opinion about your financial statements. This *opinion* is professional in nature and is based on acceptable standards found in GAAP and GAAS. Your auditor issues a formal report stating his opinion after he completes his review of your nonprofit's finances. Minor findings are reported to management in a management letter.

You can then use the auditor's report as a tool when reporting financial information to your constituents. The auditor's opinion can attract donors, investors, and grant makers to your nonprofit, or it can deter them. These days, people place a good amount of emphasis on having audited financial information, so many donors won't even consider investing in your organization without looking at audited financial statements.

Identifying the types of auditor opinions you can receive

After the auditor evaluates your nonprofit's financial statements, the accounting firm where the auditor works issues a report about your records and gives an opinion. *Note:* Only a CPA can issue a valid opinion about your financial statements. The auditor expresses his opinion in a traditional seven-part report. The report has a letter that includes the report title, address, introductory paragraph, scope paragraph, opinion paragraph, name of the CPA firm, and the report date.

Just receiving the opinion isn't enough. You need to know what it means and what to do with it.

Included in the report will be *findings,* which are conclusions the auditor reaches after reviewing your financial statements. Some audit findings are considered common because they have no significant material effect on your organization. Common findings include suggesting ways to implement better bookkeeping and accounting methods.

The following sections point out the different types of opinions you can receive from an auditor and what you need to know about each one to help your nonprofit improve its condition.

Unqualified opinion

The *unqualified opinion* means that your auditor believes the financial statements are free from material misstatements and are in accordance with GAAP. This is the most desirable type of report to receive, because it means your organization's financial condition is fairly represented in the financial statements.

If you receive this opinion from your auditor, congratulations. Your nonprofit's financial status is a clean bill of health. You don't have to worry if the IRS comes knocking.

Qualified opinion

Just by looking at the name, you'd think this would be the most desirable opinion, but it's not. A *qualified opinion* means the auditor saw one of two things:

- ✔ You deviated from GAAP in one or more areas of the financial statements.
- ✔ The auditor couldn't verify a certain area because you didn't have the information.

For instance, say that you gave your auditor a list of donors, but the contact information was missing, so the auditor couldn't verify the donors' gifts. Everything else presented was in accordance with GAAP. Therefore, the auditor will state in the report that your financial statements were presented fairly, with the exception of the donors' gifts, which couldn't be audited.

Having a qualified opinion isn't a bad report; everything that the auditor looked at checked out okay. But something was missing that wouldn't allow the auditor to verify or test your records. If you had this missing element, you probably would've checked out with an unqualified opinion report.

If you receive a qualified opinion, your auditor will make suggestions about how to avoid losing important information needed to audit your records. You should take the necessary steps to correct your problems. Then the next time your records are audited, you'll pass the test.

Adverse opinion

An *adverse opinion* is issued when your financial statements have material misstatement and don't conform to GAAP. Think of an adverse opinion as the exact opposite of the unqualified opinion.

If you receive an adverse opinion, you need to get your act together. Your auditor will give you a list of things to do and make several suggestions about how to fix your problems. Just follow his professional opinion by cleaning up your act.

Disclaimer of opinion

If you get a *disclaimer of opinion* report, it means the auditor can't form an opinion or refuses to issue one. Usually this happens when the auditor can't finish the work necessary to complete an audit. Certain situations warrant a disclaimer:

✔ **A lack of independence or conflict of interest exists between your nonprofit and the auditor:** Unless your auditor is independent, he shouldn't issue an opinion about your financial statements. If you're related to your auditor, this presents a conflict of interest.

✔ **A lack of evidence on which to perform procedures:** There is just not enough documented information available to do the audit.

✔ **Based on the information presented, your nonprofit won't exist much longer:** The *going concern concept* states that your organization should continue to operate for future accounting periods. In other words, an auditor can't issue an opinion if it violates GAAP principles.

✔ **If you hide or withhold information from your auditor:** If your auditor suspects that he doesn't have all the information he needs to conduct a thorough audit, he'll have to issue a disclaimer of opinion.

If you receive a disclaimer, I suggest you call an emergency board meeting and work aggressively to fix your situation. An auditor won't place his stamp of approval on anything that's not valid, so you have some serious bookkeeping and accounting issues to resolve.

If You Get Audited by the IRS

Because you've received tax-exempt status from the IRS to operate your nonprofit, you may be required to get an independent auditor to audit your financial statements. The IRS also expects you to practice good bookkeeping and accounting practices in compliance with GAAP (generally accepted accounting principles) and GAAS (generally accepted auditing standards).

According to the IRS, about 1.9 million nonprofits have been formed in the United States. With nonprofits popping up like popcorn, the IRS is trying to control the nonprofit population. One way that it keeps tabs on organizations is by conducting an IRS audit.

Just like with your personal taxes, your nonprofit may be selected for an audit at random. You may also be audited if someone reports you to the IRS for questionable activity or if the IRS suspects something fishy is going on.

Head to www.irs.gov/pub/irs-pdf/p892.pdf to check out IRS Publication 892, Exempt Organization Appeal Procedures for Unagreed Issues, for more about your nonprofit's rights when it comes to the IRS audit.

Unless the IRS suspects that you've committed a crime, the IRS usually notifies you by mail that you're going to be audited. If you've committed a crime or are under criminal investigation, the feds may just show up and take your records. (This is rare, but it happens. Usually, serious violations are suspected or have been reported when this occurs.)

I hope you never get that dreaded letter from the IRS, but if you do, don't turn on the shredder and start getting rid of stuff. Instead, call the accounting firm that did your audit and tell your auditor you're being audited. Get some help because you don't want to face Uncle Sam alone.

If you've played by the rules, then you have nothing to worry about, right? Well, that depends. Sometimes not knowing the rules will get you some mercy, but then the IRS has to decide whether what you did was intentional, fraudulent, or careless oversight.

Recent reports indicate that the IRS is not as mean as it used to be. Now the agency is willing to work with you. Even if you're savvy enough to read the fine print and work through the red tape, I still advise you to seek professional help from a CPA.

Part V
The Part of Tens

The 5th Wave   By Rich Tennant

"Cooked books? Let me just say you could serve this statement of activities with a fruity zinfandel and not be out of place."

In this part . . .

No matter how much you know, good advice is priceless! Like every *For Dummies* book, this part includes some fun and simple advice you can use on a daily basis. Here you can find ten tips on how to keep your organization operating according to accounting standards. Taking advantage of these tips can lend you the accountability you need to pass an audit and meet the federal guidelines that relate to your organization. You can also find ten pointers to remember when keeping your books to ensure everything balances and your nonprofit remains solvent.

Chapter 21

Ten Important Things to Know When Keeping Nonprofit Books

In This Chapter

▶ Safeguarding your assets

▶ Documenting donations

▶ Getting help

As the executive director or manager of a nonprofit, your job is to make sure your organization's books are in order. You want to make sure your staff follows the guidelines set in the generally accepted accounting principles (GAAP). You also want to verify that you and your staff are following these guidelines through detailed documentation.

This chapter reviews the ten most important things you need to know when keeping your nonprofit's books. Ignoring any of these items can negatively impact your nonprofit's books and the success or future of your organization.

Watch Cash Contributions

Cash is the most liquid and volatile asset because it's the hardest asset to track after you exchange or receive it. To prevent any potential problems, your organization needs to have an in-house policy that describes how to receive and handle cash. When you establish your policy, remember that the same person should never both receive the cash and pay the bills. Accountants refer to policies like this example of segregation of duties as *internal controls*.

Another example of internal controls: You can put up a sign on your clerk's desk reminding donors that they should receive receipts for all donations. Without this receipt policy (and sign), you increase the risk that the clerk may pocket the money because your nonprofit has no record of the transaction without physical documentation.

Keep a Donors List

Making a donors list and checking it twice pays off. A *donors list* is simply a complete and up-to-date list of all the people who have donated to your organization, including their names, phone numbers, and addresses, along with the dates they donated and the amounts they contributed. Updating this list is important because the IRS may need to verify a donor's list. For example, when someone deducts a charitable donation from his income taxes, the IRS sometimes tracks this donation back to the organization that received it to verify that person's donation. Your up-to-date donors list can provide the verification the IRS is looking for.

When your CPA audits your books, he requires a donors list. During the audit, your CPA performs a random test by contacting some of the people on your donors list to verify contributions.

Balance Your Nonprofit Checkbook

Every organization needs a system of checks and balances. Your checkbook is the first place to start when you're trying to get a handle on your finances. Even if your checkbook is out of balance, you still need to know how much money you have, how much you have spent, and how much you need.

Because banks make mistakes, you must keep an eye on your checking account to make sure you and the bank are on the same page at all times. If possible, get online banking and review your account often.

Leave a Paper Trail

Document and keep copies of everything that takes place in your organization — services and programs offered, celebrations had, salaries paid, and so on. Keep copies of every receipt, invoice, and bill paid. Make copies of all the checks your organization writes to justify and verify your expenses. Every transaction that occurs in your organization has to leave a clear path that explains when it happens, why it happens, and how it happens.

When you have supporting documentation to justify every transaction that takes place in your nonprofit, you maintain your accountability. Plus, complete documentation allows you to clearly and accurately show why you did what you did, who gave you what, when things happened, and how you kept up with them. Your auditor will want to see invoices, receipts, and other documents to verify your financial activities.

Protect Your Nonprofit from Employee Theft

Unfortunately, nonprofits face a similar problem that for-profits face — employees who steal from their own organizations. You can lessen the impact of employee theft by protecting yourself. Take the following simple actions to help protect your assets:

- ✔ **Give your potential employees a standard test.** By having potential employees answer certain questions, you can gauge the likelihood that they may steal. These tests are usually electronic and include multiple-choice questions that ask potential employees what they would do in certain scenarios. For example, one question may ask what you would do if you witnessed another employee stealing from the organization. Answers to questions like this one are good indicators of personal values, ethics, and attitudes.

- ✔ **Segregate duties.** Segregating duties means not putting the same person in charge of making decisions about purchases, writing checks to pay for the same purchases, receiving the purchases, and keeping up with inventory. When you don't segregate duties, you make yourself vulnerable to potential employee theft because if the same employee is in charge of all duties regarding a particular purchase, she can steal the purchase, and no one would know. After all, no one else may even know the purchase was made.

- ✔ **Place security cameras in your building.** Security cameras protect you from outside threats as well as internal threats by recording what happens in your building at all times.

- ✔ **Do background checks on potential employees.** In some states, employers have to do background checks on volunteers and employees who may work with children. Check with your attorney general's office or state department of public safety for information about how to get a background check of a potential employee. Always get prior signed approval from the potential employee before doing a background check. Sometimes you can even get the potential employee to pay for it. Do a little homework before you choose a company to do your background checks because fees vary.

- ✔ **Reference a potential employee's credit reports.** Pulling a potential employee's credit history can help you gauge that person's character. Responsible individuals usually pay their bills on time. Make sure you get signed approval from the potential employee before running a credit history.

Talk to your auditor about other protective measures you can take to safeguard your assets. Check out Chapter 2 for more about protecting your organization's assets.

Consider Your Constituency

Your *constituencies* are your donors and the people you serve. In the nonprofit world, your constituencies are your *stakeholders* — individuals who have a vested interest in your outcome to make a positive difference in the lives of the people in your community. Your stakeholders are very important to the livelihood of your organization because your organization can't survive without the people who donate money or the people who use your services. Therefore, before making any major decision, always consider the impact it will have on your constituency.

Stay in Compliance

In exchange for your tax-exempt status, you have certain obligations to fulfill to the state and federal governments. You can stay within the guidelines the IRS gives you by filing all necessary paperwork in a timely fashion. You have to follow the IRS's rules regarding how you should operate and run your program on a daily basis to maintain your tax-exempt status. In addition, if your nonprofit receives federal grants, you should have received a list of policies along with your grant award that you need to follow to continue to receive your grant funds.

Three of the most important rules you need to stay in compliance with are

- ✔ **File your 990 on time.** If you forget to file Form 990 for three years in a row, you lose your nonprofit tax-exempt status.
- ✔ **Avoid commercial activities.** If you start operating like a for-profit entity, you can lose your nonprofit status.
- ✔ **Stay out of politics.** If you start campaigning and encouraging others who benefit from your services to vote a certain way, you can jeopardize your tax-exempt status with the IRS.

Check out Chapter 9 for more on staying in compliance with the IRS.

Track the Truth in the Books

When you and your staff are keeping track of your nonprofit's books, don't cook your books. Show your numbers just as they are because honesty is always the best policy. Plus, if you plan to be around for the long haul, you need to build a solid reputation for yourself and your organization.

Executive directors are required to sign off on financial statements stating that the records are presented accurately according to accounting records. Your signature means that the statements are a fair representation of your true financial position. If you lie about your financial position, you'll likely lose your credibility in other areas, too. You may even lose your job or your organization. You don't want to end up going down the same path that Enron and others who falsified their books followed, do you?

Keep Charities and Politics Separate

Remember, you can encourage the public to vote, but if you're not an advocacy group, don't rock the boat by rallying and campaigning for candidates. Also, never use your Web site, newsletters, or any other form of advertisement to persuade people to vote for a particular candidate.

You have only one vote — yours, not your organization's — and although you have the right to exercise that vote, you don't have the right to use your nonprofit organization to persuade other people how to exercise their votes. Using your organization to sway beneficiaries to vote for a specific candidate is something you can't do if you want to keep your tax-exempt status, as well as maintain a positive image for both you and your organization.

Get Free Support

Running a nonprofit definitely has its challenges. One way to make everything a tad easier is to rely on the free support available. I suggest you start with the following two services first:

- **IRS:** Although you may not realize this fact, the IRS actually does want to help you. The IRS offers many free classes to assist you with operating your nonprofit. For convenience, many courses are offered online, and conference calls can be scheduled to discuss issues that directly affect your organization.

  For example, the IRS offers several free training courses to assist you with filling out and complying with Form 990. If you require help with your payroll or tax forms, or if you have other burning tax-related questions, you can contact the IRS for answers. For more information about training provided by the IRS, visit www.irs.gov.

- **SCORE:** Assess your organization's weaknesses and search for ways to strengthen its capacity by taking advantage of the many free services offered by SCORE, a nonprofit association that counsels small businesses in America. If you need a little help with the overall operations of your nonprofit, contact SCORE online at www.score.org.

Chapter 22

Ten Tips to Keep Your Nonprofit Viable

In This Chapter

▶ Managing day-to-day operations

▶ Strategizing your future

▶ Working your network

Accountability is more important than ever in the nonprofit sector. People think very hard about where to invest their hard-earned dollars, and to maintain good standing in your books, you need people to see your organization as a solid investment option. Long gone are the days when a man's word was his bond. Today you have to prove that you're a good steward if you want to receive donations; after all, people aren't going to give money because of what you say but rather because of what you do and stand for.

Consider changing your mindset of doing business as usual. The fundraising method you've been using for years may not appeal to donors today. Every gift you receive is an investment in your programs and services, so letting donors know that you're valid and trustworthy is important.

Although your community programs and services are the reason behind your nonprofit, its daily operation depends on much more than just these programs to survive. Clearly, the organization can't flourish without finances; after all, money is the oil that keeps the wheels turning. This chapter gives you a few tips to help keep your head above water. It addresses the importance of balancing your books, maintaining a positive reputation, planning your future, and making the right connections.

Keeping Your Books Balanced

A good financial manager wants to evaluate how she's doing at the end of each month. To keep a good handle on your income and expenses, have your bookkeeper do monthly financial reports. One thing you definitely want to watch in these reports is how your operating budget compares to what's actually taking place in your organization. (For more information about how to compare your actual results to what you planned, see Chapter 8.)

Not keeping balanced books can cost you some hefty overdraft banking fees and cause you to lose your credibility with creditors and vendors. As a result, your organization may receive a bad credit rating, which can affect your organization's financial future. See Chapter 7 for how to balance your organization's checkbook.

You need to set up your accounting system to make updates to your books automatically. When you enter or change something in one field, your system should be able to show the results of that change in terms of your overall financial situation. For more information about setting up your accounting system, see Chapter 4.

Waiting until the end of the year to put your books in order isn't good financial management. Suppose you have an emergency situation to resolve (like an unexpected computer crash or a pipe that bursts), and you need to quickly evaluate how much money you have and compare that to how much money you need to correct your problem. Keeping your books balanced can save you a lot of time during an emergency, not to mention during tax season.

File Paperwork with the IRS

No matter the size of your nonprofit, you have to file the appropriate paperwork with the IRS to keep your nonprofit status active. The IRS occasionally changes the threshold amounts that determine which form your organization needs to file, so visit www.irs.gov/charities/article to stay current. For example, for tax years prior to 2010, nonprofits that generated $25,000 or less in gross revenue can file Form 990-N (e-Postcard). Beginning with the 2010 tax year, this amount changes to $50,000 or less.

If your organization generates more than $25,000 in gross receipts per year (or more than $50,000 in the 2010 tax year), but less than $1 million (or $500,000 in the 2009 tax year or $200,000 in the 2010 tax year), you get to choose whether to file Form 990-EZ or Form 990. If your gross receipts are more than $1 million (or $500,000 in the 2009 tax year or $200,000 in the 2010 tax year), you have to file Form 990.

In summary, the decision about whether to file Form 990-N, Form 990-EZ, or Form 990 is based on the gross receipts your organization generates in a given year and your total assets for that year. For the most up-to-date info about which form to file, go to `www.irs.gov/charities/article/0,,id=184445,00.html`. Check out Chapter 14 for more on the specific paperwork you need to file with the IRS.

Pay Bills on Time

Your organization has a reputation, and you have to do whatever you can to maintain its good name. To keep a good reputation (and to keep your books accurate and up to date), pay your utilities, rent, employees, vendors, creditors, and all other bills on time.

Just as paying bills on time is important for your own personal credit score, paying bills is also important for your organization's credit score. If you find that you can't meet your obligations, call your creditors. Many of them may be willing to work out some type of arrangement to keep you as a customer.

Use reminders, such as your wall calendar, cellphone or PDA, and computer calendar, to help you remember to pay your bills on time. Nowadays, you have no excuse for forgetting to be on time.

Explore New Fundraising Ideas

No matter how large or small your nonprofit is, you don't want your fundraising efforts to become stagnant. Without fundraising money coming in, your nonprofit's bottom line can suffer. To keep fundraising fresh, consider new ideas.

The best way to come up with new ideas is to brainstorm with your staff and board members to generate innovative ways to bring funding to your nonprofit. Forget about what everyone else is doing and figure out your own approach. Have your staff and board members list any ideas that come to mind. Remember that no idea is bad. You'd be surprised at the types of innovative ways to keep your head above water in terms of fundraising. After you finish brainstorming, break down the list and look at the ideas to determine which ones work best for your nonprofit.

Watch Your Nonprofit's Bottom Line

Pay close attention to giving trends and track your nonprofit's budget on a monthly basis. Compare what happens to what you expected to happen and take note of the differences. By doing so, you can identify signs and signals that may indicate a problem — these signs can be very helpful in the future.

Keeping a close eye on your nonprofit's bottom line is key to survival. You may not be running the nonprofit to make money, but you can't function without it. You need money to run programs, to pay employees, and to keep the lights on. Make sure you know how much money your nonprofit has at all times (for more information on how to keep track of your expenses and donations, see Chapter 7).

Analyze, Plan, and Project Future Funding Streams

Believe it or not, your nonprofit is a business. Your board needs to have a clear vision about the future of your organization. To do so, you and your board need to know where you're going, how you can get there, and how much money you need to get there. Make sure you do the following:

- **Analyze.** Assess where you are now and where you want your nonprofit to be in three to five years. This is called *ongoing concern*. A good manager keeps the day-to-day operations functioning while also preparing for tomorrow's expansion and growth.

- **Plan.** Create a *business plan* or strategic plan that clearly sets the path for your future.

- **Evaluate.** Assess where you are and project future resources to evaluate whether your nonprofit is meeting its plan.

Check out Chapter 8 for more in-depth information about these three points.

Get Grant-Writing Training

Federal grants provide an important way for your nonprofit to receive money to pay for its programs. However, you can't receive federal grants if you don't know how to correctly apply for and request the grant money, so knowing how to write grants is to your advantage. Your nonprofit helps your community by supporting people through services, and because you qualified for nonprofit status, you're eligible for grant funding.

Find out where to find grants, how to apply for grants, and how the federal grant system works by getting some training. Contact your local university or United Way office to find out where training is available. If you prefer online classes, you can get quality online training through Education To Go (ed2go);

find a list of online courses at www.ed2go.com/. Or, if you prefer books over computer screens, take a look at *Grant Writing For Dummies,* 3rd Edition, by Beverly A. Browning (Wiley).

If you prefer more personal attention, consider hiring a grant consultant to mentor and coach you through the grant-writing process. A grant consultant can give you insight about the process from the perspectives of both the granting agency and your organization. Knowing more about grant writing increases your chances of receiving grants and placing your nonprofit on the government's grant map.

Gain the knowledge you need to relieve some of your financial worries by getting some help. Put together a team within your organization to find out more about how corporations, foundations, and government agencies award grants. Take advantage of the information available to you at www.grants.gov. Read the information on that site about how to narrow your search for grants before you start going down the crowded grant highway. Check out Chapter 10 for more.

Get an Independent Audit

Getting an independent financial audit is not an option, it's a requirement. An *independent auditor* is a certified public accountant (CPA) who audits your organization's financial records and offers a professional opinion about whether your records are prepared according to national accounting standards. Your independent auditor must be unbiased in the view and performance of professional services. For more about selecting and hiring an independent auditor, see Chapter 20.

Get Acquainted with Elected Officials

Wouldn't you like your organization to be a line item in the government's budget? To have a government appropriation set aside just for your nonprofit is a director's dream. Well, sometimes dreams do come true.

Knowing your elected officials is definitely to your benefit, but even more important is making sure they know you and your organization — what you do and how the community benefits from your existence. By knowing your elected officials, you gain strong advocates who can help you secure funding for your organization. Notify your senators before you submit a federal grant application and get letters of support from them. Your senators can rally for you and your organization only if they know about you.

Plus, when you're applying directly to federal agencies for grants, you want to make sure your elected officials are aware of what your needs are so they can rally for you when related topics come up for discussion. Building relationships with your elected officials isn't supporting one candidate over another; it's putting your already-elected officials to work for you.

Attend Networking Activities

To have a viable and fluid nonprofit, you have to network with the important people and organizations in your community. In other words, you need to reach out to your city's chamber of commerce, United Way office, city councilmen and women, representatives, congressmen and women, governor, and other key people and organizations.

The reason is simple. These organizations and people, such as the chamber of commerce and the governor, have a good understanding of the direction in which your city is moving, in terms of new industries and other forms of growth. You need to know which new companies are coming to your city so you can present your cause to them and, hopefully, solicit their support. Furthermore, other organizations, such as United Way, usually know most of the other nonprofits in your state. Using their resources, you can find out more about your competition. However, don't think of this as a turf war of us against them; instead, think of your competition as your allies.

After all, your organization isn't about you; it's about the people you serve. I see too many small nonprofits fighting among themselves for the crumbs (minigrants of $25,000 or less) and missing the big picture — coming together to help better serve the community as a whole.

Index

SINESS, CAREERS & PERSONAL FINANCE

ounting For Dummies, 4th Edition*
0-470-24600-9

kkeeping Workbook For Dummies†
0-470-16983-4

nmodities For Dummies
0-470-04928-0

ng Business in China For Dummies
0-470-04929-7

E-Mail Marketing For Dummies
978-0-470-19087-6

Job Interviews For Dummies, 3rd Edition*†
978-0-470-17748-8

Personal Finance Workbook For Dummies*†
978-0-470-09933-9

Real Estate License Exams For Dummies
978-0-7645-7623-2

Six Sigma For Dummies
978-0-7645-6798-8

Small Business Kit For Dummies,
2nd Edition*†
978-0-7645-5984-6

Telephone Sales For Dummies
978-0-470-16836-3

SINESS PRODUCTIVITY & MICROSOFT OFFICE

ess 2007 For Dummies
0-470-03649-5

el 2007 For Dummies
0-470-03737-9

ice 2007 For Dummies
0-470-00923-9

look 2007 For Dummies
0-470-03830-7

PowerPoint 2007 For Dummies
978-0-470-04059-1

Project 2007 For Dummies
978-0-470-03651-8

QuickBooks 2008 For Dummies
978-0-470-18470-7

Quicken 2008 For Dummies
978-0-470-17473-9

Salesforce.com For Dummies,
2nd Edition
978-0-470-04893-1

Word 2007 For Dummies
978-0-470-03658-7

UCATION, HISTORY, REFERENCE & TEST PREPARATION

can American History For Dummies
0-7645-5469-8

ebra For Dummies
0-7645-5325-7

ebra Workbook For Dummies
0-7645-8467-1

History For Dummies
0-470-09910-0

ASVAB For Dummies, 2nd Edition
978-0-470-10671-6

British Military History For Dummies
978-0-470-03213-8

Calculus For Dummies
978-0-7645-2498-1

Canadian History For Dummies, 2nd Edition
978-0-470-83656-9

Geometry Workbook For Dummies
978-0-471-79940-5

The SAT I For Dummies, 6th Edition
978-0-7645-7193-0

Series 7 Exam For Dummies
978-0-470-09932-2

World History For Dummies
978-0-7645-5242-7

OD, GARDEN, HOBBIES & HOME

lge For Dummies, 2nd Edition
0-471-92426-5

n Collecting For Dummies, 2nd Edition
0-470-22275-1

king Basics For Dummies, 3rd Edition
0-7645-7206-7

Drawing For Dummies
978-0-7645-5476-6

Etiquette For Dummies, 2nd Edition
978-0-470-10672-3

Gardening Basics For Dummies*†
978-0-470-03749-2

Knitting Patterns For Dummies
978-0-470-04556-5

Living Gluten-Free For Dummies†
978-0-471-77383-2

Painting Do-It-Yourself For Dummies
978-0-470-17533-0

ALTH, SELF-HELP, PARENTING & PETS

er Management For Dummies
0-470-03715-7

iety & Depression Workbook
Dummies
0-7645-9793-0

ting For Dummies, 2nd Edition
0-7645-4149-0

Training For Dummies, 2nd Edition
0-7645-8418-3

Horseback Riding For Dummies
978-0-470-09719-9

Infertility For Dummies†
978-0-470-11518-3

Meditation For Dummies with CD-ROM,
2nd Edition
978-0-471-77774-8

Post-Traumatic Stress Disorder For Dummies
978-0-470-04922-8

Puppies For Dummies, 2nd Edition
978-0-470-03717-1

Thyroid For Dummies, 2nd Edition†
978-0-471-78755-6

Type 1 Diabetes For Dummies*†
978-0-470-17811-9

 **WILEY**

INTERNET & DIGITAL MEDIA

AdWords For Dummies
978-0-470-15252-2

Blogging For Dummies, 2nd Edition
978-0-470-23017-6

Digital Photography All-in-One Desk Reference For Dummies, 3rd Edition
978-0-470-03743-0

Digital Photography For Dummies, 5th Edition
978-0-7645-9802-9

Digital SLR Cameras & Photography For Dummies, 2nd Edition
978-0-470-14927-0

eBay Business All-in-One Desk Reference For Dummies
978-0-7645-8438-1

eBay For Dummies, 5th Edition*
978-0-470-04529-9

eBay Listings That Sell For Dummies
978-0-471-78912-3

Facebook For Dummies
978-0-470-26273-3

The Internet For Dummies, 11th Edition
978-0-470-12174-0

Investing Online For Dummies, 5th Edition
978-0-7645-8456-5

iPod & iTunes For Dummies, 5th Edit
978-0-470-17474-6

MySpace For Dummies
978-0-470-09529-4

Podcasting For Dummies
978-0-471-74898-4

Search Engine Optimization For Dummies, 2nd Edition
978-0-471-97998-2

Second Life For Dummies
978-0-470-18025-9

Starting an eBay Business For Dumm 3rd Edition†
978-0-470-14924-9

GRAPHICS, DESIGN & WEB DEVELOPMENT

Adobe Creative Suite 3 Design Premium All-in-One Desk Reference For Dummies
978-0-470-11724-8

Adobe Web Suite CS3 All-in-One Desk Reference For Dummies
978-0-470-12099-6

AutoCAD 2008 For Dummies
978-0-470-11650-0

Building a Web Site For Dummies, 3rd Edition
978-0-470-14928-7

Creating Web Pages All-in-One Desk Reference For Dummies, 3rd Edition
978-0-470-09629-1

Creating Web Pages For Dummies, 8th Edition
978-0-470-08030-6

Dreamweaver CS3 For Dummies
978-0-470-11490-2

Flash CS3 For Dummies
978-0-470-12100-9

Google SketchUp For Dummies
978-0-470-13744-4

InDesign CS3 For Dummies
978-0-470-11865-8

Photoshop CS3 All-in-One Desk Reference For Dummies
978-0-470-11195-6

Photoshop CS3 For Dummies
978-0-470-11193-2

Photoshop Elements 5 For Dummi
978-0-470-09810-3

SolidWorks For Dummies
978-0-7645-9555-4

Visio 2007 For Dummies
978-0-470-08983-5

Web Design For Dummies, 2nd Edi
978-0-471-78117-2

Web Sites Do-It-Yourself For Dumm
978-0-470-16903-2

Web Stores Do-It-Yourself For Dumm
978-0-470-17443-2

LANGUAGES, RELIGION & SPIRITUALITY

Arabic For Dummies
978-0-471-77270-5

Chinese For Dummies, Audio Set
978-0-470-12766-7

French For Dummies
978-0-7645-5193-2

German For Dummies
978-0-7645-5195-6

Hebrew For Dummies
978-0-7645-5489-6

Ingles Para Dummies
978-0-7645-5427-8

Italian For Dummies, Audio Set
978-0-470-09586-7

Italian Verbs For Dummies
978-0-471-77389-4

Japanese For Dummies
978-0-7645-5429-2

Latin For Dummies
978-0-7645-5431-5

Portuguese For Dummies
978-0-471-78738-9

Russian For Dummies
978-0-471-78001-4

Spanish Phrases For Dummies
978-0-7645-7204-3

Spanish For Dummies
978-0-7645-5194-9

Spanish For Dummies, Audio Set
978-0-470-09585-0

The Bible For Dummies
978-0-7645-5296-0

Catholicism For Dummies
978-0-7645-5391-2

The Historical Jesus For Dummies
978-0-470-16785-4

Islam For Dummies
978-0-7645-5503-9

Spirituality For Dummies, 2nd Edition
978-0-470-19142-2

NETWORKING AND PROGRAMMING

ASP.NET 3.5 For Dummies
978-0-470-19592-5

C# 2008 For Dummies
978-0-470-19109-5

Hacking For Dummies, 2nd Edition
978-0-470-05235-8

Home Networking For Dummies, 4th Edition
978-0-470-11806-1

Java For Dummies, 4th Edition
978-0-470-08716-9

Microsoft® SQL Server™ 2008 All-in-One Desk Reference For Dummies
978-0-470-17954-3

Networking All-in-One Desk Reference For Dummies, 2nd Edition
978-0-7645-9939-2

Networking For Dummies, 8th Edition
978-0-470-05620-2

SharePoint 2007 For Dummies
978-0-470-09941-4

Wireless Home Networking For Dummies, 2nd Edition
978-0-471-74940-0

OPERATING SYSTEMS & COMPUTER BASICS

Mac For Dummies, 5th Edition
978-0-7645-8458-9

Laptops For Dummies, 2nd Edition
978-0-470-05432-1

Linux For Dummies, 8th Edition
978-0-470-11649-4

MacBook For Dummies
978-0-470-04859-7

Mac OS X Leopard All-in-One
Desk Reference For Dummies
978-0-470-05434-5

Mac OS X Leopard For Dummies
978-0-470-05433-8

Macs For Dummies, 9th Edition
978-0-470-04849-8

PCs For Dummies, 11th Edition
978-0-470-13728-4

Windows® Home Server For Dummies
978-0-470-18592-6

Windows Server 2008 For Dummies
978-0-470-18043-3

Windows Vista All-in-One
Desk Reference For Dummies
978-0-471-74941-7

Windows Vista For Dummies
978-0-471-75421-3

Windows Vista Security For Dummies
978-0-470-11805-4

SPORTS, FITNESS & MUSIC

Coaching Hockey For Dummies
978-0-470-83685-9

Coaching Soccer For Dummies
978-0-471-77381-8

Fitness For Dummies, 3rd Edition
978-0-7645-7851-9

Football For Dummies, 3rd Edition
978-0-470-12536-6

GarageBand For Dummies
978-0-7645-7323-1

Golf For Dummies, 3rd Edition
978-0-471-76871-5

Guitar For Dummies, 2nd Edition
978-0-7645-9904-0

Home Recording For Musicians
For Dummies, 2nd Edition
978-0-7645-8884-6

iPod & iTunes For Dummies,
5th Edition
978-0-470-17474-6

Music Theory For Dummies
978-0-7645-7838-0

Stretching For Dummies
978-0-470-06741-3

Get smart @ dummies.com®

- Find a full list of Dummies titles
- Look into loads of FREE on-site articles
- Sign up for FREE eTips e-mailed to you weekly
- See what other products carry the Dummies name
- Shop directly from the Dummies bookstore
- Enter to win new prizes every month!

* Separate Canadian edition also available
** Separate U.K. edition also available

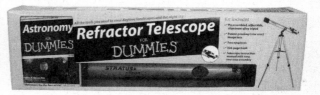